The Role of the Defense Lawyer

The Role of the Defense Lawyer

Conceptions and Perceptions within a Changing System

Ed Johnston

LEXINGTON BOOKS
Lanham • Boulder • New York • London

Published by Lexington Books
An imprint of The Rowman & Littlefield Publishing Group, Inc.
4501 Forbes Boulevard, Suite 200, Lanham, Maryland 20706
www.rowman.com

6 Tinworth Street, London SE11 5AL, United Kingdom

British Library Cataloguing in Publication Information Available

Library of Congress Cataloging-in-Publication Data

Names: Johnston, Ed, author.
Title: The role of the defense lawyer : conceptions and perceptions within a changing system / Ed Johnston.
Description: Lanham : Lexington Books, [2021] | Based on author's thesis (doctoral - University of West England, Bristol, 2019) issued under title: The defence lawyer in the modern era . | Includes bibliographical references and index. | Summary: "The adversarial criminal trial is changing, as are the roles of the actors within the process. This book examines the implications of such change"— Provided by publisher.
Identifiers: LCCN 2021021319 (print) | LCCN 2021021320 (ebook) | ISBN 9781793612922 (cloth) | ISBN 9781793612939 (epub)
Subjects: LCSH: Defense (Criminal procedure)—England.
Classification: LCC KD8358 .J64 2021 (print) | LCC KD8358 (ebook) | DDC 345.42/05044—dc23
LC record available at https://lccn.loc.gov/2021021319
LC ebook record available at https://lccn.loc.gov/2021021320

This book is dedicated to the memory of Leanne Phillips. A beautiful Wife, Mother, Sister, friend, teacher, and cousin. I will miss you forever.

Leanne Phillips
(1980–2020)

Contents

Acknowledgments

This monograph is based on my PhD thesis. I am forever indebted to the excellent supervision from Professors Ed Cape and Phil Rumney. I would also like to thank Professor Nic Ryder who supervised me through the post-viva stage of the PhD. Thank you all. Without your guidance, I would not be able to complete the PhD journey and this book would never have come to fruition.

I would like to thank my friends and colleagues, Dan Jasinski and Tom Smith. Both of you have been massive shoulders to lean on and helped balance our working commitments around my writing. I owe you both more than a beer. I would also like to thank my good friend, Paul Cuff. You were a brilliant distraction—although those PES breaks were not as stress-free as I envisaged.

I also owe my family a huge debt, my loving partner Wolfy and our beautiful children, Erin and Jacob. You have sacrificed so much to allow me to steal away evenings to complete this book. You have listened intently to my ideas, offered advice, and supported me when I was shattered (which was frequently). This book is as much yours as it is mine.

I would like to thank my Mum, Shelia. Your passion for the "right thing" set me on the path of criminal justice when I was a much younger man than today. You are a constant source of inspiration and strength. I love you very much.

Finally, I would like to thank my editors, Becca Beurer and Carter Moran, for all their support and answering my many questions throughout the writing of this book.

Thank you one and all.

Foreword

David S. Rudolf

What is the appropriate, indeed necessary, role of the defense lawyer in the Anglo-American system of criminal justice? To whom does the defense lawyer owe her primary duty of loyalty, to the client or to the justice system itself? In the event a conflict arises between the two, how should it be resolved?

In England and Wales in 2021, these are no longer merely philosophical questions. The passage and implementation of the Police and Criminal Evidence Act 1984 and the Criminal Procedure and Investigations Act 1996 have made conflict between the duty of the defense lawyer to the client and his or her duty to the court and the justice system an inevitable and everyday occurrence. To those of us who represent people charged with crimes in the United States, this is an ominous development. While we owe a duty not to actively mislead a court or take other actions that undermine the basic integrity of the criminal justice system, we do not owe a duty to "grease the wheels" of the system, or to make the prosecution's burden of overcoming the presumption of innocence, and proving guilt beyond a reasonable doubt, any less difficult or onerous.

Our job as defense lawyers is not to make the process more "efficient" at the expense of a true adversarial system, in which our role is, and ought to remain, preventing the abuse of power by those in positions of authority, and ensuring that the rule of law is followed no matter how heinous the accusation, or the reality of the crime. Because once defense lawyers become simply a cog in the criminal justice system, whose function is to enhance cooperation and efficiency, rather than to serve as the last line of defense for the rights of those accused of crimes, our clients, and the citizenry as a whole, will rightly have no faith in our ability, and willingness, to jealously protect their rights.

With the rise of right wing, and even fascistic, governments all over the world, governments that are far more concerned with protecting their own power than they are with protecting the rights of their citizens, even those of us living in free and democratic societies must be careful to retain the trust of the people. When those accused of crimes feel that their criminal defense lawyers are no longer their protectors, but rather just a part of a system that elevates efficiency over their rights, they will lose faith in the criminal justice system itself. When that happens, when the people come to believe that the system no longer serves to protect them against the abuse of power by the government and the majority, the justice system itself loses its moral authority.

Efficiency cannot be the only, or even the primary, goal of the justice system. The primary goal, indeed the overriding goal, must be the belief of the citizens that the system is designed to protect the rights of all who are subjected to its power.

This book highlights these very issues.

David S. Rudolf
Criminal Defense Attorney
April 2021

Introduction

This monograph is based on the author's PhD thesis which was successfully defended in August 2017. The empirical findings were gathered from twenty-six semi-structured interviews with practicing defense lawyers in England and Wales. The findings were transcribed and coded and provided an answer to the question: What is the role of the defense lawyer in the modern era?

The criminal defense lawyer and access to a defense lawyer are considered vital components of an accused person's right to a fair trial.[1] If a person is arrested in England and Wales, they are entitled to a defense lawyer (free of charge) to advance their best interest during the police interview.[2] However, questions remain as to what are the duties of the criminal defense lawyer? Is the lawyer the "mouthpiece for his client, is he an officer of the court or is he[3] the zealous protector of their rights?"[4] This monograph seeks to answer this very question. The monograph aims to examine the role of the defense lawyer in the modern era. For the purpose of this monograph, the modern era will be defined as post-1996. The monograph has adopted 1996 as the genesis of the "modern era" as it was then that defense pretrial disclosure obligations were overhauled and enhanced. Prior to 1996, the defense had to disclose little to the prosecution in advance of trial, save for alibi witness evidence[5] and the evidence of any expert witnesses[6] the defense intended to call at trial. However, the Criminal Procedure and Investigations Act 1996 (hereafter, CPIA 1996) placed an obligation on the defense to disclose a defense case statement which outlined the nature of the accused's case, including any defenses he wished to rely on.[7] This obligation is mandatory in the Crown Court but merely voluntary in the magistrates' court.[8] However, the advent of the Criminal Procedure Rules (CrimPR) in 2003[9] effectively circumvents this statutory provision and places an obligation on the defense to assist in satisfying the overriding objective of the CrimPR of "dealing with cases justly"[10] by identifying "the real issues."[11] This effectively renders the defense disclosure obligations compulsory.

However, an argument exists that the modern era should start two years earlier with the advent of the silence provisions under the Criminal Justice and Public Order Act 1994. Quirk suggests that the provisions represent the "price" paid for the due process safeguards afforded to suspect in the Police and Criminal Evidence Act 1984.[12] However, this monograph is concerned with the post-charge, pretrial disclosure obligations which manifest itself in the CPIA 1996 and CrimPR. Furthermore, the monograph argues that the CPIA 1996 allowed for the creation of what is referred to in this monograph as a "new regime." This is a term coined for this monograph; it encapsulates the rise of a defense disclosure regime under both the CPIA 1996 and CrimPR which in turn have increased the managerialist goals of desired by the justice system, as well as enforcing cooperation between the defense and prosecution; something that is distinctly non-adversarial. This regime has managerialist goals at its heart and looks to ensure the criminal justice process eliminates waste and focuses on efficiency.

While it is arguable that the silence provisions were the genesis for this efficiency driver, the CPIA1996 reinvented the disclosure regime. This new regime was also extended to the magistrates' court where the disclosure provisions were previously only voluntary. This change represents a serious threat to adversarialism and have a far-reaching effect for all connected to the criminal justice process. As such, for the purposes of this monograph, this is the start of the modern era is 1996. Arguably, the disclosure developments have led to a culture of cooperation and notification has led to a departure from traditional adversarial values. This monograph aims to examine the role of the defense lawyer by critically exploring academic expressions of the role and empirically exploring the competing duties and tensions faced by this fundamental part of the adversarial criminal justice process. Furthermore, this monograph will explore the arena in which the defense lawyer practices. Arguably, this arena is one that has become distinctly non-adversarial; the ramifications of which will be explored throughout.

WHY EXPLORE THIS?

The culture of defense work has undergone significant change over the course of the last twenty-five years. These changes may have generated confusion and uncertainty concerning the role of the defense lawyer in the modern era. If the lawyer is confused as to his role, is it possible to zealously advance the best interests of his client? Furthermore, if the lawyer is confused, how does he reconcile any confusion? The advent of the CrimPR and the implicit creation of a criminal justice process that prioritizes the managerialist aims of economy, efficiency, and effectiveness has gone relatively under-researched.[13] While the role of the defense has been explored through the culture of their law firms, the individualized role of the defense lawyer is something that has not been exposed to scrutiny. The work of Michael McConville,[14] Max Travers[15] and Daniel Newman[16] all examined how lawyers interact with and treat their clients. This monograph differs from the aforementioned studies, exploring how lawyers view their own individual role in the context of the changed obligations introduced by the CPIA 1996 and the CrimPR. These views will be examined through the lens of a theoretical conception of an adversarial defense lawyer, which will be established in this monograph. This approach will permit the monograph to draw conclusions regarding the role of the defense lawyer in the modern era.

It has been argued that the changes made over the last twenty-five years have led to a departure from traditional adversarial values. McConville and Marsh argue that the CrimPR place pressure on role of defense lawyer that ultimately leads to the erosion of the adversarial criminal justice process.[17] If criminal justice is in transition,[18] what are the implications for the defense lawyer? This dilution of adversarialism and the enhanced pretrial obligations has left England and Wales with process that is akin to the "Accused Speaks" trial of the seventeenth century. Here, the accused is unaware of the charge laid against him and he "speaks" to assist the court in discovering the truth of the allegation. The monograph aims to illuminate the idea that adversarialism in England and Wales is returning to the "accused speaks" format; whereby the defense lawyer plays almost no role in the trial process. However, in the modern era, the accused "speaks" via the medium of his disclosure obligations rather than making oral admissions at trial. The focus of this monograph is centered on the defense lawyer in the magistrates' court. Primarily, this is because the vast majority of cases take place in the magistrates' court.[19] The changes to the disclosure provisions have led to the establishment of what this monograph terms "The New Regime," whereby there is now a normative expectation that the defendant will disclose his defense prior to trial. While the CPIA 1996 had a voluntary disclosure regime in the magistrates' court, the defendant is now co-opted into the process by completing the case management forms under the umbrella of the overriding objective of the CrimPR to deal with cases justly. This significantly alters the culture and nature of the criminal trial.

The New Regime of efficiency and cooperation means the defendant is compelled to be an active participant in proceedings by having to divulge more information than ever before. Lord Justice Auld's Review *of the Criminal Courts of England and Wales*[20] provided a cornerstone in the drive for efficiency. He stated that "fairness, efficiency and effectiveness of the criminal justice system demand that its procedures should be simple, accessible and so far as practicable, the same for every level and type of criminal jurisdiction."[21] A fundamental element of this uniformed approach is the case management provisions. However, in the post-*Review* era, the courts had already started "managing" cases[22] but the framework contained within the rules co-opts the defendant into active participation, allows the court to sanction noncompliance and effectively redesigning the culture of the adversarial criminal trial. The case management provisions of the CrimPR extended the CPIA 1996 disclosure regime and the New Regime poses a great threat to the very notion of adversarialism and fundamental fair trial rights. The monograph explores these points and finds that there has been a departure from the traditional model of adversarialism and has given rise to a new form of process that is anchored in managerialist goals. However, little thought is given to the in-built due process protections afforded by classic adversarialism. This monograph will explore the impact of this change.

RESEARCH QUESTIONS

The monograph has one overarching question:

What is the role of the defense lawyer in the modern era?

However, to comprehensively answer this question, the monograph has three guiding research questions:

1. What relevant legislation has changed over the last twenty years? The monograph will concentrate on the following changes: the evolution of the rules of disclosure[23] the explicit pretrial obligations on both the defense and the accused and finally, the changing function of the judiciary. All three aspects of change have potential implications for the role of the defense lawyer and for the adversarial nature of the criminal process in England and Wales.
2. What are the theoretical and practical consequences of the changing legislation for the defense lawyer?

   The traditional role of the defense lawyer is to be his client's mouthpiece, an officer of the court and a zealous protector of the defendant's rights.[24] It is of paramount importance to permit the defense lawyer to act in a fearless manner; in *Rondel v Worsley*,[25] it was held that "Counsel has a fearless duty to raise every issue, advance every argument, ask every question . . . that will advance his client's case. But as an officer of the court, he has an overriding objective to the standards of his profession and to the public."[26] Effectively, the defense lawyer operates on the "horns of a trilemma"[27] in which he has to balance the three competing duties espoused by Lord Reid. This question leads to an examination of whether the classic conception of the role of the lawyer exists in practice today or whether it has been eroded by the legislative changes.

3. What are the implications of the developments for both the lawyer-client relationship and the notion of adversarialism in England and Wales?

   This final question will examine how the legislative changes have impacted on the lawyer-client relationship. If a culture of cooperation exists between the two opposing sides, does this alter the lawyer-client relationship? Does the very nature of cooperation create tension between the lawyer and his client? Furthermore, how have these changes impacted the notion of adversarialism in England and Wales? The adversarial process in England and Wales has been characterized as a "legally regulated debate between the [two] parties, with the trial as its centerpiece."[28] The adversarial process has two opposing parties who gather and select the pretrial evidence before each side presents their evidence at trial. The court is adjudicative in nature rather than possessing any investigative function.[29] Zander described the traditional role of judge as "a passive umpire, as in a tennis match."[30] Can it be claimed that this sufficiently represents the adversarial trial process in the modern era? This monograph will address this question and provide a comprehensive account of the modern day adversarial criminal justice process.

Analytical Models

During both the empirical analysis in chapter 6 and the conclusions contained within chapter 7, the monograph will use both existing studies and analytical models to examine the changing obligations faced by the defense lawyer. The seminal text on how the defense lawyer operates can be found in McConville et al.'s *Standing Accused*.[31] However, there are distinct differences between that work and this study. As such, the work is used as a lens for analysis as opposed to a direct comparative tool. The work of McConville et al. described the working practices, values systems, and organization of solicitors who are engaged in criminal defense work. In essence, his study examined "the nature and quality of the legal defense and 'representation' they provide to their clients."[32] This monograph is rather different but the influence of McConville's work will permeate the monograph. Whereas McConville examined the nature and quality of the work and the organizational influence of the defense firm, this monograph will examine how the defense lawyer operates on a daily basis and seeks to examine what influences their prioritization of duties. This prioritization is thematically coded and differing categories of lawyer shall emerge; all of which will have, to some degree, different prioritizes and goals.

Further to McConville's work, the work of Herbert Packer will be used to examine the impact the changed legislation and obligations has had for the traditional notion of adversarialism in England and Wales. Packer created two models of the criminal process and they represent "an attempt to abstract two separate value systems that compete for priority in the operation of the criminal process."[33] While the Crime Control and Due Process models should not be viewed as absolute, one can ascertain where on a spectrum, between the two models, the current criminal process resides. By analyzing the piecemeal changes to the disclosure obligations since the introduction of alibi disclosure in 1967,[34] the monograph can examine the values that underpin the changes and ascertain whether there has been a drift from due process values to a more crime control-focused agenda or vice versa.

Methodological Overview

To answer the questions posed by the monograph, a mixed methodological approach was used. To adequately answer the overarching question, the study required a full examination of both current and past legislation relevant to the defense lawyer in defending a client in criminal proceedings. In order to do this, a doctrinal approach was employed. However, in order not to be "disadvantaged by the intellectual straight-jacket [of] the traditional legal method,"[35] the monograph also adopted a socio-legal approach to research. The empirical research took the form of semi-structured interviews. The interviews offered insights into the impact of the changing legislation. Furthermore, the empirical study provided insight into how their role is perceived by lawyers themselves.

There were two distinct stages of research. Firstly, desk-based research was undertaken. The first research question seeks to examine what legislation has changed over the last twenty years. The disclosure regime first introduced by the CPIA 1996 was a highly significant change and this was chosen to be the start point of the modern era. Until 1996, the defense had to make minimal disclosure in advance of trial.[36] The era of minimal prosecution disclosure faded; the CPIA 1996 insisted, for trials on indictment, that the defendant outline the general nature of his defense, what issues he takes with the prosecution's case and why he takes issue.[37] This was then amplified by the CrimPR, requiring the defendant to disclose a defense case statement in both Crown Court and magistrates' court cases.

The desk-based research yielded a picture of substantial change to the relevant legislation over the last twenty years, albeit in a piecemeal fashion. With the changing legislation analyzed, these findings would now underpin the second research question, concerning the theoretical and practical consequences of the disclosure legislation. Prior to answering this question, it was important to understand what was meant by the term "defense lawyer." As such, a classic conception of the defense lawyer was conceived. This conception was built from a wealth of academic literature, predominately from the United States, which highlighted the core functions and traits illustrated by the defense lawyer. This conception highlighted that there were three core duties of the lawyer—the duty to the client, to the court, and to the administration of justice. However, it was clear that no clear priority of duties existed. Although there was no priority of duties, it was clear that the duties offered a great deal of conflict. Once the theoretical consequences for both the lawyer and the general notion of adversarialism was established, the interview *pro forma* was created, in essence this would tease out the practical consequences of the disclosure legislation.

With the completion of the first part of the desk-based research and the creation of the research instrument, the empirical aspect of the study could be undertaken and the answer to both the theoretical and practical implications of the changes could be answered. The semi-structured interview was chosen because the primary goal of the study was to obtain an understanding of the processes, thoughts, and perceptions of defense lawyers.[38] With the completion of the empirical study, a return to desk-based research would answer the final research question. By examining both the theoretical and practical implications of the CPIA 1996 and CrimPR, the study can draw conclusions about both the impact on the lawyer-client relationship and the impact for the traditional notion of adversarialism in England and Wales.

NOTES

1. Article 6 of the "European Convention on Human Rights" has legislative effect through the Human Rights Act 1998 and guarantees access to a defense lawyer.
2. S.58(1) PACE 1984 states "A person arrested and held in custody in a police station or other premises shall be entitled, if he so requests, to consult a solicitor privately at any time."
3. This monograph follows the convention in many law publications and that "he" refers to both male and female lawyers unless indicated otherwise.
4. M. Blake and A. Ashworth, "Ethics and the Criminal Defense Lawyer" [2004] *Legal Ethics* Vol 7, 167–190, 167.
5. S.11 Criminal Justice Act 1967.
6. S.2(1) Criminal Justice Act 1987.
7. S.5 Criminal Procedure and Investigations Act 1996.
8. S. 6 Criminal Procedure and Investigations Act 1996.

9. The Criminal Procedure Rules were first introduced in 2003. Since then, they have been revised on a number of occasions. Unless stated otherwise, the use of CrimPR makes reference to the current Rules which were introduced in October 2016.

10. Rule 1.1 Criminal Procedure Rules 2016.

11. Rule 3.2(2)(a) Criminal Procedure Rules 2016.

12. H. Quirk, "Twenty years on, the right of silence and legal advice: the spiraling costs of an unfair exchange" [2013] Vol 64 (4):465–484 at 466.

13. With the exception of Professor McEwan's work, research on the impact of the CrimPR is scant. See J. McEwan, "Truth, Efficiency and Co-operation in Modern Criminal Justice" [2013] *Current Legal Problems*, Vol 1, 66(1), 203–232, Oxford University Press; J. McEwan and F. Garland, "Embracing the Overriding Objective: Difficulties and Dilemmas in the New Criminal Climate" [2012] *International Journal of Evidence and Proof*, Vol 16(3), Vathek, 233–262 and J. McEwan, "From Adversarialism to Managerialism: Criminal Justice in Transition" [2011] *Legal Studies*, Vol 31(3), Wiley, 519–546.

14. M. McConville, J. Hodgson, L. Bridges and A. Pavlovic, *Standing Accused* (Oxford University Press: Oxford, 1994).

15. M. Travers, *The Reality of Law* (Ashgate: Dartmouth, 1997).

16. D. Newman, *Legal Aid Lawyers and the Quest for Justice* (Hart: Oxford, 2013).

17. M. McConville and L. Marsh, "Adversarialism Goes West: Case Management in Criminal Courts" [2015] E&P, Vol 19(3), 172–189.

18. J. McEwan, From Adversarialism to Managerialism: Criminal Justice in Transition, [2011] *Legal Studies*, Vol 31(3), Wiley, 519–546.

19. S.6 CPIA 1996 states that disclosure in the magistrates' court is voluntary. For the year ending 2018. Approximately 94 percent of all criminal cases were heard in the magistrates' courts in England and Wales. For further information see, House of Commons Briefing Paper, Court Statistics for England and Wales, December 2019, at p. 3.

20. R. Auld, *A Review of the Criminal Courts of England and Wales* (2001). https://www.criminal-courts-review.org.uk/auldconts.htm.

21. Ibid., Chapter Ten, Paragraph 271.

22. The monograph will analyze the impact of *Chaaban* [2003] EWCA Crim 1012, *Jisl* [2004] EWCA Crim 696 and *Gleeson* [2004] 1. Cr. App. R 29

23. For the purpose of this monograph, it is important to distinguish prosecution from defense disclosure. The primary focus will be the evolution of defense disclosure. The distinction will enable the monograph to analyze the impact of the changing legislation on both the role of the defense lawyer and the legal system in England and Wales.

24. Blake and Ashworth, Ethics and the Criminal Defense Lawyer, Legal Ethics 167.

25. [1969] 1 AC 191 HL.

26. Ibid., at pp. 227–228.

27. M. Freedman "Professional Responsibility and the Criminal Defense Lawyer" (1966) 64 Mich. L. Rev. 153.

28. J. Hodgson *Conceptions of the Trial in Inquisitorial and Adversarial Procedure* in A. Duff, *The Trial on Trial Volume 1, Truth and Due Process* (1st Edition, Hart: Oxford, 2001).

29. Ibid., at p. 224.

30. M. Zander, *Cases and Materials on the English Legal System* (10th Edition, CUP, Cambridge) 2007.

31. M. McConville, J. Hodgson, L. Bridges and A. Pavlovic *Standing Accused* (Clarendon Press: Oxford, 1994).

32. Ibid., at p. 1.

33. H. Packer, *The Limits of the Criminal Sanction* (California: Stanford University Press, 1968) at p. 153.

34. s.11 Criminal Justice Act 1967.

35. A. Bradney, *How to Study Law* (5th edition, London: Sweet and Maxwell, 2005) p. 47.

36. s.11 Criminal Justice Act 1967 compelled the defense to disclose any alibi evidence they intended to use. This was further enhanced by Criminal Justice Act 1987.

37. S.6(a)-(c) Criminal Procedure and Investigations Act 1996. It is important to remember that this provision was only voluntary in the magistrates' courts. However, this monograph will establish that the voluntary nature of the provision has been replaced with compulsion due to the advent of the case management provisions of the CrimPR.

38. S. Arber, *Designing Samples*, in N. Gilbert (ed.) *Researching Social Life* (California: Sage, 1993) at p. 73.

Chapter 1

Theories of Criminal Justice

This chapter will examine the evolution of the adversarial criminal process in England and Wales up until the mid-1990s. To analyze the position of the criminal justice process until the mid-1990s, two key aspects will be examined. Firstly, the chapter will examine adversarial and inquisitorial theory, before examining the purpose of the criminal trial, the role of the judiciary within the criminal trial process and, finally, the role of the prosecutor. Chapter 8 will examine whether the roles and purpose have altered in the modern era. Each aspect will be examined on an independent level. While the predominant focus of the chapter is the adversarial nature of the criminal justice process, the inquisitorial ideology will be used as a foil to the adversarial ideology. While the models in this chapter are based on theory, the make-up of each model will permit an analysis to ascertain whether the legislative changes have led to deviation from the traditional concept of adversarialism in England and Wales. This chapter will identify that there is an emergence of a new form of procedure, the managerialist approach.

The role of the defense lawyer is purposively omitted from any analysis in this chapter. The defense lawyer's role will be examined in chapter 2. The purpose of the trial, and the roles of the judge and prosecutor, provide a contextual element for examining the role of the defense lawyer.

TRADITIONAL ADVERSARIAL AND INQUISITORIAL IDEOLOGY

There are two main approaches to criminal procedure[1]: the adversarial and inquisitorial approaches.[2] However, these terms merely refer to the model of each approach; no system of criminal procedure is a pure embodiment of either model.[3] Concerns have been raised that the models are somewhat outdated.[4] Despite the reservations concerning the contemporary value of the models, they provide a useful starting point for this chapter. The chapter will utilize the classic concept of the adversarial criminal process as its starting point to ascertain whether England and Wales have departed or deviated from this classic concept. In 1993, the Royal Commission on Criminal Justice described the adversarial legal system of England and Wales as: "a system which has the judge as an umpire, who leaves the presentation of the case to the parties (the prosecution and defense) on each side. They separately prepare their case and call, examine and cross-examine witnesses."[5]

The adversarial process in England and Wales has been characterized as a "legally regulated debate between [two] parties with the trial as its centerpiece."[6] The adversarial process has two opposing parties who gather and select the relevant pretrial evidence before each side presents their evidence at trial. Traditional adversarial ideology is centered on the notion that "the truth is best discovered by powerful statements on each side of the argument."[7] Both the prosecution and defense are responsible for gathering their evidence, building and presenting their case at trial, in a light that best favors their desired result—a conviction for the prosecution or an acquittal for the defense.[8] The court is adjudicative in nature and does not possess any investigative function. Zander described the traditional role of the adversarial judge as "a passive umpire, as in a tennis match."[9] As he will listen to the evidence offered by both sides and ensure that the rules and procedures of the court are adhered to. In order to maintain a passive and neutral stance, the decision-makers do not conduct an active role in proceedings. If the neutral decision-maker does become overtly active in proceedings, he runs the risk of compromising his ability to "neutrally evaluate the adversaries' presentations."[10] The pretrial preparation is motivated by self-interest rather than public interest and the preparation is geared toward mounting the evidence in the best possible light to achieve each side's desired result. Adversarial theory holds that by allowing both sides to fully investigate the issue and permitting both sides to present their own interpretation of the facts the real truth will emerge.[11]

In an archetypal adversarial system, the accused is armed with tools to defend himself from the "oppressive state"; these tools include his right to refuse to testify or to cooperate.[12] The adversarial model appears to be content to sacrifice speed and efficiency in order to enhance the integrity of the deliberations. In theory, the system is happy to allow each side to have an opportunity to present their facts. Upon resting their case, the neutral adjudicator can take his time in order to reach a satisfactory and correct conclusion on the defendant's guilt or innocence.

Both models seek to ascertain the truth. However, the two models employ vastly different mechanisms to reach the point of deciding upon the "truth." In the inquisitorial model, the onus does not fall on the partisan parties to conduct the pretrial investigation; instead the responsibility falls on a "central judicial authority whose role is to act in the wider public interest in the search for the truth."[13] As Ellison states, "[t]he trust in the adversary system on partisan parties, to bring facts to light, is replaced by faith in the integrity and capacity of public officials to pursue the 'truth.' "[14] In theory, the person who conducts the pretrial investigation is a member of the judiciary, either an examining magistrate or a prosecutor. The judiciary will investigate all the evidence, both exculpatory and inculpatory. The model is based on the concept that the truth can only be discovered from an investigative procedure.[15] As it may be in the best interests of each party to conceal the truth, the inquisitorial process is premised on the notion that it is the state that is best equipped to carry out the investigation. An examining judge or prosecutor creates a dossier. The dossier is passed to a judge in preparation for trial; it will be for the judge to decide on what witnesses to call and it is the judge who will also conduct any examination of the witnesses. The role of the prosecution and the defense is less significant than their adversarial counterparts and both sides play a subsidiary role to the judge.

In general, pretrial investigation of the most serious offences will be the responsibility of an examining magistrate. However, in most other cases the police, under the supervision of the prosecutor, will conduct the pretrial investigation. Inquisitorial theory holds that the best person equipped to conduct the investigation is the benevolent state[16] and the judicial supervision is a safeguard from abuse of power by state officials. The pretrial investigation culminates in the creation of a dossier of evidence; it is this dossier and pretrial investigation that is the centerpiece of the inquisitorial model.[17] Writing in 1977, Goldstein and Marcus claimed that uncontested inquisitorial trials merely serve as perfunctory proceedings and often, in the French Correctional Court, not a single corroborating witness is called. The accused makes his statement, the lawyers make their speeches and sentencing swiftly follows.[18] Essentially, the public trial element of the inquisitorial process is an evaluation of the evidence in the dossier, rather than a forum for an oral contest.[19] Both the adversarial and inquisitorial models reflect the ideology of their respective society's stance on the allocation of power. This illustrates that the adversarial process attaches less weight to the goal of fact-finding.[20] The weighting is not because adversarial ideology values fact-finding as unimportant but because it acknowledges the importance of other aims, such as the protection of the citizen from the overzealous state. There are various safeguards in place to prohibit the state from abusing its powers. The use of lay people in the criminal justice system and the passivity of the judge are examples of the safeguards afforded to the accused against oppressive or abusive behavior from state officials. Further safeguards are afforded to the suspect at the investigative stage. These safeguards include a limitation on the duration of time the suspect can remain in police detention without charge, the right not to incriminate oneself and the right to legal representation.

Whereas the adversarial model embodies the belief that state power is best kept in check, the inquisitorial model believes that the state is best equipped to carry out the investigation and as such, state officials should be provided with broad tools of investigation. The adversarial safeguard of the defense lawyer plays a reduced role in the inquisitorial model. It is the duty of the inquisitorial defense lawyer to ensure that the state's representatives adhere to the procedural rules of investigation. The defense can suggest to the prosecutor certain avenues of investigation that benefit the case of the accused, but he cannot conduct his own investigation. The dossier has also been described as a safeguard: it not only forms the basis of the trial, but also a coherent system of supervision and control.[21]

MODELS OF CRIMINAL PROCEDURE

The adversarial and inquisitorial models of criminal process are not universally accepted as providing a comprehensive account of the differing approaches to the criminal process. While the monograph will not examine the alternative frameworks in great detail, it is appropriate to briefly mention them. In order to analyze the shifts in procedural ideology, it is important to use analytical models to examine any particular shifts in the justice system. The models are helpful because they provide a useful way to examine and understand complex procedural ideals. Ericson suggests that multiple models are helpful because they represent multiple versions of what is occurring and they can account in different ways for the system's operation.[22] Models can also provide a normative account of what values ought to influence the criminal justice process.[23] The models that will assist with the analysis are Packer's Crime Control and Due Process models, Damaska's Coordinate and Hierarchical Models, and Summers' theory of a European Tradition. While the models are introduced here, the analysis of using the models to analyze the contemporary state of the adversarial process will be undertaken in chapter 8.

In 1964, Herbert Packer created arguably the most influential models of criminal procedure; the crime control and Due Process models. The crime control models holds that the repression of criminal activity is the most important function that the criminal process undertakes and very little should stand in the way of this goal.[24] In order to successfully achieve this goal, the model requires that full trust is given to investigators and guilt is largely assumed. The model intends to achieve a high rate of both detection and conviction. There is a premium on efficiency and the process should effectively resemble a conveyor belt. Limited challenges to the court's decision should be allowed and the pretrial investigation should be prioritized. It is here where the facts can be discovered and guilt established. The model rejects the importance of the actual trial. Unsurprisingly, the Due Process model represents the other end of the spectrum. If the crime control model is like a conveyor belt, the Due Process model represents an obstacle course, with a number of hurdles in the way of a successful prosecution holding that there is no presumption of guilt. The model holds that there is a chance of a high degree of error in the pretrial investigation and as such, it emphasizes the importance of safeguards and the criminal trial.

While Damaska does not reject the traditional adversarial or inquisitorial ideologies, he believes the understanding of their intricate workings can be better understood if they are explored in more explanatory terms. As such, he created two explanatory models: the coordinate and hierarchical models. The coordinate model is likened to the adversarial model. It places great reliance on oral testimony and use of lay officials, and the process concludes in a trial that is "packed with excitement and drama . . . surprises and unpredictable turns of events are commonplace."[25] The hierarchical model is likened to the inquisitorial approach to criminal procedure that is favored in parts of Europe. The hierarchical ideal is multilayered and consists of a number of different levels in a pyramid of authority; each stage is allotted a different task or responsibility. One stage may be responsible for the gathering and organization of the relevant material, another responsible for the initial decision-making, and another stage for hierarchical review. The completion of each stage is merely one episode in a continuing sequence. The hierarchical review is both comprehensive and regular. Once a lower official has completed his duties, his procedural episode comes to a close. The correction of decisions made by lower officials can only be completed by those in the higher echelons of authority. It is this supervision and correction of decision-making that guarantees a fair and orderly administration of justice.[26]

In her book *Fair Trials and Procedural Tradition in Europe*, Sarah Summers claims that the classic use of the adversarial and inquisitorial models should be abandoned. She argues that since the nineteenth century, criminal procedure in Europe can be described as a single tradition.[27] In order to establish an alternative conceptual framework for the development of the single criminal procedure in Europe, Summers's book proceeds in two halves; firstly, it challenges and rejects the established opinion that criminal procedure in Europe should be viewed through the lens of the adversarial and inquisitorial models. After rejecting this idea, she seeks to "identify a common European concept of criminal procedure."[28] She uncovers an "emerging European discourse"[29] among jurists in the nineteenth century. It was thought that criminal proceedings should be based around the notion of the "accusatorial trinity."[30] The trinity was the defense, prosecution, and an impartial judge.

THE PURPOSE(S) OF THE CRIMINAL TRIAL

Defining one meaning of the purpose of the criminal trial has proven to be quite troublesome. It is commonly assumed that the purpose of the criminal trial is to determine the guilt or innocence of the defendant. However, if the purpose of the trial is deconstructed, it is clear to see that the criminal trial serves many different purposes. This subsection will utilize many different sources to try and identify a clear purpose of the trial. The subsection will examine the role that the trial plays in the search for the truth, the airing of conflicts, a forum to allocate punishment, and the cathartic effect of the trial. It will close with a comment on how the inquisitorial trial operates; this contrast will aid the final thoughts on what the purpose of the adversarial criminal trial.

The Search for the Truth

Upon researching this subsection, a common theme was discovered in a large number of sources; the adversarial trial is less committed to the discovery of the truth than its inquisitorial counterpart.[31] The prosecution and defense are charged with the responsibility of examining the facets of each other's account and exposing any weaknesses discovered during the public forum of the trial. It is during the trial that advocates endeavor to "reveal to the tribunal which witnesses can be relied upon and which can be cast aside."[32]

Despite the search for the truth being central to the adversarial process, this search is balanced against various other considerations including maintaining the integrity of the system. The prosecution's case will only succeed should it be able to present enough evidence to convince the jury in Crown Court cases, or the magistrates or district judge in summary trials, that the defendant is guilty of the alleged offence beyond reasonable doubt. Procedural safeguards not only protect the defendant but also help maintain the integrity of the system. These safeguards may also inhibit the search for the truth; for example, if evidence was obtained inappropriately, it should be excluded from trial.[33] This exclusion of evidence protects the defendant from any abuse of state power. However, this exclusion may render a truthful confession inadmissible owing to how it was extracted from the defendant. The skill, knowledge, and experience of the advocate may also inhibit the search for the truth. The prosecution and defense lawyers present their version of an alleged incident. They attempt to convince the jury or the magistrates' court that their version is the "truth"; which can be dependent on the skill and experience of the advocate presenting the case as well as the quality and temperament of the witnesses. The art and skill of advocacy is "a highly refined one whose very best practitioners may manage to persuade in the face of facts [tending against their case]."[34] Whereas a more inexperienced, less eloquent practitioner may not be able to convince the jury or magistrates' court that his version of events is the truth. Further to the skill and art of the advocate, the performance of a witness may also inhibit the search for the truth. If the witness is weak, inarticulate or unwilling to answer questions it may mean a case flounders despite its merits.[35]

The Trial and Finality

The allocation of punishment is a common feature of all trials where the defendant has been convicted. If a defendant enters a guilty plea, the truth-finding, conflict airing, dispute-resolving aspects of the trial are redundant. In essence, the trial will merely serve as a forum to allocate punishment for a certain offence. If the conviction is the moment of condemnation for a particular act, sentencing is its refinement and elaboration.[36] The act of sentencing communicates to the defendant and to the wider community as a whole the precise condemnation and punishment for committing a certain act.[37] The sentencing stage can be seen to communicate societal disapproval and sends out powerful statements concerning issues such as expected societal norms, morals, values, and expectations of each and every citizen. Furthermore, the sentencing stage illustrates where authority lies in society, what acts constitute a threat to this authority and who maintains order, as well as illustrating how this order is maintained. The sentencing stage of trial is the symbolic means of upholding the dignity of the criminal justice process. By passing sentencing, the trial judge is demanding that the law is respected and that those that breach the law can expect to be punished.[38] This message of demanding respect is conveyed not only by the trial judge but further conveyed by the media. The media will carry snippets of judicial comment when reporting on sentencing; this reporting will amplify the public debate on appropriateness or controversy surrounding a sentence. Ultimately it builds societal expectations of what is right and wrong.

In the second half of the eighteenth century, there was a growing aversion to capital punishment. Langbein states that capital punishment was overprescribed and the function of the trial was to "winnow down the number of persons actually executed from the much larger cohort of culprits whom the

'Bloody Code' threatened with death"[39] Langbein added that during the latter half of the eighteenth century, "too much truth meant too much death."[40] The objective of winnowing down the number of people executed illustrates an early indication that the criminal trial operates as a dynamic rather than static platform. Furthermore, this also illustrates that the trial can be truth-defeating as opposed to being a forum that exclusively seeks to discover the truth. This desire for "finality" not only applies to the victims and witnesses but also to the defendant. Article 6 of the ECHR states that when charged with the commission of a criminal offence, the accused is entitled to a fair and public hearing within a reasonable time by an independent and impartial tribunal.[41] This requirement ensures that the fate of the defendant does not remain uncertain for too long a period. The requirement also ensures that the alleged incident is fresh in the memory of witnesses and therefore minimizes the potential for memory loss.

The notion of finality is in conflict with the notion of the trial representing the search for the truth. If the search for the truth were the primary aim of the trial, the quest to reach the truth would not be restricted by finality. Furthermore, to reach the truth the system would need recourse to quash a conviction should new evidence come to light regarding the potential wrongful conviction of a suspect. In essence, the search for the truth may not lead to finality at all.

DETERRENCE OR REHABILITATION? THE INQUISITORIAL TRIAL

According to Duff, the aim of the criminal trial is to "not merely reach an accurate judgement on the defendant's past conduct; it is to communicate and justify that judgment—to demonstrate its justice—to him and others."[42] The trial may also be seen as part of the rehabilitation of the accused. It is not enough to merely punish an offender; he needs to learn what society thinks justice should be. In a study of the French inquisitorial criminal process, Stewart Field identified an interesting contrast between adversarial and inquisitorial criminal trials. Here, the French judge spent a vast amount of time questioning the accused about his private life, education, history, sexual relationships, and hobbies.[43] Field noted that French criminal proceedings were not only designed to discover if the particular individual committed the particular offence; there were further aims to ascertain in detail who did what, when, how, and why within the context of a set of general norms about the life of the ordinary French citizen. Field stated that "these assumptions seemed to be part of a set of reciprocal expectations between the individual on the one hand and the state and community on the other."[44] By conducting this examination of the accused's educational and social weaknesses or failings, Field remarked that he had the impression that the offence in question was not only being judged but also the life of the defendant, according to a positive and fairly developed notion of what a French citizen ought to be.[45]

The French inquisitorial trial places great emphasis on character evidence. Evidence of both good and bad character is heard prior to pronouncing judgment. In the adversarial trial in England and Wales, the use of character evidence is less significant in determining the culpability of the defendant. It is acceptable for character evidence to be considered at the sentencing stage but at the trial stage, the adversarial process does not permit the use of character evidence to the extent of its inquisitorial counterpart. This is to ensure that the guilt of the defendant relates to the particular offence in question and not to a broad-ranging judgment of the standing of the accused in the community.[46] However, this stance toward character evidence has not always been the norm in England and Wales. Prior to the emergence of the adversarial trial in the last quarter of the eighteenth century, the trial and sentencing stages were less distinct.[47] The sentencing stage would immediately follow the conclusion of the trial and it was during the sentencing proceedings that juries would sometimes return a partial verdict, which is where the defendant was convicted on a lesser charge which carried a lesser penalty.[48]

Field believes that the criminal trial in France is part of the process of rehabilitating the accused as a reformed citizen of the state. The trial acts as a positive concept of the citizen in which it is deemed appropriate to judge the character and life of the accused.[49] Furthermore, the "dominance in France of the fact-finding by the professional judiciary changes the attitudes to the social prejudice generated by character evidence."[50] The adversarial criminal trial presents a far narrower image of the relationship between state and citizens than its inquisitorial counterpart; as such the adversarial criminal law is more distanced from social expectations of the citizen.[51]

It is clear that one single purpose of the criminal trial does not exist and there is no set definition of the trial in either the adversarial or inquisitorial jurisdictions. What has been discovered illustrates that the criminal trial is a dynamic institution; this can be seen from the eighteenth century where the discovery of the truth was, at times, treated as a secondary goal in order to reduce the number of defendants executed. The trial also has rehabilitative functions, as can be seen in Stewart Field's inquisitorial study in which the use of character evidence is employed? All of these points emphasize the idea that there are many facets to the purpose of the criminal trial and that the trial is constantly evolving.

The Actors in the Criminal Justice Process

In order to fully understand the role of the defense lawyer, there is a need to examine both the arena in which he operates and the other actors in the process. This section will examine the roles of the prosecution and judiciary in both the adversarial and inquisitorial traditions.

The Adversarial Prosecutor

The Royal Commission established in 1962[52] recommended that a separate body should be created to separate the investigative and prosecution stage of proceedings. This added layer of independence would ensure that tension between the two stages would not arise. However, this recommendation was not implemented and many police forces continued to prosecute their own cases in magistrates' courts. For cases that would be heard in the Crown Court, the police instructed solicitors and barristers to prosecute cases on their behalf.[53] As this situation evolved, the police gradually started to employ their own in-house prosecuting solicitors who would act on the instructions of the police.[54] The prosecutor would have little recourse if the police wanted to go ahead and prosecute a weak case or "overcharge" a suspect.

This arrangement between the police and the prosecution came under attack in the report on the "Confait Affair."[55] This case raised questions about the procedures followed by the police during the interrogation of three youths, suspected of the murder of a male prostitute. The interrogation led the youths to falsely confess to the murder of Maxwell Confait. In 1977, an inquiry into the investigation was opened and recommended many of the provisions contained within PACE 1984, as well as establishing the Crown Prosecution Service, under the Prosecution of Offenders Act 1975. Both changes dramatically altered pretrial investigation. The report revealed that the officer in charge of the investigation was willing to breach the judges' rules and put severe pressure on the suspects when questioning them. The prosecutor was deemed unable or unwilling to act independently from the police and the youths were wrongly convicted of murder.[56] The report, chaired by Sir Henry Fisher, proposed a number of recommendations; that the judges' rules should be overhauled, and that the safeguards provided to suspects, such as having a right to have a solicitor present during interrogation and the right of young people to have an appropriate adult present, should be made clearer.[57]

Following this case, the Royal Commission on Criminal Procedure (the Phillips Commission) proposed that an independent body be created to take over cases that the police decided to prosecute. If the prosecutor did not believe the case should be taken to court, then the prosecutor would have the authority to discontinue the case, have the charges changed or have the police investigate further in order to obtain more evidence.[58] The government accepted the majority of the recommendations made by the Phillips Commission. As highlighted above, this resulted in the Prosecution of Offenders Act 1985 and established the Crown Prosecution Service (CPS). The head of the CPS would be the Director of Public Prosecutions (DPP). The director's position was not a new creation; it was initially created in the late nineteenth century to advise the police on criminal matters and handle serious cases. Despite the CPS having a national identity, prosecutors were based locally, and the CPS was organized into areas that matched police forces, each headed by a chief prosecutor.

The Inquisitorial Prosecutor

In inquisitorial theory, the adversarial battle is replaced in the inquisitorial model by a pursuit of the truth that is unprompted by partisan party allegiances.[59] The inquisitorial prosecutor is responsible for the creation of a dossier of evidence that is used as the basis for the criminal trial at a later date. The prosecutor ensures that both inculpatory and exculpatory evidence is included. Should a prosecutor not act upon defense requests for further lines of enquiry to be followed up, the trial judge can postpone the trial until the investigation has been concluded.[60] A postponement in proceedings would cause a great deal of professional embarrassment to the prosecutor; they do not seek to establish themselves as one of the contending parties but as "dignitaries of the court."[61] Unlike his adversarial counterpart, the prosecutor and defense lawyer are not considered equal parties, whose contributions are both given an equal standing. The prosecutor is said to represent the wider public interest at both the trial and pretrial stage; he ensures that both the rights of the defendant and the effectiveness of the investigation are protected. The evidence submitted by the prosecutor is a result of the pretrial investigation; the argument submitted by the defense lawyer is seen to only represent the narrow interests of the accused.[62]

In the French legal system, the *juge d'instruction* is a mandatory form of supervision for the most serious of crimes.[63] However, this form of supervision is almost as rare as the adversarial jury trial in England and Wales.[64] The opening of "an information" is the prelude to instructing an examining magistrate, and this is only opened in 8 percent of criminal proceedings. Therefore, the police under the supervision of the *procureur* will investigate the vast majority of crimes. The police inform the *procureur* of all offences. There are three categories of offence in France: *crimes*, *délits*, and *contraventions*. Crimes are categorized as the most serious offences, such as murder. A *délits* offence is a less serious offence such as burglary or assault and *contraventions* are the least serious of offences. If the investigation concerns the most serious offence, an *information* is opened on the authority of the *procureur* and the case is passed to the *juge d'instruction* to supervise the investigation. In all other instances, the police are supervised by the *procureur*.[65]

The *procureur* is responsible for the investigation and prosecution of offences. In order to carry out this role, the *procureur* directs the police investigation and will supervise the garde à vue. However, despite being responsible for the supervision of the investigation, the interrogation of the suspect will often have already been carried out by the police[66] and therefore this renders any supervision retrospective. The *procureur* has the authority to release the suspect, extend the period of detention, or charge the suspect.

The Adversarial Judge: Less Investigator More interventionist?

The classic adversarial position of the judge is one who is both passive and impartial.[67] In the case of *Jones v National Coal Board*,[68] Lord Denning gave what is generally accepted as the classic premise of the position of the adversarial judge: "The judge's part is to hearken to the evidence, only asking questions of witnesses when it is necessary to clear up any point that has been overlooked . . . to see that advocates behave themselves and keep to rules laid down by law . . . to discourage repetition . . . if he goes beyond this, he drops the mantle of a judge and assumes the robe of an advocate."[69]

Lord Greene in *Yuill v Yuill*[70] stated that if a judge was to speak, "he . . . is liable to have his vision clouded by the dust of conflict." Both Lord Greene and Lord Denning appear to be clarifying the importance of the judge remaining impartial and passive. The common law in England and Wales states that it is the duty of the prosecution and defense to conduct the examination of all witnesses. The judge does not examine the witnesses himself, save for the fact that he may pose supplementary questions to the witness. The passive habit stems from the Middle Ages and it was once the original method of conducting criminal trials in all European countries. However, this procedure was abandoned in the twelfth century in favor of the inquisitorial procedure in many countries.[71] This notion of the impartial and passive judge ensures that he is free from any bias, and by remaining passive he will be able to perform his duty correctly: "[t]he duty most appropriate . . . is to attentively listen to all that is said on both sides. After performing the duty patiently and fully he is in a position to give a jury the full benefit of his thoughts on the subject."[72] However, with regard to the rights of the defendant, the judge can question a witness at some length. Lord Goddard stated that "if a judge thinks the case has not been thoroughly explored he is entitled to put as many questions as he likes."[73] However, there are limits to this provision. When a judge has intervened too frequently, the Court of Appeal has moved to quash the conviction in order to ensure that the notion of impartiality and passivity is retained. In

Gunning,[74] the defendant's conviction was quashed because of the number of judicial interventions; counsel asked 172 questions and the judge asked 165.

Further to questioning a witness, the judge does have the authority to call a witness. Despite having this authority, this power is rarely used although it can be used when its purpose is to assist the defense.[75] However, if the calling of a witness will, in effect, assume the role of the prosecution then this may lead to a quashed conviction. This situation occurred in the case of *Grafton*.[76] The Court of Appeal held that the judge had to remain impartial, his role was to direct the jury on points of law. By calling the witness, the judge had acted as if he had assumed the mantle of the prosecution. In the 1993 Crown Court Study, approximately 19 percent of judges questioned were aware of important witnesses who were not called by either side.[77] The Phillips Commission recommended that when judges are aware that an important witness has not been called, they should ask counsel to explain the absence of the witness, and if deemed necessary, the judge should urge counsel to rectify the situation. As a last resort, judges should be prepared to exercise their power to call witnesses.[78] However, as Zander notes, there is no evidence to suggest that either recommendation has been adopted.[79]

The danger posed by an intervening judge is clear to see; if a judge is overly interventionist, he runs the risk of appearing to favor one side over the other. In *R v Sharp*,[80] the Court of Appeal held that the judge "may be in danger of seeming to enter the arena in the sense that he may appear partial to one side or other. This may arise from a hostile tone of questioning or implied criticism of counsel who is conducting the examination or cross-examination." Thus, power to intervene should only be used to satisfy the minimal case management responsibilities of the judge. By making use of proper interventions, the judge is, in essence, managing the criminal trial. He is ensuring that proceedings are kept orderly and the rules of evidence and procedures are being followed. When intervening, the judge needs to ensure that the truth-finding process is not put at risk by his interventions, as can be seen by the case law illustrated; the judge's interventions may affect the fair trial process.

The Inquisitorial Judiciary

Despite the similarity in titles, the traditional concept of the role of the judiciary in the inquisitorial model is vastly different from his adversarial counterpart. The inquisitorial judge is viewed as the guarantor of individual liberties.[81] In order to fulfil this function, the judge has a broad range of tasks for which he is responsible. The judge may be responsible for the investigation, adjudication to determine the culpability of the accused, and the authorization of coercive measures that directly impinge on individual liberty; such measures can include telephone tapping or extending the period the suspect is remanded in custody without charge. Historically, the functions of investigation, prosecution, and trial were all the responsibility of a single individual[82] and in theory this remains the case today. In order to determine the culpability of the accused, the function of the *magistrate* is not merely to pass judgment on the evidence presented, but to conduct his own enquiries to determine the guilt or innocence of the defendant. This investigation may be conducted via direct questioning of the defendant or by insisting that the police carry out further investigations.

The judge is not only charged with the responsibility for the investigation but is also responsible for the discovery of the truth and therefore is charged with discovering both exculpatory and inculpatory evidence; he is, therefore, cast in more neutral terms than the *procurer*.[83] The inquisitorial model holds that the truth is best discovered by nonpartisan investigation, conducted by the judiciary. All other interests, including that of the accused, are subordinate to this theory. The inquisitorial theory holds that the truth cannot be discovered by a party contest that contains checks and balances. The truth is best discovered by "a concentration of power in the hands of one person, who represents neither the narrow interests of the defense or prosecution but what are claimed to be the wider interests of society."[84]

However, Hodgson found that the role of the judge is not as impartial in practice as it is in theory: "The guilt of the suspect is presumed, and denials are rejected. Evidence of violence committed against the suspect by the police was ignored and left for the defense to raise . . . the word of the victim or of the police was consistently preferred to that of the suspect; serious cases means an almost automatic request for a remand in custody, even where evidence is thin."[85]

Despite many jurisdictions implementing the position of an investigating judge, there is a danger that corruption or bias may infiltrate the judiciary. Jackson states that, over time, some officials may come to favor certain kinds of litigants than others. Psychological insight suggests that it is difficult for active investigators to suspend judgment and weigh up evidence dispassionately; ultimately this will allow that particular hypothesis to be pursued to the exclusion of others.[86] One *juge* interviewed by Hodgson was very proud of his record of only two cases he had been sent in ten years resulting in acquittals.[87] However, despite the efficiency of the *juge*, Germany abolished the role of examining magistrate in 1975 over doubts about the role, and, in 1988, Italy abolished the role after a corruption scandal.[88]

This section has sought to ascertain the position and function of the adversarial judge until the mid-1990s. In this period, the judge largely remained passive throughout proceedings. Despite having the authority to call and examine witnesses, neither power was invoked consistently or with any frequency. The accounts of the use of this particular authority are very few. In general, the judiciary appeared to remain true to the depiction of the passive umpire. At times, the judge had to dismiss this mantle and become interwoven in proceedings, but this was largely confined to the voir dire procedure. Despite sharing the same title, the role and the position of the inquisitorial judge is vastly different from that of his adversarial counterpart. The inquisitorial judge is deeply interwoven into the criminal proceedings. He possesses more investigative powers and he is charged with the responsibility of investigating the criminal offence. Throughout the course of this judicial investigation, all evidence will be considered, both inculpatory and exculpatory. In providing this account of the role of the judiciary in both an adversarial and inquisitorial setting, it will become clear how the changes in legislation in England and Wales over the last twenty years have altered the role of the judiciary. Chapter 7 will examine the extent to which the changes have affected the judiciary. In asking this pertinent question, the foundation established in this subchapter and its findings will be called upon.

CONCLUSION

This chapter has provided an account of the adversarial and inquisitorial approaches to criminal procedure, and the various roles within them. It was necessary to identify the key facets of both models and how they work in practice. This foundation will provide a basis for explaining and analyzing the impact of the CPIA 1996 and the CrimPR, both in respect of the role of criminal defense lawyers, and in relation to the characterization of the criminal process in England and Wales as "adversarial." With the adversarial trial being of such symbolic significance, any deviation from this viewpoint could have ramifications for the notion of justice itself. As such, this chapter explains the purpose of the criminal trial and the various actors who have different roles to play depending on the particular jurisdiction in which they work. This means that it is very difficult to transplant adversarial values into an inquisitorial procedure and vice versa. Therefore, any departure from a particular procedure will hold ramifications for all of the actors involved in the process.

NOTES

1. It is important to note that there are other approaches to criminal justice that exist outside the scope of adversarialism and inquisitorialism. However, the French approach is generally seen as the exemplar of the procedural tradition and as such that is why the inquisitorial procedure is viewed through the French lens.

For further reading on alternative models of criminal procedure, see R. Vogler, *A World View of Criminal Justice* (Aldershot: Ashgate Publishing, 2005) See Part III (p. 197) The Popular Justice Tradition, the model depends upon common sense understanding rather than upon law or regulation and it is a collective practice. The model is informal and the lack of procedural and evidential norms facilitates the direct involvement of the participants. The modern popular tradition can be divided into two broad categories, the *unmediated* and *mediated.* In the former, the power of the community to investigate and punish deviancy is absolute and uncontrolled by external influences. The *unmediated* is operated in a framework derived from other traditions such as adversarialism and inquisitorialism. For further examples, see F. Pakes *Comparative Criminal Justice* (2nd Edition, London: Willan Publishing, 2010) Chapters 5 & 6, P. L. Reichel, *Comparative Criminal Justice Systems: A Topical Approach* (4th Edition, New Jersey: Prentice Hall, 2004) Chapter 4, J Griffiths, "Ideology in Criminal Procedure or a Third model of criminal process. 1970 79 Yale LJ 359 and K, Roach, 'Four Models of Criminal Process" (1999) 89 *J Crim law and Criminology* 671.

2. C. M. Bradley, 'The Convergence of the Continental and Common Law Model of Criminal Procedure,' [1996], *7 Criminal Law Forum* Vol 471, 471.

3. L. Ellison, *The Adversarial Process and the Vulnerable Witness* (Oxford: Oxford University Press, 2001) at p. 142.

4. See Louise Ellison's comments in 'The Protection of Vulnerable witnesses in Court: An Anglo-Dutch Comparison' [1999] *International Journal of Evidence and Proof* Vol 3, 1.

5. Royal Commission on Criminal Justice, *Report* (London: HMSO, 1993), para 10.

6. J. Hodgson *Conceptions of the Trial in Inquisitorial and Adversarial Procedure* in A. Duff, *The Trial on Trial Volume 1, Truth and Due Process* (1st edition, Oxford: Hart, 2001) at p. 224.

7. As per Lord Eldon LC in ex p Lloyd (1822) Mont 70 at 72.

8. Although in certain instances, the defense will not seek an acquittal but a conviction for a lesser offence. For example, in the case of homicide, the defense may attempt to seek a conviction for involuntary manslaughter rather than murder.

9. M. Zander, *Cases and Materials on the English Legal System* (10th Edition, Cambridge: Cambridge University Press, 2007).

10. S. Landsman "The Decline of the Adversary System: How the Rhetoric of Swift and Certain Justice has Affected Adjudication in American Courts" [1980] *Buffalo Law Review* Vol 29(3), 487–529, 491.

11. L. Fuller, "The Forms and Limits of Adjudication" [1978] 92 Harv LR 353 at p. 383.

12. Ibid., at p. 48.

13. See Ellison, 'The Protection of Vulnerable Witnesses in Court' [1999] *The International Journal of Evidence & Proof* Vol 3(1), 29–43.

14. Ibid.

15. W. H. Simon, "The Ideology of Advocacy: Procedural Justice and Professional Ethics" [1978] *Wis LR* Vol 29, 43.

16. Ibid.

17. G. S. Moohr, "Prosecutorial Power in an Adversarial System: Lessons from Current White Collar Cases and the Inquisitorial Model" [2004] *Buffalo Law Review*, Vol 8, 193.

18. A. S. Goldstein and M. Marcus, "The Myth of Judicial Supervision in Three 'Inquisitorial' Systems: France, Italy and Germany" [1997] *Yale Law Journal* Vol 240, 268.

19. N. Jorg, S. Field and C. Brants, Are Inquisitorial and Adversarial Systems Converging? in *Criminal Justice in Europe: A Comparative Study* (Clarendon Press, Oxford, 1995) at p. 50.

20. A. Sanders and R. Young, *Criminal Justice* (3rd Edition, Oxford, Oxford University Press, 2007) at p. 14.

21. For discussion, see J. Hodgson *Conceptions of the Trial in Inquisitorial and Adversarial Procedure* in A. Duff, *The Trial on Trial Volume 1, Truth and Due Process* (Oxford: Hart, 2001).

22. See R. Ericson, *The State and Criminal Justice Reform* in R. Ratner and J. McMullan (eds), *State Control* (Vancouver: University of British Columbia Press, 1987).

23. K. Roach, "Four Models of the Criminal Process" [1999] *Journal of Criminal Law and Criminology* Vol 89(2), 672.

24. H. L. Packer, *The Limits of the Criminal Sanction* (California: Stanford University Press, 1968) at pp. 158–163.

25. M. R. Damaska, *The Faces of Justice and State Authority: A Comparative Approach to the Legal Process* (New Haven: Yale University Press, 1986) at pp. 57–62.

26. Ibid., at p. 50.

27. S. Summers, *Fair Trials and Procedural Tradition in Europe* (Oxford: Hart Publishing, 2007) at p. 29

28. Ibid., p. xix.

29. Ibid., p. 22.

30. Ibid., p. 27.

31. Because the model insists that both inculpatory and exculpatory evidence is included in the dossier.

32. S. Solley, The Role of the Advocate in M. McConville and Wilson (eds), *The Handbook of the Criminal Justice Process* (Oxford: Oxford University Press, 2002) at p. 312.

33. S.78(1) states that in any proceedings the court may refuse to allow evidence on which the prosecution proposes to rely to be given if it appears to the court that, having regard to all the circumstances, including the circumstances in which the evidence was obtained, the admission of the evidence would have such an adverse effect on the fairness of the proceedings that the court ought not to admit it.

34. L. Zedner, *Criminal Justice* (Oxford: Oxford University Press, 2004) at p. 169.

35. A. Sanders, *Victims with Learning Disabilities* (Oxford: Centre for Criminological Research, 1997) at p. 312.

36. J. McEwan, The Adversarial and Inquisitorial Models of Criminal Trial in *The Trial on Trial* Vol 1: Truth and Due Process (Oxford: Hart: Oxford, 2004) at p. 171.

37. S.141(1) Criminal Justice Act 2003 outlines the purposes of sentencing.

38. Ibid., at p. 172.

39. J. H. Langbein, *The Origins of the Adversary Criminal Trial* (Oxford University Press, 2003) at p. 6.

40. Ibid.

41. Article 6(1) European Convention on Human Rights

42. R Duff, *Trials and Punishments* (Cambridge: Cambridge University Press, 1986).

43. S. Field, "State Citizen and Character in French Criminal Process" [2006] *Journal of Law and Society* Vol 33(4), 523.

44. Ibid., at pp. 523–524.

45. Ibid., at p. 524.

46. Ibid., at p. 544.

47. J. Beattie, *Crime and the Courts in England 1660–1800* (New Jersey: Princeton University Press, 1986) at p. 253.

48. Ibid., at p. 58.

49. R. Duff, *Trials and Punishments* (Cambridge: Cambridge University Press, 1986) at p. 545.

50. Ibid., at p. 544.

51. Ibid.

52. The Royal Commission on the Police Cmnd. 1728 (London: HMSO, 1962).

53. For a further discussion on the police's use of solicitors and barristers in 1970s see Sigler J 'Public Prosecutions in England and Wales' [1974] Crim LR 642.

54. The Investigation of Criminal Offences in England and Wales: The Law and Procedure (Cmnd 8092-1) (London: HMSO, 1981) at pp. 49–52.

55. See Inquiry into the Circumstances leading to the Trial of Three Persons on Charges arising from the Death of Maxwell Confait (HCP 90) (London: HMSO, 1977).

56. Ibid.

57. For a further in-depth account of the Confait affair and the recommendations made by Sir Henry Fisher please see ibid.

58. Ibid., at Ch. 7.

59. M. Maguire, *Researching Street Criminals,* in R. D. King and E. Wincup, *Doing Research on Crime and Justice* (Oxford: Oxford University Press, 2008) at p. 142.

60. Ibid., at p. 143.

61. S. Field, P. Alldridge, and N. Jorg, "Prosecutors, Examining Judges and the Control of the Police Investigations" in C. Harding, P. Fennel, N. Jorg, and B. Swart, *Criminal Justice in Europe: A Comparative Study* (Oxford: Clarendon Press, 1995) at p. 234.

62. J. Hodgson, Conceptions of the Trial in Inquisitorial and Adversarial Procedure in *The Trial on Trial vol 1* (Oxford: Hart Publishing, 2001) at p. 232.

63. It is important to note that this section is primarily referring to France. In a number of inquisitorial jurisdictions, the role of the *juge* has been abolished. Germany abolished the role in 1974 and Italy followed suit in 1988. In the main, the role was seen to be "needless . . . and time consuming." See M. Delmas-Marty and J. Spencer, *European Criminal Procedures,* (Cambridge University Press: Cambridge, 2002) at p. 11.

64. Chapter 1 highlighted that approximately 94 percent of all criminal cases are heard in the magistrates' court.

65. J. Hodgson, "The Police, The Prosecutor and the Juge D'instruction: Judicial Supervision in France, theory and Practice" [2001] *British Journal of Criminology* Vol 41, 342–361 at 344.

66. Ibid., at pp. 343–346.

67. Langbein J, "The Criminal Trial Before Lawyers"; (1978) 45 U Ch LR 263 at p. 314.

68. [1957] 2 QB 55.

69. Ibid., at para 64

70. [1945] 1 All ER 183, 61 TLR 176.

71. G. Williams, *The Proof of Guilt* (London: Stevens and Sons, 1963) at p. 24.

72. Sir James Fitzjames Stephen, *History of the Criminal Law* (Kessinger Publishing, 1883) as cited in ibid. p. 26.

73. As Per Lord Goddard C. J. in Williams, *The Times*, April 26, 1955.

74. [1980] Crim LR 592.

75. See *R v Haringey Justices*, ex p DPP [1996], 1 All RT 828 and *Olivia* [1965] 1 WLR 1028.

76. [1992] Crim LR 826.

77. M. Zander and P. Henderson, *The Crown Court Study* (Royal Commission on Criminal Justice, Research Study No 19, 1993) section 4.3.12.

78. Ibid., p. 123.

79. M. Zander, Cases and Materials on the English Legal System, Tenth Edition, (Cambridge University Press, Cambridge, 2007) at p. 383.

80. [1993] 3 All ER 225, 235.

81. D. Salas "The Role of the Judge" in M. Delmas-Marty and J. R. Spencer (ed), *European Criminal Procedures'* (Cambridge: Cambridge University Press, 2002).

82. J. Hodgson, Conceptions of the Trial in Inquisitorial and Adversarial Procedure in the *The Trial on Trial* Volume 1 (Oxford: Hart Publishing, 2004) at p. 230.

83. J. Hodgson, "The Police, The Prosecutor and the Juge d'instruction: Judicial Supervision in France, Theory and Practice" [2001] *British Journal of Criminology*, Vol. 41, 342–361 at 357 at 347.

84. Ibid., at p. 356.

85. Ibid., at p. 357.

86. J. Jackson and S. Doran *Judge Without Jury* (Oxford: Clarendon Press, 1995) at p. 68.

87. See J. Hodgson, "The Police, the Prosecutor and the juge d'instruction: Judicial Supervision in France Theory and Practice" [2001] *British Journal of Criminology* Vol. 41, 342–367 at 357.

88. For an in-depth discussion on the rationale behind the abolition of the examining magistrate in Germany and Italy please R. Vogler *A World View of Criminal Justice* (Aldershot: Ashgate Publishing, 2005) at p. 166.

Chapter 2

The Genesis of Adversarialism

Before an examination of the defense lawyer's role can begin, it is important to analyze the forum in which he operates. Whilst the previous chapter analyzed the purpose(s) of the criminal trial, this chapter will look at how the trial has organically evolved and allowed the defense lawyer to become one of, if not the, central actors in the process. The chapter will begin with an historical account of the adversarial criminal trial in England and Wales; this subsection will chart the origins of the criminal trial and follow its transformation into the modern adversarial trial. This examination will also analyze the initial rationale for the prohibition on defense counsel in the criminal trial that existed until the early eighteenth century. Furthermore, the chapter will examine how he exerted his influence in court to transform himself from an unwanted outcast to becoming one of the key actors in the criminal justice process. Similarly, the structure of this chapter will utilize 1996 as the genesis of the modern era, as discussed in the introduction.

THE ALTERCATION: THE VICTIM VERSUS THE ACCUSED

One of the earliest views on the modern criminal trial is stated by Langbein to be Thomas Smith's *De Republica Anglorum*, written in 1565.[1] Smith depicts a hypothetical felony trial held in a provincial assize court. Here the victim, and witnesses supporting the victim's version of the alleged incident, engage the defendant in a confrontational dialogue about the circumstances of the offence. At the end of the altercation between the two, the question for the jury was whether the accused had adequately explained away the evidence adduced against him.[2] Owing to the lack of counsel, the trial judge organized the admission and presentation of the evidence in court. It was he who examined both the prisoner and witnesses and he would make comments on their testimony as it was being given. Thus, the judge would effectively act as both examiner and cross-examiner.[3] At times the judge may have consulted the pretrial examinations of the witnesses and the accused that the committing magistrate would have prepared and filed with the court. The power to conduct an early form of the committal hearing was permitted by the Statutes of Philip and Mary of 1554 and 1555 (also known as the Marian statutes). This statute allowed the Justice of the Peace (hereafter, JP) to take the statements of suspects and witnesses in the cases of petty crime.[4] The JP would compel the victim and witnesses to attend trial to testify against the accused and would also question the prisoner. In essence, the JP was freezing the evidence so that it remained accurate and fresh for trial. This practice restricted the scope for any doubt or inconsistency to seep into the mind of the witnesses.

The Marian system injected a strong prosecutorial bias into the legal system. The JP did not serve as a neutral investigator of an incident; it was his job to aid the accuser in building their case against the accused. A day or so prior to the trial, a grand jury would decide whether or not to approve the prosecution's case, in a process known as the Prosecutor's Bill. To support the bill, the prosecution witnesses would testify in front of the grand jury. If the grand jury decided to approve the bill, it was then sent for trial. If the bill appeared groundless or insubstantial it would be rejected, and the defendant was saved from the humiliation of a public trial. In essence, the grand jury acted as a filtering mechanism to weed out the weak cases that held little substance. The Marian statute did not allow any disclosure of the prosecution's case to the accused; it was thought that the truth would be revealed by the unprepared answers of the accused hearing the allegations for the first time. The jury's decision of guilt or innocence would be based on his immediate and unprepared responses. It was thought that the ignorance of the accused was essential to the trial process.[5] The defense lawyer played no part in the early development of the criminal trial. It seems to have been generally agreed that it was best for the accused to be unrepresented at trial, as this gave the greatest opportunity for discovering the "truth." Furthermore, the sincerity of his denials would further demonstrate his innocence for the jury to see.[6]

Cases of High Treason

The late seventeenth century was a period of great instability in English politics and three major treason trials from 1678 to 1685 would prove to be landmark events. These trials led to subsequent criminal procedural reform that culminated in lifting the prohibition on defense counsel at trial and the defense lawyer entered the trial arena. The Popish Plot was an alleged conspiracy on the part of Catholics to murder King Charles II. Titus Oates claimed he had overheard a plot to murder the king whilst he was in France. Upon hearing these accusations, William Bedloe came forward and confirmed and embellished the accusations made by Oates. Upon his death, his brother, James, would succeed Charles as king. It was James's personal secretary, Edward Coleman, who was the alleged ringleader for the assassination. Oates had sworn his testimony to London Magistrate Sir Edmund Berry Godfrey, who then mysteriously disappeared and was later found dead in circumstances that indicated murder and ultimately confirmed the plot to kill the king. The treason trial lasted from 1678 to 1680 and the trials were described as "six memorable failures of justice, involving the sacrifice of no less than fourteen innocent lives."[7] As the trials wore on, Oates's web of lies and deceit become uncontrollable. He was eventually prosecuted for perjury and although the sanction did permit the death penalty, the judge claimed Oates's crime was "infinitely more odious than common murder."[8]

The enactment of the Treason Act 1696 marked the first step in permitting the defendant to be represented by defense counsel. During the Popish Trials it was said that "the prisoner is half or more than half, proved to be an enemy of the King, and that, in the struggle between the King and the suspected men, all advantages are to be secured for the King."[9] The preamble of the Treason Act 1696 took a different approach to the assumed guilt of the suspects, and raised the notion that the defendant may be innocent; "[N]othing is more just and reasonable than that person prosecuted for High Treason . . . should not be debarred of all just and equal means for the defense of their innocence in such cases."[10] The Act permitted those accused of treason to have the assistance of defense counsel at both the pretrial and trial stages. The Act also granted the accused the right to obtain "a true copy of the whole indictment but not the names of the witnesses [at least] five days at least before [the trial]."[11] Linked to the disclosure of the indictment was the right to speak to counsel during the pretrial process.[12] By disclosing this information, the defendant could speak to his counsel to plan his defense. Section 1 of the Act also permitted the defendant to "advise with Counsel thereupon, to plead and make their defense." Coupled with this right to seek an advanced copy of the indictment, the defendant would be better prepared for questions as defense counsel could probe the legal sufficiency of the prosecution's case. Further to the disclosure of the prosecution's case and the pretrial preparation, the Act also allowed the defendant to receive a "full defense" at trial. However, defense counsel was only permitted in cases of treason; counsel was still not permitted to enter ordinary felony cases.[13] If a case would be tried as a *felony*, the prosecution would also not be represented by counsel. There were five reasons that ensured treason trials were demarcated as a procedural world of their own:[14]

1. Prosecutorial Imbalance: The late Stuart cases, outlined above, indicated there was a potential imbalance between the prosecuting lawyer and the unrepresented accused. This notion of imbalance stemmed from prosecutorial misconduct, such as reliance on perjured testimony and the inequality of the procedure to convict the defendant. The prosecution was permitted to hire as many members of counsel as required, whereas the defendant was left unrepresented. In an ordinary *felony* case, the victim or kin of the victim acted as the prosecutor and he was not the beneficiary of vast state resources funding the search for witnesses and other evidence to support the prosecution's story.
2. Judicial Bias: The subservience of the court to the king was a problem perceived to be specific to treason trials. Most treason trials took place in London under the watchful gaze of the Crown, and the judges were handpicked for the trials. Langbein states that whilst the Crown had an acute interest in the outcome of a treason trial, it had no direct interest in whether a defendant was found guilty of stealing sheep.[15] As such, defense representation at trial was thought to be necessary.
3. The Complexity: Ordinary crimes were thought to involve more reliable proofs. Murder, burglary, stealing sheep are examples of crimes that would leave eye-witnesses or other physical evidence. The evidence that was used in treason trials was generally as simple as someone overhearing a plot to kill the king. The case of the Popish Plot underlined the dangers of false testimony being admitted and therefore a greater propensity of evidential probing by counsel was required. It would be impossible to think an unrepresented defendant, who has no knowledge of the charge, would be able to comprehend and probe the evidence the prosecution had advanced. Hence, the defense lawyer was allowed into the trial process.
4. Preserving the "Accused Speaks" Trial: As treason trials were relatively rare, there was no threat that permitting the defense lawyer into the court would diminish the traditional "Accused Speaks" trial. As such the defendant would not lose his voice in the courtroom.[16] Further to this, the courts desire to find the "truth" would also not be lost.
5. Evening Up: By permitting the defendant to be represented by defense counsel, the Treason Act was evening up the playing field because the Crown was represented by the prosecution. The preamble of the Act states that a defendant "should not be debarred of all just and equal means."

It is clear from the drafting of the Act that its intention was to afford safeguards to the defendant by way of pretrial disclosure and representation by counsel. However, whilst being mindful to protect the defendant from further miscarriages of justice, the drafters carefully restricted the right to defense representation to treason trials alone. This chapter moves on to examine how the defense lawyer became a part of not only treason trials but of all criminal trials.

Enter the Lawyer: From Lawyer Free to Lawyer-Dominated Trials

During the latter part of the sixteenth century, judges resolutely enforced the prohibition on defense counsel, despite some emphatic comments from the juristic literature of the period. One Elizabethan writer explained that even in cases where the prosecution is represented by counsel "no man is suffered to defend, instruct or speak for the accused: which is the greatest injustice that can be devised; and no doubt but innocent infinite blood is shed by this means, and lyeth upon the heads of our judges [and] juries."[17] The victim of the alleged crime acted as the prosecution and, in cases of homicide, the victim's kin or the local coroner assumed the role of prosecutor.[18] The prohibition on defense counsel in felony trials applied to matters of fact as opposed to matters of law.[19] A prisoner would be assigned defense counsel when the court recognized that a legal question would require discussion. The defense counsel was not viewed as a partisan advocate of his client's rights; he acted as an *amicus curiae* rather than the representative of the accused.[20] However, the vast majority of defendants raised no objections at this stage and entered a plea of not guilty. Sir Edward Coke explained that the defendant only entered the trial process after he had entered a plea, "which goeth to the fact best known to the [accused] . . . shall [he] have no counsel to give evidence, or allege any matter for him."[21] It was thought that it was to the accused's advantage to argue his own case as he would know more about the facts of the incident than any lawyer. William Hawkins best encapsulated this notion when he claimed: "[I]t requires no manner of skill to make a plain and honest defense [because] the simplicity and innocence, artless and ingenuous behavior of one whose conscience acquits him, ha[s] something in it more moving and convincing than the highest eloquence of persons speaking in a cause not their own."[22]

If the defendant was also represented at trial, it would inhibit the court from treating the accused as an informational resource. Judges and juristic writers feared that counsel would speak for the accused and thereby diminish his worth as an informational resource. Furthermore, there were concerns that the defensive tactics of defense lawyers could impair the ability of the court to adjudicate accurately.[23] However, it would not be long until the defense lawyer entered the court room as an advocate for the accused in all crimes.

Departure from the Prohibition of Defense Counsel

During the 1730s,[24] the judiciary began to depart from the rule that prohibited defense counsel in ordinary felony cases. Counsel was permitted at trial for the limited purpose of examining and cross-examining witnesses. However, defense counsel was denied the opportunity to address the jury. This forced him to either do nothing or to cross-examine the witness. This act was somewhat futile as the defense counsel did not possess an evidential base on which he could effectively challenge or discredit the prosecution witnesses, as they were not entitled to copies of the witnesses' depositions.[25] The lack of opportunity to address the jury further inhibited the role of the defense counsel because the lawyer could not explain the significance of the witnesses' answer, therefore, the significance had to be clear from the question and answer itself. This led to counsel asking leading questions throughout the cross-examination and Fitzjames Stephen suggested that "the cross-examination tended to become a speech thrown into the form of questions."[26]

Defense lawyers were keen to maximize their opportunity to address the jury at trial, despite being prohibited from doing so. William Garrow, a defense lawyer at the Old Bailey, successfully circumvent the limits on defense lawyers. He became renowned for his intimidating and aggressive cross-examinations.[27] Garrow used cross-examination in order to address the jury, despite the prohibition on such behavior. He told the court, "I had a right, if I could, indirectly to convey observations to the fact; and whatever other people may say, I shall certainly take the liberty of doing it; for what the law of England will not permit me to do directly, I will do indirectly, where I can."[28] What Garrow is effectively saying is "I will do anything I can get away with."[29] The notion of the defense lawyer acting as a zealous advocate for his client was advanced by another Old Bailey practitioner, John Silvester, when he stated, "My Lord, it is my duty standing here as a counsel for the prisoner to take every objection that lays in my power for a man standing in his unfortunate situation."[30]

It is at this moment that the criminal trial takes its first steps in departing from the "accused speaks" mode of trial to what has become the modern form of adversarial criminal trial. The removal of the prohibition on defense lawyers in criminal trials did not come without restrictions. By 1780, the accused's counsel was playing a greater role in the trial proceedings. In one instance, the court told the accused if there were "any questions omitted you think proper to have your counsel ask, write them down and send them over . . . [D]o not (you) put the questions yourself, but hand it to your counsel."[31] The late seventeenth and early eighteenth centuries were pivotal in transforming the criminal trial from the "accused speaks" to a more lawyer-dominated trial. Those early adversarial battles provided an early example of a conflict of interests that the contemporary defense lawyer is faced with. The ethos of the adversarial battle conflicted with the notion that fidelity to the truth should place bounds upon counsel's service to his client.[32] When the judges of the 1730s first permitted defense counsel to act as a safeguard against the prospect of a mistaken conviction, they limited his role by permitting him only to examine and cross-examine witnesses. It was thought that he would supplement the accused conducting his own defense and the "accused speaks" trial would live on. The defense lawyer slowly encroached into the domain of the trial; the role evolved into one where the counsel would write statements for the prisoner and ask questions in court on his behalf. As such, the accused speaks trial was unofficially dead.

Lifting the Restrictions on the Role of the Defense Lawyer

Between 1821 and 1837, Parliament debated the role of the defense lawyer and his role in the criminal trial. This debate resulted in the Trials for Felonies Act 1836 (this is more commonly known as the Prisoner's Counsel Act) and the Judicial Practice Memorandum of 1837. These two provisions abolished the restriction on the role of the defense lawyer; all prisoners were now entitled to a defense lawyer and the defense lawyer was not constrained by the restriction to only conduct the cross-examination and examination of witnesses. The second major change made by this legislation was the right acquired by prisoners to demand copies of the depositions made by prosecutorial witnesses. Here, we can see the evolution of the adversarial criminal process; not only were prisoners afforded representation, but they also now receive a form of pretrial disclosure. The issue of the prisoner being afforded the right to a full defense[33] had been debated a number of times in Parliament. The first phase of debate started with the introduction of the Capital Crimes Bill in 1821. However, from 1821 to 1826, the bill could not gain sufficient support to be passed by the House of Commons. The trial still viewed as an "investigation for the truth" and the full introduction of defense counsel would render the trial as a "war of wit, ingenuity and eloquence" all of which are incompatible with the criminal trial.[34] Cairns believes supporters of the bill were of the opinion that ingenuity and eloquence were conducive to the discovery of truth by presenting a forum where the facts of the case could be fully discussed by either side. The relationship between the truth and advocacy emerged as the major issue in Prisoner's Counsel Act debate.[35]

In 1836, the *Second Report* of the Criminal Law Commissioners[36] was published. This report fully endorsed a full right to defense counsel. The commissioners criticized the traditional stance that the truth of the offence would manifest from the prisoner's unprepared testimony as both "strange and unreasonable." The Prisoner's Counsel Act brought about an immediate and far-reaching transformation of criminal procedure. The Act replaced "the rough-and-ready procedure of the eighteenth and early nineteenth centuries into the scrupulous adversarial trial of today."[37] The Act permitted all persons who were tried for felonies to be granted permission to a full defense by a lawyer.[38] The Act also permitted a person bailed or committed to prison to be entitled, on demand, to copies of the examination of witnesses on whose deposition they have been held for the sum of three and a half pence for each folio of ninety words.[39]

The introduction of defense counsel to the criminal trial disentangled two activities that were previously the sole responsibility of the unrepresented defendant; it was the duty of the defense lawyer to probe whether the prosecution had submitted a tenable case, and the lawyer would offer evidence of a defensive nature to rebut the prosecution's allegations. The defense lawyer was able to insist on asking on the judge whether the prosecution had discharged their burden of adducing sufficient evidence to support a verdict in its favor. The defense lawyer would typically move for a verdict of an acquittal at the conclusion of the prosecution's evidence. If a judge overruled this, the defense would then present its evidence.[40] Further, the inclusion of the defense lawyer changed the structure of the trial; he broke up the dual roles of speaking and defending that had previously been the responsibility of the accused. He assumed the role of defender; he insisted on prosecutorial burdens of proof and largely shut down the role of the accused.[41] The trial had evolved; the new "lawyer-dominated" trials were no longer the place the accused merely aired his response to the charge, but became the forum in which the accused's defense counsel tested the prosecution's case and adversarialism was born.

The Accused Speaks Again?

Although the central purpose of the criminal trial was to use the accused as an informational resource and therefore to hear him "speak," he was not considered a witness because he spoke unsworn at trial. The disqualification on sworn testimony of the accused was lifted by the Criminal Evidence Act 1898.[42] The Act was enacted during a period of the widespread use of capital punishment. In Parliament, repeated references were made that compelling the accused to testify at trial was putting him in a position to put a noose around his own neck as the prisoner would be compelled to answer "a question [that may lead him] to convict himself, and thus put the noose round his neck by his own word of mouth."[43] Parliamentary debates continued and concerns were raised that compelling the accused to speak at trial would bring English law in line with the inquisitorial approach to the trial as adopted in France. Here, there were mounting concerns that prisoners could be turned "inside out, to supplement a case that the [prosecution] have not been able to prove."[44]

The Twentieth-Century Defense Lawyer

The early twentieth century saw the continuation of the "testing the prosecution's case" form of trial. The defense lawyer was firmly established as a key actor in the criminal justice process. In fact, the position and role of the defense lawyer gained further importance as access to legal representation was increased. The Poor Prisoner's Defense Act 1903 established that legal aid would be provided for trials on indictment for serious offences, where this would be in the interests of justice. It was not only the defense lawyer's role at trial that grew in importance during the early part of the twentieth century; the defense lawyer was also becoming more active at the pretrial stage. The Judges' Rules 1912 stated that suspects should be able to consult with a solicitor, albeit with a caveat that this caused the police no unreasonable hindrance.[45] This reaffirmed the position of the "testing of the prosecution's case" in favor of replacing the "accused speaks" trial.

Whilst the availability of defense representation via legal aid was increased by the Poor Prisoners Act 1903, judges were encouraged not to actively advertise that access to legal advice was readily available.[46] However, attempts to keep the right to legal advice under wraps were effectively removed by the advent of the Legal Aid and Advice Act 1949. In theory, the Act would have a great impact on the defense lawyer's role: the Act provided for legal representation for all except those who could not by any reasonable view be regarded as appropriate for state aid at all. In 1950, the Council of Europe recognized the importance of the defense lawyer's role in the criminal justice process in the European Convention on Human Rights.[47] This is an international treaty that protects the human rights and fundamental freedoms of citizens of member states of the Council of Europe. Article 6 is the provision that protects the right to a fair trial. In particular, Article 6(3)(c) allows a defendant to either defend himself or be defended through legal assistance of his choosing. Should he not be able to afford legal assistance, it is to be given to him free when it is in the interests of justice. If a case exhibits one or more of these features, then it is a case that prima facie is one in which the interests of justice require that legal representation be provided.[48] Following the recommendations, the Criminal Justice Act 1967[49] set out the guidelines governing when the use of legal aid should be authorized. Section 75(1) stated that the court shall grant legal aid when it is desirable in the interests of justice and the court should make such an order where a person is committed to court on a charge of murder,[50] or where the prosecutor appeals or applies for leave to appeal from the Criminal Division of the Court of Appeal, or from the Courts Martial Appeal Court to the House of Lords.[51] The 1967 Act also imposed a disclosure obligation on the defense lawyer; should the accused be relying on an alibi as part of the defense, Section 11 of the Act states he must inform the police of this in advance of trial so this can be checked. This will be further analyzed later in the book, when the evolution of the disclosure regime is analyzed. For context, it was important to outline the beginnings of a statutory regime here.

Despite the growing influence of the defense lawyer, it was found that defense representation in the magistrates' courts was still very much a minority activity. A report by Justice in 1971 called for a greater role for the defense in the criminal justice process as some 96 percent of defendants in the magistrates' court were unrepresented.[52] The importance of defense representation was highlighted by the Widgery Committee when it said that "the object of the legal aid system should be to secure that injustice does not arise though an accused person being prevented by lack of means from bringing effectively before the court matters which may constitute a defense to the charge or mitigate the gravity of the offence."[53]

The Justice report highlighted the dangers faced by unrepresented defendants. The report stated that a "majority of defendants sentenced to the most serious penalties available to the magistrates are unrepresented."[54] In order to rectify the disproportionate treatment of unrepresented defendants, Justice called for the establishment of a Duty Solicitor Scheme. The Widgery Committee considered the merits of such a scheme but arrived at the conclusion that such a scheme was impractical considering the scale that would be necessary for its implementation in England and Wales.[55] The Justice report was not persuaded by this and stated that the scheme had many merits; primarily it would provide assistance to a large number of defendants who would otherwise not receive any legal advice. This advice would be offered at the first stage of legal proceedings, where the suspect was still in a position to make up his mind how he wished to plead. The duty solicitor could help make up their mind by offering professional advice as opposed to rumor, suspicion or police pressure and imagined fear of consequences.[56]

A Theoretical Conception of the Defense Lawyer

As the introduction to this chapter stated, there is not one standard definition of the role of the defense lawyer. Thus, a coherent account of the role of the criminal defense lawyer will be developed using a variety of sources, and this theoretical ideal will be tested in subsequent chapters when comparisons are drawn with the workings of the defense lawyer in practice. This comparison will allow a conclusion to be drawn regarding the differences between the theoretical role of the defense lawyer and the role in practice in the context of the disclosure legislation and the CrimPR.

This section will attempt to clarify the theoretical position of the defense lawyer starting in the eighteenth and nineteenth centuries. However, details on the theoretical conception of the lawyer during this period are scant. In fact, it was not until the 1960s that academic writing concentrated on the theoretical conception of the defense lawyer and that collection of literature originated in the United States. Between the 1960s until the early 1980s, there was a great deal of scholarly work concerning the theory behind the role of the adversarial defense lawyer. As such, a great deal of this work is used to establish my own "classic conception" of the defense lawyer's role. Whilst in practice, there is some question as to whether the adversarial defense lawyer may actually exist, the theory provides a useful starting point for analysis, as this classic conception can be tested against the empirical fieldwork later in the book. It will provide a baseline for what an adversarial defense lawyer should do and look like. The empirical findings can examine if this type of lawyer exists and if they do not exist; the findings can extrapolate traits from this defense to classify what the lawyers look like. As previously discussed, the criminal defense lawyer in the seventeenth century was seen as an unnecessary addition to the criminal process; as this chapter has illustrated, the court was deemed to be better suited to protecting the accused than any lawyer. To emphasize the point that the lawyer was deemed superfluous, Sir Edward Coke observed that "it is far better for a prisoner to have a judge's opinion for him, than many counsellors at the Bar. The judges . . . have special care of the indictment and see that justice be done to the party."[57] In this statement, Coke is effectively reinforcing the notion that the defense lawyer is an unnecessary addition to the trial; the judge can carry out the role that a prisoner would want a lawyer to carry out. In the early eighteenth century, there was growing unease about the reliability of the evidence generated by both the prosecution and defense counsel.[58] There are examples of the defense lawyer being cast in a shady or murky light. Langbein cites an example of a lawyer who, with three other people, concocted a false highway robbery in order to claim the reward of £40. One witness claimed that the lawyer told him that it was his business to "set people together by the Ears and foment Law-Suits."[59] It is clear from these examples that the common notion of the defense lawyer in the seventeenth and eighteenth centuries was someone who may not be trustworthy and certainly someone who did not have the interests of justice in the forefront of their mind; they would rather further their own selfish goals of self-gain instead of dealing with their clients justly. This chapter will now address how the theoretical conception of the defense lawyer has evolved over time.

The Defense Lawyer's Role: The Zealous Advocate?

When considering the role of the defense lawyer, there is a danger oversimplifying it as one that merely advances the interests of the client. This simplified view does not allow any room for other values that, at times, the defense lawyer may have to promote ahead of his client's interests. The role of the defense lawyer can be seen to operate on three interwoven levels: firstly, he is the mouthpiece of his client; secondly, he is an officer of the court; and finally, he acts as a zealous protector of the rights of his client.[60] Despite being charged with advancing his client's case, the defense lawyer's obligation to his client is, at times, tempered by obligations owed to other parties in the criminal justice process; this notion was expressed by Lord Reid in the case of *Rondel v Worsley*:[61]

> Counsel has a duty to fearlessly raise every issue, advance every argument and ask every question, however distasteful, which he thinks will help his client's case. But as an officer of the court concerned with the administration of justice, he has an overriding duty to the court, to the standards of his profession and to the public, which may and often lead to a conflict with his client's wishes.[62]

It is clear from this statement that the role of the defense lawyer is not as clear-cut as merely advancing the case of his client and acting in his best interest. At times, he will be charged with actively engaging in ethical decision-making. These ethical obligations will be discussed at a later stage; this initial stage is attempting to construct a theoretical conception of the defense lawyer. It has been claimed that the defense lawyer operates on the horns of a trilemma: he needs to accumulate as much knowledge about the case as possible; to hold it in confidence; and yet to never mislead the courts.[63] The adversarial criminal process in England and Wales is rooted in the image of the defense lawyer acting as the accused's shield from the powerful state; this notion has in turn cultivated the ideal of neutral partisanship becoming a central tenet of the role of the defense lawyer.[64] This duty of neutral partisanship reflects a dual part of the adversarial ethos; the accused is to be adequately protected from the "oppressive" state, and the truth is best discovered by arguments on both sides of the question.[65] Despite this notion of "zealous advocacy" being the root of the adversarial process and the best way to discover the truth, very little is said on how the ethical implications should underpin the role of the defense lawyer. Does the notion of zealous advocacy permit the lawyer to take advantage of any legal point that favors his client; should the defense lawyer be so aggressive in challenging the prosecution's witnesses that their evidence is rendered weak, muddled, or confusing?[66] It is clear that part of the defense lawyer's role is to act as a zealous advocate in advancing his client's best interests, but how is this primary goal tempered by various obligations to other parties? To answer that, the obligations placed on the defense lawyer will be examined to ascertain how they impact the role.

Following Lord Reid's judgement in *Rondel v Worsley*, the obligations of the lawyer's role can be deconstructed into three core duties:

1. The duty to the client
2. The duty to the court and the administration of justice
3. The duty to the public

The Duty to the Client

The defense lawyer's duty to the client is well recognized and the sources used to research this chapter have given numerous symbolic illustrations of the role of the defense lawyer. He is seen to be the "gladiator of the accused,"[67] a "fearless knight,"[68] and the "hired gun."[69] These epithets express the notion that the defense lawyer acts as the accused's fearless protector, unafraid to protect the accused from the "over-zealous" state and ready at will to advance his client's case. In theory, the defense lawyer becomes an "extension of the client's will"[70] as it is the defense lawyer who presents the facts of the accused's case to the court. In essence, the lawyer says, "all that the client would say for himself (were he able to do so)."[71]

The Partisan Defense Lawyer

An example of a partisan defense lawyer can be identified from Lord Reid's speech in *Rondel v Worsley*;[72] he is one who fearlessly raises every issue, advances every argument and asks every question, however distasteful, which he thinks will help his client's case. Coupling this quote with the symbolic illustrations above, a common thread occurs; the defense lawyer's loyalty to his client. This basic level of loyalty is well illustrated by O'Dair when he says that the duty of the defense lawyer is to present the facts of the case "as persuasively as he can . . . as seen from the standpoint of his client's interests."[73] By presenting the facts as persuasively as he can, the lawyer transforms himself into a part of his client's will. The issues he raises and the presentation of facts favor his client's perspective; they are presented in a way that his client would present, if he could.

The notion of fearlessness and partisanship are often interwoven. In order to give a full defense to a suspect, the defense lawyer must be fearless in his approach to protection. The client will often meet a lawyer post-arrest and therefore he is already in the police station, which can be viewed as a hostile environment for a suspect. The police will interrogate the suspect in order to extract a confession from him; this can then be used as a basis for the trial.

The questioning may well be hostile and, as such, the defense lawyer will need to act with both "courage and devotion"[74] in order to protect his client. As Lord Reid identified, a partisan defense lawyer must do all he can to advance his client's case, which also includes being prepared to do "whatever it takes to improve the client's position."[75] As such, he may offend others who may be uncomfortable with his actions; he may have to ignore certain evidence in order to present his client's case in a more favorable light and to induce the jury or judge to find a verdict that is favorable to the client. This is one example of the tension and conflict that the defense lawyer faces; as a partisan defender of the accused, he is not concerned with seeking the truth. He has an aim of what will best serve his client and then he attempts to persuade others to reach a decision that will fulfil that aim. This potential truth-defeating goal may run counter to the other duties owed by the defense lawyer to the other actors and participants in the criminal justice process. Despite causing a potential conflict with the defense lawyer's other obligations, the principle of partisanship is described as the "virtue that trumps all other values and virtues."[76] Therefore, the obligation of partisanship takes precedence over the other obligations the defense lawyer has; namely, to the court and the public. This notion is supported by Charles Curtis, who said that the "lawyer's official duty . . . is to devote himself to the client. The [duty to the] court comes second."[77]

A key element of being a fearless partisan advocate is assertiveness; this is clear when the lawyer is faced with a prosecution witness. In these circumstances, the priority of the defense is clear; at times he may have to " go after the [witness] aggressively—to destroy [their] credibility or even reputation—when the alternative is that the client will be hurt."[78] Another aggressive tactic the partisan defense lawyer has at his disposal is the weapon of an ambush defense. This occurs when a defense lawyer introduces evidence at trial at the last possible moment; it does not allow the prosecution a chance to rebut, so this evidence may result in an acquittal. For example, if a defense lawyer spots a flaw in the prosecution's case, he should point it out to the judge or jury. However, not pointing the flaw out, whilst possibly being beneficial to the client, is frowned upon by the court: "to look the other way and not point it out . . . is to violate your commitment as a lawyer."[79] These tactics can be used as effective weapons for the partisan criminal defense lawyer in the fight to protect his client and further their interests. It is clear, though, that these weapons may conflict with the other obligations the lawyer owes to both the court and to the public.

The notion of partisanship is permitted in an adversarial environment; a long-standing ethic of adversarial justice is that it is better to allow a number of criminals to go free rather than to subject one innocent individual to be wrongfully convicted.[80] This cornerstone principle of the adversary justice system gives rise to the notion of partisan representation because "the criminal justice system is less a device for discovering the truth than it is a series of 'screens' designed to make it exceedingly difficult for the innocent to be convicted."[81] Therefore, by the permitting of a rigorous, aggressive, partisan defense, wrongful convictions should be rare in their occurrence as the prosecution's case has to pass through the many "screens." The process becomes more expansive, transparent, and in theory protects the innocent and only allows convictions to be based on comprehensively examined evidence. Without the partisan participation of the defense lawyer, the adversarial justice system would mirror its inquisitorial counterpart, which has far fewer "screens" for a conviction to pass through.

The Duty to the Court and the Administration of Justice

In *Rondel v Worsley*, Lord Reid explained that the lawyer not only owes a duty to his client but also to other interested parties. The second duty owed by the defense lawyer that will be used to illustrate the theoretical conception of the defense lawyer is the duty to the court. It is important to explain that in this context the duty owed to the court will encompass more than a duty to the physical courtroom. For the purpose of this chapter, the "court" shall include other "officers of the court" namely the prosecution, judge, and jurors. Therefore, when the term "court" is used in this section, it is including those other actors as outlined. The defense lawyer is not interested in the moral truth of a matter, he is said to owe "an allegiance to the higher cause of truth, justice and the public interest."[82] The term "higher cause" gives the impression that the allegiance owed to truth, justice, and the public interest should override other duties the defense lawyer has. Truth and justice are interwoven elements of the adversarial process, but they are not the same. "Truth" may represent what "actually" happened in relation to a criminal offence. Truth is defined by the *Oxford English Dictionary* as "that which is true or in accordance with fact or reality."[83] The adversary system is based on the notion that the "truth is best discovered by powerful statements on both sides of the question."[84] This very definition accepts that whilst powerful statements aid in answering the question, it accepts that both the defense and prosecution's version of events may not be entirely truthful. The *Oxford English Dictionary* defines "justice" as "the quality of being fair and reasonable."[85] Therefore, the term "justice" is more concerned with the fairness of the procedural process rather than ascertaining the truth of what actually happened. How the defense lawyer assists the court to arrive at the point of achieving both truth and justice is what will aid the construction of this theoretical conception of the defense lawyer.

It is clear that securing both truth and justice is at the forefront of the defense lawyer's responsibilities. The defense lawyer may "not do everything legally permissible to promote his client's cause."[86] As such, it appears that the duty to the court is paramount and the lawyer's duty to the client is secondary to fulfilling the obligation to the court. If the duty to the client should be the primary duty the defense lawyer owes, he would be permitted to do anything, so long as it was legal, to advance the case of the client. However, this is not the case and the duty owed to the court appears to take precedence over the other duties. Therefore, the lawyer cannot look to delay proceedings by manufacturing a situation that would lead to a delay; therefore, he must ensure that the procedural justice system runs efficiently.

An ambush defense is an acceptable tactic to employ when furthering a client's case as part of being a partisan advocate; however, when furthering the duty to the court, an ambush defense is strongly discouraged. It is thought that an ambush approach allows the defense a strategic advantage but it "denies the fundamental principles of fairness."[87] Tactics to delay proceedings and ambush defenses are tools that the partisan defense lawyer can employ but they do not necessarily advance the client's case. As an officer of the court, the defense lawyer must take steps to ensure that he is not blinded by partisanship.[88] Despite the duty the defense lawyer owes to the client, the duty to the court should be the primary duty owed by the lawyer: "the criminal trial is not a sporting contest and the fair determination of an individual's guilt and the protection of society are both important objectives of criminal law."[89] This statement further emphasizes the notion that despite owing a duty to his client, the defense lawyer's primary concern should be achieving a fair and just verdict, which is not necessarily a verdict that favors the client. This notion creates tension in the theoretical role of the defense lawyer; how does he balance his responsibility to the court with furthering the case of his client. It is clear that the duty to the court severely tempers the ability of the defense lawyer to solely advance the best interest of the client.

The Duty to the Public

The final duty from Lord Reid's statement in *Rondell v Worsley* is the duty to the public. This duty obliges the defense lawyer to consider the implications of his actions upon the public; he must have regard to the requirements of the society for which the system serves. The criminal defense lawyer is a public servant and as such there is a requirement for him to protect the integrity of the legal system; in protecting the values and integrity of the legal system, the defense lawyer fulfils his duty to the public. He satisfies this aim by not "degrading" himself in order to achieve the desired result for their client.[90] The duty to the public may be seen as restricting the defense lawyer's duty to his client. A partisan approach to defending a client is tempered by the principle that the lawyer should act, throughout his dealings with the client, as "a good person should act."[91] The lawyer should remember that a partisan duty to his client does not replace his ideas of what behavior is right and wrong. Should a client propose a course of action that is unjust, the lawyer should advise the client to take the action that is morally correct; it is important to remember that the action and direction of the defense lawyer will have ramifications for society and the general public. The duty to the client renders the defense lawyer as an "instrument of justice and not a worker of injustice."[92] This means the lawyer, whilst acting as a partisan representative of the accused, has other obligations that he has to acknowledge. Without this duty to the public, the client would have an unrestricted and unchecked defense; this may encourage dishonest, deceitful, and distracting practices that will allow the defense lawyer to keep his opponent from presenting their case effectively.[93] The duty to the public acts as a check to ensure the lawyer acts in an ethically correct manner and in a way that would not cause the public to lose confidence or faith in the criminal justice process. Furthermore, by ensuring that the process is conducted ethically, it ensures that both sides play fair and, ultimately, it ensures that the criminal justice process is fair.

CONCLUSION

As this chapter outlined at the start, there is not one settled definition of the role of the defense lawyer. This chapter has sought to build a conception of the archetypal defense lawyer. Whilst this chapter has relied heavily on the use of literature from the United States in the 1960s and 1970s, the chapter does not accept that there is one particular view of the defense lawyer that should be adopted. Instead, the chapter contends that there are many differing facets that need to be considered when building a theoretical conception of a defense lawyer. This chapter attempted to mold a conception of the defense lawyer, and the obligations faced. The role of the defense lawyer is greater than merely advancing the case of his client. Whilst the duty to his client involves acting in a partisan manner, the notion of partisanship is heavily impinged by duties to the court and the administration of justice, as well as a duty to the public. The duty to the court and the administration of justice frowns upon certain acts that may be beneficial to the client, such as ambush defenses, which despite being legitimate are discouraged by the court for fear that they distort the search for the truth. The duty to the public ensures that the behavior of the lawyer is ethically and morally correct. The literature used for this classic conception suggests that the defense lawyer has a paramount duty to his client, despite acknowledging that other duties exist; they do so with lesser priority than the duty to the client. Terms such as "zealous advocate" and "hired gun" suggest that this duty should be prioritized by the defense lawyer, above the other competing duties. However, this places the defense lawyer with a conundrum; the theoretical literature suggests that the duty to the client is the paramount duty. However, this conception offers little guidance on how the lawyer should deal with obligations that may conflict with this duty and this is what the empirical study aims to achieve.

NOTES

1. J. H. Langbein, *The Origins of the Adversary Criminal Trial* (Oxford University Press: Oxford, 2005) at p. 13.
2. Ibid., at p. 14.
3. J. Beattie, *Crime and the Courts in England 1660-1800* (Princeton University Press: Princeton, 1986) at p. 342.
4. For an in-depth analysis of the role of the Justices of the peace, please see J. Langbein, *Prosecuting Crime in the Renaissance* (Cambridge: Harvard University Press, 1974) chapter 3.
5. J. H. Langbein, *The Origins of the Adversary Criminal Trial* (Oxford University Press: Oxford, 2005) at pp. 62–63.
6. J. H. Langbein, *Prosecuting Crime in the Renaissance* (Cambridge: Harvard University Press, 1974) at p. 272.
7. J. H. Langbein, *The Origins of the Adversary Criminal Trial* (Oxford University Press: Oxford, 2005) at p. 71 and Sir James Fitzjames Steven, *A History of the Criminal Law in England* (Macmillan: London, 1883), Vol. 1 at p. 392.
8. *R v Titus Oates* 10, St. Tr 1079 (K.B 1685) at 1300 as cited in Ibid., at pp. 62–63.
9. Sir James Fitzjames Steven, *A History of the Criminal Law in England* (Macmillan: London, 1883), Vol. 1 at p. 392.
10. Treason Act 1696 Act, preamble.
11. S.1 Treason Act 1696
12. Ibid.
13. A crime classed as a *felony* is any serious crime other than treason.
14. J. H. Langbein, *The Origins of the Adversary Criminal Trial* (Oxford University Press: Oxford, 2005) at p. 98.
15. Ibid., at p. 99.
16. This notion is discussed at length in the next section, it is briefly mentioned here to contextualize the rationale for permitting defense lawyers in treason trials yet prohibiting them in all other offences.
17. An unnamed Elizabethan writer in A Memorial of the Reformation of England (1596), published as *The Jesuit's Memorial for the Intended Reformation of England* 250 (London) 1690 as cited in J. H. Langbein, *The Origins of the Adversary Criminal Trial* (Oxford University Press: Oxford, 2005).
18. R. F. Hunnisett, Eighteenth-Century Coroners and Their Clerks, 76 Wiltshire Archaeological Natural History Mag. 123 (1982).
19. The accused was allowed counsel to argue matters of law even in cases of treason or felony. These cases were however infrequent, David Seipp identified several

cases in the fourteenth and fifteenth centuries in which counsel acts for the defense. See D. J. Seipp, *Crime in the Year Books*, in Law Reporting in England 15,22 (Chatal Stebbings ed.) (1995).

20. An amicus curiae means "friend of the court." He is someone who is not a party to proceedings but assists the court in the furtherance of their goals by offering advice and expertise. For more see, D. J. A Cairns *Advocacy and the Making of the Adversarial Criminal Trial 1800–1865* (Clarendon Press, 1998), at p. 47.

21. E. Coke, *The Third Part of the Institutes of the Laws of England: Concerning High Treason and Other Pleas of the Crown, and Criminal Causes*, 137 (London, 1644) as cited in Ibid. *https://books.google.co.uk/books?id=_Ik0AAAAIAAJ&pg=PP9&source=gbs_selected_pages&cad=2#v=onepage&q&f=false.*

22. See W. Hawkins, *A Treatise of the Pleas of the Crown*, 400 (London, 1716, 1721) (2 Volumes). https://www.lawbookexchange.com/pages/books/54020/william-hawkins/a-treatise-of-the-pleas-of-the-crown-or-a-system-of-the-principal.

23. J. H. Langbein, *The Origins of the Adversary Criminal Trial* (Oxford University Press: Oxford, 2005) at p. 26.

24. Langbein explains that the deviation from the prohibition on defense counsel occurred in early eighteenth century. However, Cairns suggests that the lifting of the prohibition occurred in the nineteenth century.

25. E. Coke, *The Third Part of the Institutes of the Laws of England: Concerning High Treason and Other Pleas of the Crown and Criminal Causes*, 137 (London: 1644), as cited in J. H. Langbein, *The Origins of the Adversary Criminal Trial* (Oxford University Press: Oxford, 2005) at p. 49.

26. J. F. Stephen, *A General View of the Criminal Law in London* (London: McMillian Publishing, 1883, Volume 2 at 431).

27. Thomas Rowlandson's cartoon "Being Nervous and Cross-Examined by Mr Garrow" from the series *Miseries of Human Life* (1808). Available here: http://art.famsf.org/thomas-rowlandson/more-miseries- being-nervous-and-cross-examined-mr-garrow-fortieth-plate-book [Last accessed February 1, 2017].

28. This statement was made at the Trial of John Taylor of Forgery at Chelmsford Assizes 11 (Chelmsford 1800) at p. 15.

29. J. H. Langbein, *The Origins of the Adversary Criminal Trial* (Oxford University Press: Oxford, 2005) at p. 307.

30. J. Lee, The Old Bailey Session Papers (Jan. 1784 No. 203) at 241, 246.

31. D. Macginniss, Old Bailey Session Papers (Jan. 1783 No. 85) at 111, 118–119.

32. See J. H. Langbein, *The Origins of the Adversary Criminal Trial* (Oxford University Press: Oxford), 2005.

33. A full defense was one where the lawyer had no restrictions on his role at trial. Currently, the lawyer is merely permitted to examine and cross-examine witnesses. A full defense would grant him full rights of the court that would include speaking for his client as well as addressing the jury.

34. This was the view of Sir John Coply who spoke out against full defense by counsel in the House of Commons in 1821, 1824, and 1826 as cited in *Supra 186* at 69.

35. Ibid., at p. 69.

36. *Second Report of the His Majesty's Commission on Criminal Law* (1836) Parl. Papers XXXVI 183 as cited in Ibid., at p. 73. Cairns states that the use of Royal

Commissions to facilitate legislative reform was a characteristic of the nineteenth century law reform and the *second report* is a classic example of this process in action

37. *Second Report of the His Majesty's Commission on Criminal Law* (1836) Parl. Papers XXXVI 11.

38. Ibid.

39. Part I—The Prisoners Counsel Act 1836 (6 & 7 Will.4, c.114) and s.3 The Prisoners Counsel Act 1836.

40. J. H. Langbein, *The Origins of the Adversary Criminal Trial* (Oxford University Press: Oxford, 2005) at p. 258.

41. Ibid., at p. 307.

42. S. 1 Criminal Evidence Act 1898.

43. Great Britain and Ireland, *Parliamentary Debates*, House of Commons, *The Parliamentary Debates (Fourth Series)* [1898] June 30, 1898, Vol. 60, 659–660 (S. Evans) as cited in C. Mosidis, *Criminal Discovery: From Truth to Proof and Back Again* (Sydney Institute of Criminology Series), 2008.

44. Great Britain and Ireland, *Parliamentary Debates*, House of Commons, *The Parliamentary Debates (Fourth Series)* [1898] April 25, 1898, Vol. 56, 1001 (Lloyd Morgan), June 27, 1898, Vol. 60, 313 (T P O'Conner) April 25, 1898, Vol. 56, 982–983 (Attorney General Richard Webster) as cited in ibid.

45. However, research shows that only 9 percent of suspects sought legal advice and only 7 percent received it. Please see P. Softly *Police Interrogation: An Observational Study in Four Police Stations,* Royal Commission on Procedure, Research Study No 4, HMSO 1980).

46. Paragraph 11 http://www.legalservices.gov.uk/docs/forms/60_Jewels_of_Information.pdf [Last Accessed May 1, 2017].

47. This was formally known as The Convention for the Protection of Human Rights and Fundamental Freedoms.

48. Ibid., at para 180.

49. S.73-84 Criminal Justice Act 1967 deals with the legal aid provisions.

50. S.75(1)(a) Criminal Justice Act 1967.

51. S.75(1)(b) Criminal Justice Act 1967.

52. Justice, *The Unrepresented Defendant in the Magistrates' Court* (London: Stevens and Son, 1971) at para 16.

53. Departmental Committee Report: Legal Aid in Criminal Proceedings, 1966, Cmnd 2934 at para 56.

54. Justice, *The Unrepresented Defendant in the Magistrates' Court* (London: Stevens and Son, 1971) at para 26.

55. Departmental Committee Report: Legal Aid in Criminal Proceedings, 1966, Cmnd 2934 at para 206–207.

56. Justice, *The Unrepresented Defendant in the Magistrates' Court* (London: Stevens and Son, 1971) at para 92.

57. *R v Walter Thomas*, 2 Bulstrode 147, 80 Eng. Rep 1022 (K.B 1613).

58. J. H. Langbein, *The Origins of the Adversary Criminal Trial* (Oxford University Press: Oxford, 2005) at p. 136.

59. These events were reported in 2 *Gentleman's Magazine* 975 (Sept. 1732) entry for September 11 as cited in Ibid., at p. 138.

60. M. Blake and A. Ashworth, "Ethics and the Criminal Defence Lawyer" [2004] *Legal* Ethics Vol. 7 167–190 at 167.

61. [1969] 1A.C. 191.

62. [1969] 1A.C. 191 at 227–228.

63. M. Blake and A. Ashworth, "Ethics and the Criminal Defence Lawyer" [2004] *Legal Ethics* Vol. 7, 167–190 at 173.

64. Ibid., at p. 169.

65. *Ex parte Lloyd* (1822) Montagu's Reports 70n, 72 per Lord Eldon.

66. See D. Napley, *The Technique of Persuasion* (4th Edition, Sweet and Maxwell: London, 1991) at p. 57.

67. R. Du Cann *The Art of the Advocate* (Penguin Publishing, 1964) at p. 46.

68. M. Cain and C. Harrington *Lawyers in the Post-Modern World* (Oxford University Press, 1994) at p. 55.

69. F. Zacahrias and B. Green, "Reconceptualizing Advocacy Ethics" [2005] 74 *The George Washington Law Review* Vol. 27, 182.

70. W. Simon, 'The Ideology of Advocacy: Procedural Justice and Professional Ethics,' [1978] *Wisconsin Law Review* Vol. 42 at page 34.

71. D. Pannick *Advocates* (Oxford: Oxford University Press, 1992) at p. 92.

72. [1967] 3 WLR 1666.

73. R. O'Dair, *Legal Ethics Text and Materials* (Butterworths, 2001) at p. 152.

74. G. Lefcourt, "Responsibilities of a Criminal Defence Attorney" [1996] *Loyola of Los Angeles Law Review*, Vol. 30, p. 61.

75. Ibid.

76. A. Smith and W. Montross, The Calling of the Criminal Defense (1998–1999) 50 Mercer L.R., 522.

77. C. Curtis, *The Ethics of Advocacy* (1951–1952) Stan.L.Rev 12.

78. Ibid., at p. 529.

79. G. Van Susteren, "Responsibility," [1996–1997] *Loyola of Los Angeles Law Review* Vol. 30, 128.

80. For further discussion please see D. Luban, "*The Adversary System Excuse*" in R. Abel, *Lawyers: A Critical Reader* (New York: The New Press, 1997), at p. 5.

81. W. Hodes, "Lord Broughman, the Dream Team and Jury Nullification of the Third Kind" [1996] *University of Colorado Law Review* Vol. 67, 1086.

82. D. Nicholson and J. Webb, *Professional Legal Ethics—Critical Interrogations* (Oxford University Press: Oxford, 1999), at p. 64.

83. http://oxforddictionaries.com/view/entry/m_en_gb0886190#m_en_gb0886190 [Last Accessed December 2020].

84. *Ex parte Lloyd* (1822) Montagu's Reports 70n, 72 per Lord Eldon.

85. http://oxforddictionaries.com/view/entry/m_en_gb0435410#m_en_gb0435410[LastAccessed December 2020].

86. F. Zacharias and B. Green, "Reconceptualizing Advocacy Ethics," [2005] *The George Washington Law Review* Vol. 74, 67.

87. G. Tomlijanovic, "Defence Disclosure: Is the Right to Full Answer the Right to Ambush?" [2002–2003] *Alta Law Review* Vol. 40, 689.

88. F. Zacharias and B. Green, 'Reconceptualizing Advocacy Ethics,' [2005] *The George Washington Law Review* Vol. 74, 28.

89. D. G. Bress, "Professional ethics in criminal trials: A view of defense counsel's responsibility" [1966] *Michigan Law Reviw*, Vol. 64(8), 1493–1498 at 1495.

90. R. Lawry, "The Central Moral Tradition of Lawyer" [1990–1991] *Hofstra Law Review*, Vol. 19, 337.

91. Ibid., at p. 337.

92. G. Archer, "Ethical Obligations of the Lawyer" in F. Zacharias and B. Green "Reconceptualizing Advocacy Ethics" [2005] *The George Washington Law Review* Vol. 74, 28.

93. A. Alschuler, "How to Win the Trial of the Century: The Ethics of Lord Broughman and the OJ Simpson Defense Team" [1997–1998] *McGeorge Law Review* Vol. 29, 299.

Chapter 3

A Departure from Adversarialism

A History of Disclosure and Case Management

This chapter will examine the evolution of the disclosure obligations and the advent of the Criminal Procedure Rules (hereafter, CrimPR) in particular, the overriding objective and the case management provisions contained within the rules. This chapter will begin with a chronological examination of the disclosure obligations for both the prosecution and defense. Owing to the way in which the law of disclosure has developed, a chronological examination is best suited for the chapter; any reform to the area of disclosure, for both prosecution and defense lawyers, has often consisted of piecemeal changes to the law. As such, the chronological examination will permit the chapter to draw out the essence of the relevant changes and allow later chapters to contextualize the impact they have on the role of the defense lawyer. To conclude, the chapter will analyze the potential impact of these obligations on the classic concept of the defense lawyer as developed in chapter 2.

THE EVOLUTION OF DISCLOSURE

Chapter 2 established that the genesis of adversarialism occurred in the nineteenth century and also established that the disclosure regime is a relatively recent creation. The Devlin Report, published in 1976, noted that until the mid-1940s, there was no duty to disclose any information prior to trial by either party.[1] *R v Bryant and Dickson*[2] is commonly regarded as the beginning of the process in which the courts began to impose a duty on the prosecution to disclose material that may lead to the acquittal of the accused.[3] The case established an obligation upon the prosecution to make available to the defense witnesses whom the prosecution knew could give material evidence. The rule in *Bryant and Dickson* was subsequently further extended by *Dallison v Caffery*.[4] Here, Lord Justice Denning sought to broaden the disclosure obligations of the prosecution: "if he [the prosecutor] knows of a credible witness who can speak [of] material facts which tends to show the prisoner to be innocent, he must either call that witness himself or make his statement available . . . it would be highly reprehensible to conceal . . . the evidence which such a witness can give."[5]

For Lord Denning, disclosure was about ensuring that justice was done and not simply following a particular rule; it was the spirit of the rule that should prevail, not its letter.[6] Until the 1960s, obligations to disclose information were placed exclusively upon the prosecution. The Criminal Justice Act 1967 was the first exception to this general rule, s.11 of which states that in trials on indictment:

1. The defendant shall not without the leave of the court adduce evidence in support of an alibi unless, before the end of the prescribed period, he gives notice of particulars of the alibi.
2. On any such trial the defendant shall not without the leave of the court call any other person to give such evidence unless—
   (a) the notice under that subsection includes the name and address of the witness, or if the name or address is not known to the defendant at the time, he gives the notice, any information in his possession which might be of material assistance in finding the witness; if the name or the address is not included in that notice, the court is satisfied that the defendant, before giving the notice, took and thereafter continued to take all reasonable steps to secure that the name or address would be ascertained.[7]

When debating the bill in Parliament, the alibi disclosure obligation found great support. Speaking in August 1966, some sixteen months prior to the implementation of the Act, Sir Richard Glyn stated that "an innocent person has nothing to lose by making a statement or going into the witness box. . . [he] has everything to gain by making the fullest possible disclosure to the police and letting them check it."[8] In June 1967, Viscount Dilhorne said that he was "greatly in favor of this proposal about disclosure of alibi defenses, and I think it would be a beneficial change to our law."[9]

The Fisher Inquiry[10] was not slow to criticize those who were involved with the prosecution of the three suspects. The report made a number of recommendations in the area of prosecutorial disclosure, including a requirement that all statements taken by the police should be disclosed by the prosecutor to the defense, in the absence of a special reason to the contrary.[11] If the statement was made by a witness who the prosecution believed the defense would call, as soon as it was clear that the defense would not call the witness, the statement should be disclosed.[12] Disclosure should not be subjected to conditions[13] and no statement should be withheld.[14] Time limits should be laid down so that the defense obtained the statements within a reasonable time prior to the commencement of the trial.[15] Finally, the committee recommended that disclosure should be made whether or not the defense asked for it.[16] The report suggested that unless and until the suggestions were implemented, the rule in *R v Bryant and Dickson*[17] should be modified; where there are a large number of witnesses, the list of witnesses supplied by the prosecution should include a summary of what evidence each witness is able to give.[18] The attorney general's guidelines were initially issued in December 1981 and were the "first attempt by the government, without recourse to statute, to comprehensively improve and overhaul the disclosure system."[19] The guidelines created a set of criteria for determining what should and should not be disclosed and established the notion of disclosing "unused material," which was defined as:

(a) Witness statements and documents not included in the committal bundle;
(b) statements of witnesses who are to be called at committal, and any documents referred to therein; and
(c) the unedited version of edited statements included in the committal bundle.[20]

In 1986, the Fraud Trials Committee published their report (hereafter, the Roskill Committee). The findings of the committee led to the second major development in the area of defense disclosure. The committee was established because, it was said, the public no longer believed the legal system was capable of bringing the perpetrators of serious frauds to book.[21] The committee found that the public was correct; the legal system was too archaic, cumbersome, and unreliable. Every stage of the legal process was an "open invitation to blatant delay and abuse."[22] Owing to this blatant abuse, the committee stated in its summary that radical reform was necessary. Although the terms of reference for the report related to fraud trials the committee argued that the changes could "be of benefit to a wider range of criminal cases."[23] The committee believed that forcing the defense to outline its case in advance of trial would make the trial both "shorter and more efficient." Furthermore, this would make the trial clearer for the jury, if they were told at the outset what part of the prosecution's case the defense intended to challenge. Requiring the defense to disclose a case outline would reduce the risk of fabricated defenses; the prosecution would be able to investigate in advance any defense claims that required investigation.[24] However, the committee admitted that they had been unable to test empirically the truth of the assertion that the jury's understanding of the case is impaired where it is not clear at the outset what the case may be.

The committee considered a number of objections to the proposal. First, it accepted that the main objection was that the proposal was an infringement of a fundamental principle of our criminal law; that the burden of proof rests with the prosecution. A further objection to the proposal was the lack of an effective sanction against a defendant who fails to comply with the provisions. To alleviate any fear that a defense disclosure regime would weaken the burden of the proof, the commission stated:

> The prosecution would still have to prepare their case fully . . . including making early disclosure of their evidence . . . we recognized that the burden of proof would be affected if the prosecution were allowed to alter the nature of their case once the defense had been disclosed. To avoid this possibility, any proposal would therefore have to involve the prosecution's case being "fixed" before the defense could show his hand. If the prosecution sought to change their ground . . . to overwhelm the case put forward by the defense, the judge might well be justified in intervening to stop the case altogether or, if it were not too late, to ensure that the prosecution adhered to the original case.[25]

By implementing the safety net of allowing the judges to intervene should the prosecution deviate from their original case, the committee believed the burden of proof would remain intact. The committee recommended three effective sanctions that could be used when a defendant failed to comply with the provision to disclose the general nature of his case in advance of trial[26]:

(a) A defendant should be refused the right to give evidence himself at trial or call any factual evidence, save for expert evidence.
(b) The sanction of costs should be used where it is clear that the failure. . . may unnecessarily prolong the trial.
(c) After comment from the prosecution and the judge, the jury should be entitled to take account of, and draw any appropriate inferences from, the defendant's failure to disclose a particular line of defense on which he relies at trial.

The committee believed that requiring the defense to provide a case outline in advance of trial would become routine in future trials. Furthermore, the occasions where the "teeth" would have an actual bite, would only occur in a small number of cases.[27] Michael Levi believed that the suggestion that the defense and prosecution should outline their cases in advance would greatly assist "the comprehension and inhibit the development of irrelevant lines or arguments in the hope of causing maximum obfuscation and uncertainty over guilt."[28] This would lead to the fraud trial being handled in a far more efficient manner. Roderick Munday stated that it would make greater sense to review the suggestion through the lens of the wider context of criminal trials, rather than narrowly focus on fraud trials alone. He accepted that if one accepts the proposals in the wider context of all criminal trials, one could no longer regard the trial as the "unique focus of legal attention."[29] He argued that the proposed defense disclosure regime would purely serve to simplify and clarify the issues for the tribunal of fact and that the defense would not be seriously harmed; the committee stated the prosecution's case is "fixed" so they would be unable to alter or deviate from their disclosed case. This provision meant the burden of proof remained sacrosanct as the prosecution would be unable to use any defense disclosure in their prima facie case.

Munday argued that it was perhaps time for the criminal trial to evolve, as the trial "ought to no longer resemble a crafty game where one side's strategy may remain artfully concealed until the last moment to no real end other than to frustrate the interests of justice"[30] and ultimately allow the guilty to walk free. Following the Roskill Committee's report, the government enacted the Criminal Justice Act 1987. The Act provided that in serious fraud cases, persons can be required to give information about and produce documents concerning the investigation. Section 2(3) allows the director of the investigation "to require the person under investigation, or any other person to produce any specified document which appear to the Director to relate to any matter relevant to the investigation."[31] The Crown Court (Advance Notice of Expert Evidence) Rules[32] provided that any statement in writing of any finding or opinion of an expert upon which a party intended to rely on had to be disclosed as soon as practicable after committal. These obligations in the mid-1980s were the first deviation from the notion that the accused does not have to outline any aspect of his defense prior to trial, save for any alibi notifications.

The genesis of the advance notice provision can be traced back to the 1981 Royal Commission on Criminal Procedure. Here the report proposed that advance notices should be extended from alibi evidence, to incorporate other spheres where it was believed the disclosure of such information would contribute to the increased efficiency of the prosecution and trial process. The commission believed the efficiency of the process would increase, as the courts would no longer have to grant an adjournment. The adjournment would be reasonable as to allow the prosecution to investigate the validity of the evidence or witness that has taken them by surprise.[33] Implicit in this proposal was the assertion that the "ambush" defense was no longer a valid weapon for the adversarial defense lawyer.[34] This notion of attempting to nullify the adversarial tactics of ambush or surprise evidence was something that would reoccur with the advent of the Criminal Procedure and Investigations Act 1996.

Furthermore, the Lord Chief Justice told the House of Commons that the prosecution was bound by a duty to be fair. This imposed a duty on the prosecution to supply the defense with any material that was inconsistent with the evidence of any prosecution witness.[35] Within a decade of their creation, the principles that were involved with the guidelines began to be developed, and shaped by the common law. In *R v Lawson*,[36] the Court of Appeal quashed the appellant's conviction on the ground that the prosecution had improperly exercised their discretion of not disclosing witness statements to the defense. At the appeal, the prosecution counsel argued that the guidelines permitted the nondisclosure. The court rejected this submission; the court preferred the approach in *Dallison and Caffery*[37] of questioning whether the nondisclosure had caused injustice to the appellant.

Following this, the next major legislative development for the law of disclosure came with the Criminal Procedure and Investigations Act 1996 (hereafter, CPIA 1996) and this held a seismic shift for the very nature of adversarial criminal justice. The Act was borne out of the recommendations made by the Royal Commission on Criminal Justice (hereafter, the Runciman Commission). The commission was established in the wake of the quashed convictions of the Birmingham Six.[38] The then home secretary, Kenneth Baker, instructed the commission to "examine the effectiveness of the criminal justice system in England and Wales."[39] The commission was of the opinion that the current regime of prosecution disclosure was so wide that it was "unduly burdensome on the prosecution"[40] and certain defense tactics could impact on the outcome of the trial.

The perceived problem of the overburden of prosecution disclosure was further exacerbated whilst the commission was sitting. A series of court decisions rapidly expanded the disclosure obligations of the prosecution. In *Ward*,[41] the court held that "non-disclosure was a potential source of injustice"[42] and it would be for the court to decide what evidence should be disclosed. If the court believed that the evidence fell within the narrow concept of Public Interest Immunity (PII), then the material would not be disclosed. However, all other materials gathered by investigators would have to be disclosed. The disclosure of unused materials should not just include: "Evidence that will obviously advance the accused's case . . . it is of help to the accused to have the opportunity of considering all the material evidence the prosecution have gathered and from which the prosecution have made their own selection."[43]

In *R v Keane*,[44] Lord Justice Taylor defined what material was required to be disclosed by the prosecution. He adopted the test pronounced by Jowitt J in *R v Melvin and Dingle*:[45] "I would judge material in the realm of disclosure that which can been seen on a sensible appraisal by the prosecution:

a) to be relevant or possibly relevant to an issue in the case
b) to raise or possibly raise a new issue whose existence is not apparent from the evidence the prosecution proposes to use
c) to hold out a real (as opposed to be fanciful) prospect of providing a lead on evidence that goes to (a) or (b)."

The prosecution must identify documents and information which are material according to the criteria set out above.[46] By requesting the police to comb through masses of material, the commission believed that requests for disclosure by the defense was too demanding. As such, the defense had the opportunity to cause a delay in proceedings or chance upon something that would induce the prosecution to drop the case rather than disclose the material concerned. The commission stated that this process was both "time consuming and wasteful of resources."[47] The law enforcement community began complaining that the judgment in *Ward* "became a charter for the criminal and had hamstrung the police in its fight against crime."[48] The Runciman Commission was of the opinion that the current disclosure burden on the prosecution "went beyond what is reasonable"[49] and this needed rebalancing. They recommended a regime that would have three elements. First, a more restricted test of disclosure, second, a compulsory element of defense disclosure, and third, a Code of Practice for the Police in carrying out their disclosure duties. The implementation of a compulsory defense disclosure regime had efficiency drivers at its heart; it was believed the regime would encourage better preparation of cases, which may well "result in the prosecution being dropped in light of the defense disclosure, an early resolution through a guilty plea, or a fixing of an earlier trial date."[50] This "better preparation" would ultimately lead to a more efficient use of resources as the length of the trial could more readily be approximated, leading to a better use of the court's time and those involved in the case.[51] Furthermore, "ambush" defenses, in which the defendant withholds his evidence until the last possible moment, hoping to confuse the jury or evade investigation of a fabricated defense, would be reduced to a minimum.[52] The commission admitted that despite the fact that the ambush defense was only used in a small minority of cases, the principle was both undesirable and unacceptable.[53] The commission suggested that the "guilty" are acquitted because the prosecution has not had time to investigate the "ambush" defense of the defendant.

Despite the admission that the problem occurred in the minority of cases, it was not as dramatic as the commission claimed, and an ambush defense was no guarantee of an acquittal. A Crown Court Study completed for the Runciman Commission found that "last minute" defenses were raised in 7–10 percent of cases, and 50 percent of those cases resulted in a conviction.[54] Roger Leng's study for the commission found that an ambush defense was raised in between 2 and 5 percent of trials, and all resulted in a conviction.[55] By examining the empirical evidence, it is difficult to argue that such a minority of cases, which often resulted in conviction anyway, deserved such onerous reform. However, the commission concluded that the system would be made more efficient by reforming the disclosure regime and implementing a compulsory aspect of defense disclosure. The commission was confident that the system would become more efficient owing to the early clarification of what was at issue in each case.

Michael Zander was the sole dissenting member of the commission in respect of this recommendation.[56] He believed that any obligation for the defendant to disclose his case undermined the principle that it is the responsibility of the defendant to respond to the case the prosecution makes at trial, not the one the prosecution says they will make. For the defendant to respond to the prosecution's case, it has to be made at trial.[57] Zander also cited the two aforementioned studies when claiming ambush defenses are indeed rare and even when they occur, they do not pose much of a problem.[58] He also commented on the effectiveness of defense statements and referred to the research conducted by Michael Levi for the commission.[59] Levi found that defense statements that were completed in relation to fraud trials proved largely ineffective because they were not sufficiently specific and therefore too generalized. Zander opined that "if it [defense disclosure] did not work in the serious fraud area, it probably will not work in other areas."[60] As this chapter will highlight, Zander was correct in that assertion.

The commission was criticized as it did not state any explicit consideration of priorities. Michael Zander stated the commission proceeded on the basis that "acquitting the innocent was the priority, with convicting the guilty second, and the effective use of resources third."[61] However, these component parts were given different weightings on varying topics and the primary weighting was not always afforded to the acquittal of the innocent.[62] This derogation from the acquittal of the innocent as the primary goal of the criminal justice system was undesirable. Stewart Field and Phillip Thomas argued that "to make acquittal of the innocent, at any point, less than the primary consideration in a system that still deploys the due-process rhetoric of preferring ten guilty going free to the single convicted innocent is an important departure."[63] The traditional adversarial ideology of the criminal justice system of England and Wales is affected by the commission's proposals; the adversarial system places great value on the built-in safeguards of oral presentation of evidence that is tested in a public court before a judge and/or jury. The judge and jury are impartial as they come to the case with no preconceptions (of the case). The commission's proposal could weaken this classic adversarial standpoint. As Field and Thomas noted, by recommending pretrial defense disclosure, the system becomes "less classically adversarial, which would reduce further the real importance of contested trials."[64] The criminal trial offers a number of in-built safeguards, yet the proposals for defense disclosure marginalize the safeguards without substituting anything in their place. Although Field and Thomas did not explicitly touch upon the implications for the role of the defense lawyer, one can assume that the implications of the commission's recommendations could also dilute the importance of his role. A key component of the role of the defense lawyer is rigorously defending his client; theoretically this includes using the weapon of the ambush defense. A regime of defense disclosure blunts this adversarial weapon.

The commission was also criticized for not addressing matters at the heart of the criminal justice system. Instead the commission adopted a "managerial" approach, which could not generate the comprehensive review that was required.[65] Whilst the aim to reduce the waste of limited resources and to increase efficiency was not to be derided, the problem with the report lies in the "absence of a general framework of priorities which would allow these issues to be considered in relation to other goals on a systemic rather than *ad-hoc* basis."[66] A common criticism rested on the following premise: no reduction in expenditure can be justified if it interferes with the right of the innocent to avoid conviction.[67] Further to this criticism, the key issue is to ensure the prosecution's burden of proving guilt beyond reasonable doubt is maintained. This burden needs to be discharged by the prosecution without the assistance of the accused. With the exception of Michael Zander's view, the commission believed that early disclosure did not erode this principle. However, the key element of the commission's proposals rests in the principle of the proposal as much as the detail of the recommendations. The commission's proposals effectively placed the accused under an obligation to assist in his own prosecution. This proposal is abhorrent to an adversarial process where the defendant is protected by the privilege against self-incrimination.

Lee Bridges and Mike McConville argue that the proposals made by the RCCJ in regards to the disclosure regime reinforced the presumption of the suspect's guilt by enforcing the suspect to provide more information by way of disclosure.[68] This notion could satisfy the political aims of the government to "correct the thirty year inbuilt bias in the criminal justice system in favor of the criminal."[69] During this process, anything that could be presented as a "contribution to cost effective crime control became an urgent political priority"[70] because it addressed political concerns. In the early 1990s, the Conservative Party was behind in the opinion polls, Prime Minister John Major was viewed as unpopular, leaving ministers jockeying for position to succeed him. The then home secretary, Michael Howard, was keen to underline his hardline right-wing credentials and effectively cannibalized the commission's report by prioritizing the implementation of the cost-effective "crime control" measures.[71]

The findings of the commission can be contrasted with those of the panel set up by Liberty and the Civil Liberties Trust in 1992. This panel was created to consider three important aspects of the criminal justice system: confession evidence, a new body to tackle miscarriages of justice, and the right to silence.[72] Over the course of three one-day hearings, with participants who included Lord Runciman and the Lord Chief Justice, the panel suggested proposals that would allow for extensive defense disclosure but would stop short of impinging on the prosecution's burden of proof. The panel suggested that any disclosure regime should consist of the following elements, for cases committed for trial: the prosecution should serve to the defense notice of the issue the case raises; in return the defense would reciprocate by responding with a single document, called a "Defense List of Issues."[73] At the beginning of the trial, both sides should briefly present their lists to the court, and should the defense depart from their list the accused could be exposed to cross-examination, with leave from the judge. The panel believed that this limited form of defense disclosure was a "positive tool that will advance both the fairness and effectiveness of the criminal process."[74]

Following the publication of the commission's findings, the government published *Disclosure: A Consultation Paper*,[75] outlining its proposals for reforming the areas of both prosecution and defense disclosure. The Consultation Paper, unsurprisingly, echoed the findings of the Runciman Commission that the current regime was very burdensome on the prosecution and the police.[76] The excessive burdens were created because the "defense can require the police and prosecution to comb through large masses of material in the hope of causing a delay or chancing upon something that will induce the prosecution to drop the case."[77] At times, the defendant sought to obscure the real issues or would sometimes create a fictitious defense. There was little or no incentive for the defendant to contribute to the process of narrowing the issues in dispute or to disclose his actual defense in advance of trial.[78] The Consultation Paper further agreed with the Royal Commission when considering the issue of defense disclosure; having no disclosure of a defense in advance of trial encouraged late preparation and the withholding of information until the last possible minute. This allowed the defendant to "surprise the prosecution by revealing its defense for the first time at trial."[79] In order to negate the possibility of an "ambush," the defense would have to provide particulars of its case which identified the issues in dispute. The paper suggested that the early disclosure of the defense case was in the interests of justice and should assist in the better management of trials.[80] Ultimately, both the commission and the government were of the opinion that the regime had to be overhauled, as the burden on the prosecution was too great. The government's defensive stance concerning the miscarriage of justice cases in the early part of the decade had been replaced by a stance that appeared to be tough on crime.

THE POLITICAL CONTEXT AND THE DRIFT FROM DUE PROCESS TO CRIME CONTROL

Whilst this chapter is concerned with evolution of disclosure and its impact on both the defense lawyer and the adversarial process of England and Wales, it is important to note that this evolution did not occur in a vacuum and a number of other changes to criminal procedure occurred in the 1980s and 1990s. The genesis of change can be traced to the Phillips Commission,[81] reporting in 1981. The commission was established in the wake of a number of miscarriages of justice that blighted the criminal justice landscape in the late 1970s. The commission rejected any notion that there should be any curtailment of current provision of the right to silence at both the pretrial and trial stage.[82] In fact, the commission reemphasized the importance of the advanced disclosure being made to the accused as "it might put strong psychological pressure on some suspects to answer questions without knowing precisely what the evidence against them was."[83] In fact, the commission appeared to enhance the due process rights of the accused and the recommended proposals that provided established PACE 1984;[84] with the focus being on stricter control on detention periods in the police station, the right to legal advice whilst detained. Quirk suggests that the Act was "momentous" and codified both parties rights in relation to stop and search, arrest, detention, questioning, and charge.[85]

The 1990s saw a succession of successful appeals on the basis of false confessions.[86] These cases "exposed a catalogue of wrongdoing in the process of . . . criminal investigation."[87] In response, the government established the Royal Commission on Criminal Justice (RCCJ) to examine potential reforms to the criminal justice process. Quirk suggests that although the Conservative Party of the early 1990s had won a fourth successive General Election, they were unpopular with the electorate.[88] As such, a governmental notion of "Law and Order" had begun to counter the rising concerns about crime. The then home secretary, Michael Howard, suggested at the 1993 Conservative Party conference that "the right to silence will be abolished. The innocent have nothing to fear."[89] This conflation of guilt and silence was endemic in both the crime control policies and political atmosphere of the time. However, the findings of the commission were widely criticized by academics. Lee Bridges suggested that the Report of the commission was a "sham."[90] He stated that the document is "[there was a lack of care with the] empirical evidence, slippery in its argumentation and shameful in its underlying political purpose."

Bridges argued that the commission should have attempted to "make substantial recommendations for new protections for the accused . . . [including] real improvements in the quality of defense services throughout the criminal justice process." Had the commission recommended this, "[it] might have at least restricted the government in its current "Law and Order" campaign."[91] The Terms of Reference of the commission referred to "convicting the guilty, acquitting the innocent and efficiency."[92] However, the report neglected to set out the balance between these three competing goals.[93] When presenting the report, Lord Runciman stated that the report "took a step toward the inquisitorial" and the aim of the report had been to "correct the excesses of the adversarial system."[94]

The excesses, inter alia, were deemed to be the systems inefficiency and the right to silence. According to the report, the majority of the judiciary believed that suspects should give an account of themselves in order that police investigations can run more efficiently. This would allow the facts of the matter to be more readily established and those suspects who were innocent, could be eliminated from suspicion. Leaving the police to investigate those whose innocence had not been established. The impact of the provision would not only combat those who are trying to avoid charge by staying silent, it would also eliminate the use of an "ambush defense" at trial where the prosecution have no time to resort to such a defense. As highlighted, the research studies used by the commission did not bare out this perceived threat. The research suggested that very few suspects stay silent in police custody and Greer suggested that those who remain silent are more, rather than less, likely to be charged and these suspects are also more, rather than less, likely to enter a plea of guilty.[95] However, despite these facts, the government pressed ahead with modifying the right to silence under the Criminal Justice and Public Order Act 1994.

The defense disclosure regime was also examined by the commission. The core issue with such a regime is ensuring that the burden of proof is not shifted from the prosecution and the accused is not pressurized to assist in the discharge of this burden. The central point of this proposal was to "bring forward the moment at which the issues that the jury will have to decide can be clearly and concisely laid out."[96] Further to this efficiency driver, there would be in-built benefits of more cases being dropped before trial, and therefore resources saved; the fixing of earlier trial dates; better estimations of trial length allowing for the better deployment of criminal justice resources, and the further eradication of the ambush defense. The proposed changes to silence and defense disclosure were designed to eradicate ambush defenses. In reality, the use of the defense did not actually seem problematic. Leng found that "the proportion of contested cases in which an ambush defense was raised was . . . at most 5 per cent,"[97] with the vast majority of those defendants being convicted at trial anyway. So, a question remains, if the use of the defense was not problematic, is it worth the cost of shifting diluting adversarialism? Michael Zander vehemently disagreed with the disclosure suggestions on the basis of five grounds:

(1) The proposal is inconsistent with the burden of proof; no obligation should be placed on the accused to assist his accusers.
    They are designed to combat ambush defenses, which the commission's evidence already established was not problematic.
(2) Advance disclosure is unlikely to streamline and make the process more efficient. He cites the example of Levi,[98] when examining disclosure in Serious Fraud Trials, where it was found that disclosures are largely ineffective because the information is specific. This is likely to cause, rather than remedy delays, as each side demands more information from the other.
(3) Should the defendant change his lawyer at the last minute, this could be even more distressing for the accused.

Finally, he suggests the sanctions would be difficult to enforce considering the judicial culture is tolerant of the more limited alibi and expert evidence disclosure.[99] Greer agreed with Zander's criticisms and found that should the regime be implemented, it would place the accused under an obligation to assist the prosecution in pursuit of his conviction and this would be incompatible with both the burden of proof and the privilege against self-incrimination.[100]

Furthermore, Field and Thomas have argued that the commission, through the proposals on disclosure, "set out to deliberately increase the pressure on the suspects to plead guilty."[101] This would lead to an increase in efficiency and ultimately a quicker process. However, this seems to conflate "justice" with "results" and just because a person enters a plea of guilty, it does not necessarily mean they have committed the offence.[102] The commission recommended that the "excesses of adversarialism" be corrected and acknowledged that the pretrial disclosure regime would not be classically adversarial and would reduce the adversarial trial, as fewer cases would be contested due to better pretrial preparation that would lead to the dropping of the charge or a guilty plea.[103] Greer suggests that rather than being based on evidence the real purpose "was to mollify a police force" in the wake of the [Police and Criminal Evidence Act 1984] . . . regime and to restore the government's tattered law and order image.[104] The Criminal Justice and Public Order Act 1994 was subsequently enacted and was swiftly followed by the CPIA 1996.[105] The provisions of the 1994 Act permit comment and the drawing of inferences should suspects fail to:

- mention when questioned or charged any feature of their defense that could reasonably have been mentioned;[106]
- testify or, having been sworn, refuse to answer questions without good cause;[107]
- answer questions relating to the presence of any substance, object or mark about their person;[108]
- answer questions relating to their presence at the scene of an offence.[109]

It was thought that the curtailment of the silence provisions was a "trade-off"[110] for the enhancement of the suspect's rights contained within PACE 1984. What followed was the "modern law and order arms race"[111] in which due process provisions were diluted and the adversarial nature of criminal justice was fundamentally altered.

The Efficient Criminal Process: The Birth of the CPIA 1996

The CPIA 1996 replaced the largely common law regime with a new statutory scheme. As recommended by the Runciman Commission, the disclosure regime had a three-stage process: primary prosecution disclosure, defense disclosure by way of a case statement that identified the issues taken with the prosecution case, and finally, secondary prosecution disclosure in response to the issues identified in the case statement. At the primary disclosure stage, the prosecution was required to disclose any unused material "which has not previously been disclosed to the accused and which in the prosecutor's opinion might undermine the case for the prosecution against the accused."[112] The second stage of prosecution disclosure was interwoven with the defense statement. The prosecution was required to disclose any material "which has not previously been disclosed to the accused and which might be reasonably expected to assist the defense of the accused, as disclosed by the defense statement."[113]

The CPIA 1996 could be described as a politically influenced piece of legislation. The Conservative government at the time was trying to take a "tough on crime" approach; when introducing the bill at the second reading, Michael Howard said the Act "is designed to restore balance in our criminal justice system—to make life tougher for the criminal and to improve the protection of the public."[114] The requirement for defense disclosure in "general terms" perhaps illustrates the tension between making the criminal process more efficient and encroaching on the traditional adversarial values of the system. However, the end result of the CPIA 1996 disclosure regime was to tip the balance more in favor of the prosecution rather than the defense.[115] Section 5 CPIA 1996 deals with the compulsory disclosure by the accused. The provisions apply when a person is charged with an indictable offence and is committed for trial.[116] The defense disclosure obligations under the CPIA 1996 are only compulsory if the accused is tried in the Crown Court. They do not apply to summary trials heard in the magistrates' courts,[117] although section 6(2) does allow the accused to voluntarily provide a defense statement to the prosecution.[118] The content of the defense statement was defined by s.5(6). It is a written statement:

a) setting out in general terms the nature of the accused's defense;
b) indicating the matters on which he takes issue with the prosecution;
c) setting out, in the case of each such matter, the reason why he takes issue with the prosecution.

If the accused is relying on alibi evidence, he must include the particulars of that evidence in the statement. This must include the names and addresses of any witnesses the accused believes can give evidence to support the alibi.[119] Furthermore, the accused must provide any information that may be of material assistance in finding any such witness, if the name and address are not known.[120] Section 12 states that the defense statement must be served within the period prescribed by the home secretary. Sanctions for noncompliance are governed by s.11 and apply when the defendant:

(a) fails to give a defense statement under that section,
(b) gives a defense statement under that section but does so after the end of the period which, by virtue of section 12, is the relevant period for section 5,
(c) sets out inconsistent defenses in a defense statement given under section 5,
(d) at his trial puts forward a defense which is different from any defense set out in a defense statement given under section 5,
(e) at his trial adduces evidence in support of an alibi without having given particulars of the alibi in a defense statement given under section 5, or
(f) at his trial calls a witness to give evidence in support of an alibi without having complied with subsection (7)(a) or (b) of section 5 as regards the witness in giving a defense statement under that section.

Under the common law, the accused was permitted to withhold any defense until trial and a judge could not make any adverse comment or invite a jury to draw an adverse inference from his pretrial silence. This was subject to two statutory exceptions; alibi evidence[121] and expert evidence.[122] In 1994, s.34 of the Criminal Justice and Public Order Act curtailed the accused's right to withhold his defense until trial. Under s.34, the court or jury can draw such inferences as appear proper from the accused's failure to mention, in the police interview any fact he later relies on in court. This was taken further by section 11 of the CPIA 1996, which sets out the circumstances in which the accused is liable to have adverse inferences drawn against him. If:

a) the defendant fails to provide a defense statement when required to do so;
b) either a compulsory or voluntary statement is provided but it is out of time;
c) the defense statement sets out inconsistent defenses;
d) a defense is put forward at trial which is different from any defense disclosed in the defense statement;
e) an alibi defense is run at trial without particulars having been disclosed in a defense statement, and;
f) an alibi witness is called without the necessary particulars of the witness having been supplied.

Should the accused fail to comply with the defense statement provisions, two sanctions are available: the court or the prosecution, with leave of the court, may make such comment as appears appropriate;[123] and/or the court or the jury may draw inferences as appear proper in deciding whether the accused is guilty of the offence concerned.[124] Despite the fact the court may draw inferences from noncompliance with the disclosure obligations, the defendant cannot be convicted by mere inferences alone.[125]

Empirical Evidence on the Disclosure Regime

In March 2000, the Crown Prosecution Service Inspectorate published their thematic review of the disclosure of unused materials. The review examined 631 contested cases that were handled by thirteen different CPS areas. The primary purpose of the review was to establish "as factually clear a picture as possible about the manner in which the CPS discharges its important statutory obligations." Although the study was primarily concerned with prosecution disclosure, the review did examine secondary disclosure. The findings of the review provided examples of the practice of defense lawyers with regards to their disclosure obligations.

The review found that in 380 Crown Court cases, a defense statement was provided in 355 cases.[126] Despite the high number of defense statements issued in Crown Court cases, prosecutors believed "they make little difference to the case."[127] Section 5(6) of the CPIA 1996 provides that the defense statement should "set out the nature of the defense in general terms" but the statement has to indicate the matters on which he takes issue with the prosecution's case, as well as the reasons why he takes issue. Despite the statutory wording of what the defense statement has to contain, the thematic review found that often, the statements would be "very brief . . . contain[ing] little more than a denial of the offence and a request for disclosure."[128] The review found that out of 344 statements examined, 85 contained insufficient detail to enable the prosecution to make an informed decision regarding secondary disclosure.[129] The review commented that the CPIA 1996 provisions make it clear what the defense statement should contain; they do not set out what the prosecution can do if the statement does not contain the necessary information.[130] The review recommended that the director of Policy draw up and issue further detailed guidance on how prosecutors should deal with inadequate defense statements.[131] Whilst the thematic review examined the issue of secondary disclosure, the report did not comment on how the issue of the defense disclosure regime could be improved.

In 2001, Joyce Plotnikoff and Richard Wolfson published their study *A Fair Balance? Evaluation of the operation of disclosure law*. The purpose of the study was to ascertain whether the disclosure provisions contained in the CPIA 1996 had met the government's objective of "bringing about the acquittal of the innocent and conviction of the guilty [and] efficiency in focusing on the key issues at trial and fairness towards all affected."[132] Among the areas covered by the study, Plotnikoff and Wolfson analyzed the effectiveness of the defense statement. They found the content of the statements was not fulfilling the requirements laid out by s.5. They found that 84 percent of statements addressed the "nature of defense" requirement, 76 percent indicated the matters they took issue with from the prosecution's case and 66 percent of statements outlined the reasons why they took issue with the prosecution's case.[133] Further findings indicated that 90 percent of judges and barristers agreed that the prosecution rarely or never adduced evidence of the contents of the defense statement at trial, other than to rebut alibi evidence.[134]

The judicial perception of the value of the defense statement was poor. None of the judges questioned for the study found the statements useful in their current guise. One judge said: "defense statements . . . are, quite properly, meaningless . . . [they] serve only to trigger the obligation to make secondary disclosure."[135] Another judge commented that the statements were " (a) complete waste of paper."[136] To improve the quality of the defense statement, the following recommendations were made to Plotnikoff and Wolfson by the judges who took part in their research:

- A demand for strict compliance with the statutory regime.
- A pro-forma that directed the defense on specific issues which it must answer.
- Amendments to the CPIA 1996 to be more detailed in defining areas under dispute. Mere denials and/or putting the Crown to proof would be deemed inadequate.

- Adverse inference sanctions.
- A requirement to amend the statement to deal with issues raised by additional evidence.[137]

In her own empirical research, Hannah Quirk concluded that the provisions were unworkable. Quirk stated the provisions were flawed due to three fundamental reasons; the lack of understanding of the role and culture of each of the participants, the inadequate allocation of responsibility, and the insufficient sanctions for noncompliance with the rules that can be imposed fairly on defendants.[138] Defense statements contained often minuscule amounts of information and were generally as vague as possible; they often served as nothing more than a denial of the charge. For example, a defense statement completed by the defense in answer to a charge of handling a stolen motor vehicle, offered the following response: "the accused denies that he dishonestly received the vehicle and that he knew or believed that the same was stolen."[139] The vagueness of this statement could potentially leave the door open for the defense to spring an ambush defense at trial.[140] The price for springing the ambush was that the defense may miss crucial material not being disclosed at the second stage of prosecution disclosure. The statement does not indicate any particular defense that the accused will rely on and therefore leaves the prosecution without any suitable guidance as to what material would be of use to the defense.

Quirk further suggests that the notion of defense disclosure and the idea of rebalancing the system fits neatly with the philosophy of managerialism.[141] Furthermore, she supports McConville's findings that there was a general lack of adversarialism and that ultimately the idea that disclosure was needed to combat "ambush defenses"[142] was misplaced. Roger Leng suggests that the threat of ambush defenses was "the single most powerful factor in the campaign to abolish the right to silence and to require the early disclosure of the defense case."[143] The mention of ambush defenses is used as a pejorative term in an adversarial setting. Although as discussed, in practice, they were relatively unproblematic. Leng's study for the RCCJ found that ambush defenses were raised in between 2 and 5 percent of trials; all of which ended in the conviction of the defendant.[144] Leng also cites the work of Block, Corbett, and Peay who observed one hundred trials and did not find one single use of an ambush defense.[145] However, Zander and Henderson's study found ambush defenses were raised in 7–10 percent of trials and half of these ended in a conviction.[146] Despite ambush defenses being relatively unproblematic for the courts and certainly not a weapon that could frustrate the interests of justice in the vast majority of cases, it is clear the government sought change. As such, the tenor and tone of the government's proposals clearly fitted the aforementioned "rebalancing" of the system. Michael Zander, who was the only academic to sit on the Runciman Commission, suggested that any obligation for the defendant to assist the prosecution is "wrong in principle."[147]

There was much criticism of the new disclosure regime: "there is no shortage of criminal lawyers——judges and practitioners alike—who consider that the disclosure provisions of the CPIA are unworkable in the interests of justice and that a return to suitably post-Ward[148] regime is the only realistic option."[149] Sprack was concerned that the reduction of prosecution disclosure and an increase in defense disclosure was likely to lead to an increase in the number of miscarriages of justice.[150] Meanwhile, Redmayne suggested that the creation of the disclosure regime "forms part of the shift towards a criminal justice system whose prime concerns are efficiency and managerialism."[151] As this book will show, these concerns have not abated, and in fact, have been expedited and enhanced with the creation of the CrimPR. Whilst it is clear that disclosure is "desirable, particularly because of its powerful potential as a tool for trial management,"[152] it has implications for both the role of the defense lawyer and for the adversarial criminal trial. With the creation of the case management provisions, it can be argued that, as suggested by Leng, we have "lost sight of the defendant"[153] and their fair trial rights contained within an adversarial system.

The Auld Review and Evolution of CPIA: The Rise of Managerialism

The *Auld Review* was part of New Labour's goal to modernize the criminal justice process of England and Wales. Tony Blair's government had the goal of eradicating inefficiencies. The criminal justice system had been tasked with the goals of diverting offenders from a life of crime; making the system more efficient by implementing a fast-track, efficient procedures from arrest to sentence; improving services to witnesses and victims; and ensuring the component parts of the system are performing to their maximum potential.[154] Clearly, the mantra of efficiency are clear in these goals; by creating a fast-track system and ensuring the different parts of the system are being as efficient as possible, it is clear New Labour wanted things to get quicker; although there is a scant discussion about the system remaining fair. These goals were consolidated in the Criminal Justice strategic plan 1999–2000, which had the goal of "dispensing justice fairly and efficiently."[155] Michael Zander believes the *Report* was somewhat flawed and the cost-savings suggested by the *report* would automatically be accepted by the government as the home secretary and Lord Chancellor made their minds up before the consultation period had closed and before time has been allowed for an assessment of the views received.[156] Furthermore, Zander expressed frustration with the consultation process itself, he termed it wholly "inadequate"[157] as it ran over from mid-October to the end of January, which would not be long enough to digest a vast report that took twenty-one months to complete, which was nine months longer than initially envisaged. Zander concludes that "major reform to the CJS is too important to be rushed through at breakneck speed."[158] It appears, at face value, that the efficiency drivers of the *Review* would be readily accepted by the government, regardless of what the consultation period offers as a response. This fits in the mantra of the government's desire to drive efficiency and reduce waste of resources.

In 2001, Lord Justice Auld was tasked to examine the workings of both the criminal justice system and the criminal courts in England and Wales with a view to considering a new structure for direction and better management of the criminal justice system. The terms of reference for the *Auld Review* were to inquire into "the practices and procedures of, and the rules of evidence applied by, the criminal courts at every level, with a view to ensuring that they deliver justice fairly, by streamlining all their processes, increasing their efficiency and strengthening the effectiveness of their relationships with others across the whole criminal justice system."[159]

In his review of the Criminal Courts of England and Wales,[160] Auld LJ said: "fairness, efficiency and effectiveness of the criminal justice system demand that its procedure should be simple, accessible and, so far as is practicable the same for every type of criminal jurisdiction."[161] He commented that the 1996 Act "was not working as Parliament intended and its operation did not command the confidence of criminal practitioners."[162] Auld reiterated that there was a high level of noncompliance by the defense in its duty of completing an adequate defense statement; this noncompliance was a major deficiency in the disclosure provisions. Despite these criticisms, Auld suggested building on and improving the current three-stage disclosure regime, rather than creating a new one. He believed that the three-stage process was both "logical and fair."[163] Auld deemed the system logical, as what is disclosed depends on what is to be an issue. He deemed the regime fair, because "all" that is required of the defendant is to disclose what facts he believes are in issue.[164] The review suggested that any test for disclosure should be anchored to the issues in the case, as the police and prosecutor know or believe them to be, and suggested the following: "material that, in the prosecutor's opinion, might reasonably affect the determination of any issue in the case of which he knows or should reasonably expect."[165]

Auld clarified this with a tautologous example, "material which in the prosecutor's opinion might reasonably weaken the prosecution case or assist that of the defense."[166] With regards to the defense statement, Auld believed the requirements were adequate as they stood. He did not believe that a general obligation to identify defense witnesses and the content of their expected evidence, save for alibi or expert evidence, should be introduced.[167]

JUSTICE published their response to the Auld Review in January 2002. The response commented that the disclosure regime contained in the CPIA 1996 provisions takes England and Wales closer to an inquisitorial approach to criminal procedure. The report states that "there can be no connection between proper disclosure by the prosecution and participation by the defense."[168] JUSTICE argued that Auld LJ did not recognize this central point, despite the widespread criticism of the CPIA regime. Furthermore, Auld failed to recognized that no matter how much the defense is cajoled or pressurized into cooperating with the prosecution, it may not wish to do so. The defense lawyer should not have to do the prosecution's work. It is for the prosecution to prove the case against the accused; a defense statement may provide the prosecution with the opportunity to investigate further and use any mistakes or admissions against the defendant. The JUSTICE response was also critical of the three-stage process that the CPIA 1996 created and which was further endorsed by Auld's review. It stated that the current regime was wrong in principle, as it legitimized the withholding of relevant information, as secondary disclosure is dependent on the submission of a defense statement. JUSTICE believed this to be incorrect because it delayed the disclosure of all relevant material to the defense. Ultimately, it may impede the defendant's chance of running a legitimate defense.[169]

In 2002, the government published its White Paper *Justice for All*.[170] The paper was built on proposals from the Auld Review and many of the White Paper's recommendations were implemented in the Criminal Justice Act 2003 (hereafter, CJA 2003). The White Paper emphasized the government's desire to rebalance the criminal justice process in favor of the victim. The current failings of the criminal justice process were summed up by the government as: "too few criminals are brought to justice, too many defendants offend on bail . . . too many guilty go unconvicted."[171] Part V of the CJA 2003 provided a comprehensive overhaul of the rules of disclosure; this overhaul impacted on both prosecution and defense disclosure. The overhaul was motivated by a dual aim; to provide more efficient case management and to minimize the chance of an ambush defense. However, as pointed out in this chapter, there is little evidence to support the notion that ambush defenses were rife. The three-stage process implemented by the CPIA 1996 was replaced by a single-stage test. Section 32 CJA, amending s. 3(1) CPIA 1996, established the following test:

The prosecutor must—

a) Disclose to the accused any prosecution material which has not been previously been disclosed to the accused and which might reasonably be considered capable of undermining the case for the prosecution against the accused or assisting the case for the accused, or

b) give the accused a written statement that there is no material of a description mentioned in paragraph (a).

Paragraph (a) is reproduced almost verbatim from Auld's suggestion of what the Act should contain. The second stage of prosecution disclosure, which was triggered by the service of a defense statement, was replaced. Under a new s.7A CPIA, inserted by s.37 CJA 2003, the prosecutor is under a continuing duty to disclose that if at any time, "there is material which might reasonably be considered capable of undermining the [prosecution's] case, it must be disclosed." The primary test for prosecution disclosure was more explicit; the prosecution had to disclose material that "might reasonably be considered capable of undermining the case for the prosecution or assisting the case for the accused."[172] This test is more objective and specifically includes the criterion of assisting the defense case.[173] The original disclosure regime under the CPIA 1996 only required disclosure of material that assisted the defense case at the secondary stage; and then only within the terms set out in the defense statement.

Section 33 CJA 2003 inserted a new s.6A CPIA 1996 setting out what is required for a defense statement. The statement needs to contain:

a) the setting out of the nature of the accused's defense, including any particular defenses on which he intends to rely;
b) indicating the matters of fact on which he takes issue with the prosecution;
c) the setting out, in the case of each such matter, as to why he takes issue with the prosecution, and an indication of any point of law (including any point as to the admissibility of evidence or an abuse of process) which he wishes to take and any authority on which he intends to rely for that purpose.

The requirements of the defense statement under the CJA 2003 provisions, inserted into the CPIA 1996, were greatly increased. Section 6A no longer requires the defense to be set out "in general terms" as per the provisions in the CPIA regime. The "nature" of the accused's defense is required to be set out. Furthermore, as per prior provisions, if the accused intends to rely on an alibi defense, the particulars of that defense have to be disclosed in the defense statement.[174] The CJA 2003 requires that the defense must give names, addresses, and dates of birth of any witness it proposes to call. Furthermore, the name and address of any expert they have consulted must be provided; regardless of whether the defense intends to call them at trial.[175]

It was widely accepted that judges were reluctant to draw adverse inference direction from faults concerning the defense statement. One reason for the reluctance was because the fault may rest with the defense lawyer as opposed[176] to the accused and the new s.6E CPIA 1996 provides that unless the contrary is proved, the defense statement is deemed to be given with the authority of the accused.

Section 37 CJA 2003 inserted a new s.11 CPIA 1996, providing for more punitive sanctions should the defense fail to comply with any of the defense disclosure rules. If the defendant fails to serve the defense statement in the permitted time or serves it out of time, the court or jury are permitted to draw such inferences as appear proper in deciding whether the accused is guilty of the offence he is charged with. If the accused calls a witness who he failed to notify or adequately identify, the court will consider whether the failure can be justified. The same applies to situations where the accused puts forward a different defense to the one mentioned in his defense statement.

The amendments made by the CJA 2003 were implemented in April 2005. The changed ideology regarding the trial and defense disclosure can be clearly seen in the Court of Appeal's judgment in *Gleeson.*[177] In that case, the defense realized it had a watertight technical defense to the charge made on the prosecution's indictment. At the end of the prosecution case, the defense made a submission of no case to answer on the basis the conspiracy charged by the prosecution was impossible. Whilst the judge agreed the defense was sound, he permitted the prosecution to redraft the indictment after closing their case to include statutory conspiracy, for which impossibility is not a defense. In his judgment, Auld LJ took the opportunity to recite a passage from his Review of the Criminal Courts of England and Wales, when he said:

> To the extent that the prosecution may legitimately wish to fill possible holes in its case once issues have been identified by the defense statement, it is understandable why as a matter of tactics a defendant might prefer to keep his case close to his chest. But that is not a valid reason for preventing a full and fair hearing on the issues canvassed at the trial. A criminal trial is not a game under which a guilty defendant should be provided with a sporting chance. It is a search for truth in accordance with the twin principles that the prosecution must prove its case and that a defendant is not obliged to inculpate himself, the object being to convict the guilty and acquit the innocent. Requiring a defendant to indicate in advance what he disputes about the prosecution case offends neither of those principles.[178]

In the judgment, Auld LJ commented on the duties of the contemporary defense lawyer:

> For defense advocates to seek to take advantage of such errors by deliberately delaying identification of an issue of fact or law in the case until the last

possible moment, is in our view, no longer acceptable, given the legislative and procedural changes to our criminal justice process in recent years.[179] Although *Gleeson* was heard prior to the implementation of the CJA 2003 provisions, it is clear from the case and the case comment that a change to the ideology of the criminal justice process was being sought and a new regime was born in England and Wales.

The New Regime: The Criminal Procedure Rules

In keeping with the recommendation of the *Auld Review*, the Criminal Procedure Rules Committee was established "to create a single and simply expressed instrument"[180] that contains a codification of criminal procedure. The rules would govern the practice and procedure to be followed in the Criminal Division of the Court of Appeal, the Crown Court and for criminal proceedings in magistrates' courts. The rules were created under the authority of s.69 of the Courts Act 2003 and the Act explicitly states that they should secure that "the criminal justice system is accessible, fair and efficient and the rules are simple and simply expressed."[181] However, the rules have far exceeded that goal and have arguably created a new regime of criminal procedure, the ramifications of which asks questions about the fairness of the process.

The rules very helpfully came with an overriding objective and Rule 1.1 explains that it is to deal with cases "justly." Rule 1.1(2) provides a non-exhaustive list of what "justly" includes:

(2) Dealing with a criminal case justly includes—

a) acquitting the innocent and convicting the guilty;
b) dealing with the prosecution and the defense fairly;
c) recognizing the rights of a defendant, particularly those under Article 6 of the European Convention on Human Rights;
d) respecting the interests of witnesses, victims, and jurors and keeping them informed of the progress of the case;
e) dealing with the case efficiently and expeditiously;
f) ensuring that appropriate information is available to the court when bail and sentence are considered; and
g) dealing with the case in ways that take into account—
    i. the gravity of the offence alleged,
    ii. the complexity of what is in issue,
    iii. the severity of the consequences for the defendant and others affected, and
    iv. the needs of other cases.

A number of these propositions have the potential to impact on the role of the defense lawyer. Proposition (a) appears, on face value at least, to give an equal weight to acquitting the innocent and convicting the guilty. This is difficult to reconcile with an adversarial criminal process that is centered on the notion that it is better for the guilty to be acquitted than the innocent be convicted. Does this proposition impact on the presumption of innocence and how does this impact upon the adversarial defense lawyer's role? It could be argued that the apparent equal weighting between the goals dilute the effectiveness of defense representation. Proposition (b) is also concerning. It appears to provide equal weight to the prosecution and defense, by requiring that they be treated fairly. This gives no thought to the equality of arms, as chapter 2 described; the state has vast resources that can be used against the accused. In the accused's corner stands the defense lawyer; it is he who is charged with defending the accused from the state. Perhaps the rules would be enhanced if they explicitly recognized the equality of arms principle. Proposition (c) is a welcome addition to the CrimPR, especially when one considers the CrimPR did not explicitly acknowledge the presumption of innocence. Proposition (d) is relatively non-contentions as it is important to respect all participants in the criminal justice process. However, there is a danger that this means that the defense lawyer cannot carry out certain lines of questioning, or that certain actions be frowned upon by jurors, which may reflect badly on the defendant Whilst this provision is welcome in the sense that respect for all parties is desirable, the proposition offers no guidance to what the real-term impact may be. Proposition (e) is directly linked into the case management provisions that will be considered at a later point in this chapter. This is an explicit obligation that aims to improve the efficiency of the criminal justice process. Proposition (f) also feeds into the "managerial" culture to ensure the system runs as efficiently as possible. By ensuring all information is presented to the court when sentencing and bail is being considered, there can be no reason for delays. This would include any reports that the court would need to make a decision. Philip Plowden argues that this is a welcome requirement for all agencies but could catch "defense lawyers who intended to make available expert or other reports at the sentencing stage."[182] Proposition (g) is interesting. At face value, it appears to be introducing a notion of proportionality into criminal proceedings. This arguably creates a culture of "justice on the cheap"; it certainly gives no thought to what the stigma of a criminal conviction can mean for a person, for example, the loss of employment or a negative perception attached to them in their local community.

The overriding objective set out in rule 1.1 applies to all participants in a criminal case. A participant is defined as "anyone involved in any way with a criminal case,"[183] which is clearly meant to include the defense lawyer. Further to complying with the overriding objective, any party must inform the court of any "significant failure" to take any step required by the rules. Duncan Atkinson and Tim Moloney explain that a significant failure is defined as "one which might hinder the court in furthering the overriding objective."[184] This could have an impact on existing professional relationships between lawyers. Should one lawyer make a significant failure, the onus would be on the other lawyer to report this to the court as a failure to do so may lead to that participant receiving a sanction from the court. Under rule 3.5(2)(i), the case management provisions of the court allow the court to "specify the consequences of failing to comply with a direction."

It is the responsibility of the court to further the overriding objective by "actively managing"[185] the case. Active case management is defined as:

Rule (2):

(a) the early identification of the real issues;
(b) the early identification of the needs of witnesses;
(c) achieving certainty as to what must be done, by whom, and when, in particular by the early setting of a timetable for the progress of the case;
(d) monitoring the progress of the case and compliance with directions;
(e) ensuring that evidence, whether disputed or not, is presented in the shortest and clearest way;
discouraging delay, dealing with as many aspects of the case as possible on the same occasion, and avoiding unnecessary hearings;

As well as (g) encouraging participants to cooperate in the progression of the case and (h) making use of technology.

Theoretically, case management provisions are nothing new to the court. Auld had already stressed the importance of case management prior to the implementation of the CrimPR. It is worth reiterating here the importance ascribed to active case management. In the case of *Jisl*,[186] Judge LJ described the starting point for any criminal case as follows:

> The starting point is simple. Justice must be done. The defendant is entitled to a fair trial: and, which is sometimes overlooked, the prosecution is equally entitled to a reasonable opportunity to present the evidence against the defendant. It is not however a concomitant of the entitlement to a fair trial that either or both sides are further entitled to take as much time as they like, or for that matter, as long as counsel and solicitors or the defendants themselves think appropriate. Resources are limited . . . time itself is a resource. Every day unnecessarily used, while the trial meanders sluggishly to its eventual conclusion, represents another day's stressful waiting for the remaining witnesses and the jurors in that particular trial, and no less important, continuing

> and increasing tension and worry for another defendant or defendants, some of whom are remanded in custody, and the witnesses in trials who are waiting their turn to be listed. It follows that the sensible use of time requires judicial management and control.[187]

This judgment occurred prior to the creation of the CrimPR, but the influence judge's statement had on the rules is clear. The statement indicates that time is a resource that is required to be managed effectively; it also gives consideration to the stress levels of the jurors, and waiting witnesses, as well as the accused. Cases are now actively managed, so what impact does that have for the defense lawyer? CrimPR rule 3.2(1)(a) requires the early identification of the real issues. What does this mean in real terms? The accused is already required to provide the prosecution with a defense statement; does an expectation exist that this provision will further widen the defense disclosure requirements? Another provision that potentially threatens to alter the fundamental fabric of the adversarial defense lawyer is Rule 3.2(1)(e). This rule is designed to ensure that the evidence is presented in the most succinct and clearest way, but who decides what is the clearest way? The defense lawyer selects the evidence to present in the way that best benefits his client. Is this now to be altered because another route of presentation is deemed more time-efficient? Could this potentially lead to a reduction in the presentation of oral evidence and place more focus on written submissions? As Auld LJ stated, the starting point is simple, "justice must be done." However, can justice be sufficiently "done" if one side of the battle is hampered by further onerous obligations; the defendant already has to indicate the matters he takes issue with the prosecution and any potential defenses he intends to rely upon. As this chapter has argued, this potentially conflicts with the adversarial theory of the English and Welsh criminal justice process; the defendant should not be required to assist the prosecution in building a case which will be used as a basis upon which to convict him.

The Case Management powers of the court can be found in rule 3.5. They are largely unsurprising in their nature, although rule 3.5(2)(i) allows the court to "specify the consequences of failing to comply with a direction." The rule does not substantiate what the sanction can be. The threat of sanctions could raise further conflict with the classic concept of the defense lawyer. Finally, the case management provisions of the CrimPR have the potential to alter the notion of the adversarial trial; as argued in chapter 2, the adversarial trial and role of the defense lawyer are inextricably linked. If there are provisions that impact on the adversarial criminal trial, they potentially impact on the role of the defense lawyer. Rule 3.10 concerns the conduct of the trial. The rules permit the court to require each party to identify:

- which witnesses he intends to give oral evidence;
- the order in which he intends those witnesses to give their evidence;
- whether he requires an order compelling the attendance of a witness;
- what arrangements, if any, he proposes to facilitate the giving of evidence by a witness;
- what arrangements, if any, he proposes to facilitate the participation of any other person, including the defendant;
- what written evidence he intends to introduce;
- what other material, if any, he intends to make available to the court in the presentation of the case;
- whether he intends to raise any point of law that could affect the conduct of the trial or appeal; and
- what timetable he proposes and expects to follow.

Does this have the effect of transforming the traditional adversarial trial, where the defense battles the prosecution, into something that more resembles a meeting that follows a strict timetable or agenda? Within rule 3.10 where is the scope for the defense lawyer to become his accused's "zealous advocate," where is the scope to be the accused's "white knight"? Do the CrimPR present a potential danger to the classic concept of the defense lawyer? Is the defense lawyer removed from his traditional partisan role and placed in a more managerial capacity, which creates pressure to conform to timetables and requirements to assist the prosecution as well as further the best interest of his client? Can the lawyer satisfy both requirements without impinging either his duty to his client or his duty to the court and the administration of justice?

The rules, as originally issued, also offered no new developments to the disclosure regime and no amendments to the existing legislation was offered. However, in May 2010, a change was made in circumstances where the defendant intends to call any persons other than himself as a witness. The defendant must give notice to both the prosecution and the court regarding the name, address, and date of birth of any proposed witness and any other information that may assist in identifying and finding the witness.[188] Failure to disclose the information about a witness may lead to that witness being subjected to cross-examination as to why the information was withheld; which may call into question their credibility.[189] This sets aside the decision in *R (Kelly) v Warley JJ*[190] where the court ruled that the general powers of case management do not extend to the defense having to identify their witnesses. Does this pose any problem in regards to any potential coercion on the part of the police to dissuade certain witnesses from giving evidence? In the case of the Guildford Four, the police "threatened" a journalist who claimed to have alibi evidence concerning one of the suspects.

He also had evidence that contradicted the police account that the bomb detonated at 20:30; he insisted the device exploded at 20:50.[191] It should also be noted the police are not necessarily looking for evidence that will exonerate or even assist the defendant as that would require "the culturally adversarial police to fulfil an effectively inquisitorial function."[192] Quirk found that the police remained "committed to prosecutorial culture"[193] and one officer suggested that they were "salesman for jails";[194] highlighting the culture and mantra of the police force. As such, if the police interviewing of defense witnesses became widespread, it could severely undermine the defense case as it could be seen to be an "invitation to poison the well by undue influence as they naturally want to get the evidence that will convict the defendant."[195]

NOTES

1. Devlin Committee Report: *Report of the Committee on Evidence of Identification in Criminal Cases*, 1976 Cmnd 338 134/135, 42 Paragraph 5.

2. [1946] 31 Cr App R 146. Prior to *Bryant and* Dickson, in the case R *v Clarke* (1930) 22 Cr App R 58 the court held that where there is a discrepancy between a witness's evidence at trial and his statements made previously to the police, the prosecution should consider if an actual copy of the witness's statement should be disclosed rather than just information given about it.

3. D. Corker and S. Parkinson, *Disclosure in Criminal Proceedings* (Oxford University Press: Oxford, 2010) at p. 3.

4. [1965] 1 QB 348.

5. Ibid., per Lord Denning M.R. at para 369.

6. Ibid.

7. This provision remained in force until it was superseded by s.74 Criminal Procedure and Investigations Act 1996.

8. Hansard HC, Vol. 733, col 1068 (August 8, 1966). Sir Richard also proposed that if a suspect refused to make a statement to the police or to give evidence at trial, counsel should be free to comment on this fact.

9. Hansard, HL, Vol. 289, col 259 (June 5, 1967).

10. "Report on an inquiry by the Hon. Sir Henry Fisher into the circumstances leading to the trial of three persons on charges arising out of the death of Maxwell Confait and the fire at 27 Doggett Road, SE6," December 12, 1977.

11. [255]Section (a) "Report on an inquiry by the Hon. Sir Henry Fisher into the circumstances leading to the trial of three persons on charges arising out of the death of Maxwell Confait and the fire at 27 Doggett Road, SE6," December 12, 1977. Paragraph 29.36. Section (b) outlines the special reasons for nondisclosure to include, national security, safety of witness and anything that might lead to a belief that an attempt might be made to mislead the court.

12. Ibid. (c).

13. (d) although counsel may impose a condition that the statement is for counsel's use only.

14. Ibid. (e).

15. Ibid. (f).

16. Ibid. (g).

17. (1946) 31 Cr App R 146.

18. Report on an inquiry by the Hon. Sir Henry Fisher into the circumstances leading to the trial of three persons on charges arising out of the death of Maxwell Confait and the fire at 27 Doggett Road.

19. D. Corker and S. Parkinson, *Disclosure in Criminal Proceedings* (Oxford: OUP, 2010) at p. 7.

20. *Guidelines for the disclosure of "unused material" to the defense in case to be tried on indictment*. (1982) 74 Cr App R 302, paragraph 1. Although the guidelines are non-statutory to all intents and purposes, they are intended to have the force of a statutory provision.

21. The Fraud Trials Committee, Chairman: The Right Honourable Lord Roskill, P.C (HMSO: 1986).

22. Ibid., at p. 1 para 1.

23. Ibid., at p. 2 at para 4. The committee did stop of recommending any proposal to anything other than fraud cases, they would leave that discussion for those with wider concerns than then own.

24. The Fraud Trials Committee, *Chairman: The Right Honorable Lord Roskill*, P. C (HMSO: 1986) p. 103 at para 6.72.

25. Ibid., at p. 104 at para 6.75.

26. Ibid., at para 6.76.

27. Ibid., at p. 106 at para 6.82. At para 6.38, the report stated that the committee could not support the suggestion that the defense should disclose the names and addresses of witnesses. They believed that the defense may not decide whether or not to call a certain witness until they have seen how the prosecution's witnesses stood up to cross-examination. Furthermore, the disclosure may lead to allegations at trial that the police have acted improperly in interviewing a witness.

28. M. Levi, "The Future of Fraud Prosecutions and Trials: Reviewing Roskill" [1986] *Company Law* Vol. 7(4), 139–146 at p. 140.

29. R. Munday "The Roskill Committee on Fraud Trials" [1986] *Cambridge Law Journal* Vol. 175–179 at p. 177.

30. Ibid., at p. 177.

31. S.2(3) Criminal Justice Act 1988.

32. SI 1987/716.

33. For a full review of the Commission's findings please see *The Royal Commission on Criminal Procedure. Report. The investigation and prosecution of criminal offences in England and Wales: the law and procedure*, Cmmd 8092 at p. 179 para 8.22.

34. See Criminal Justice Act 1987, C.L.R. 1987, Aug, 525–526.

35. House of Commons, Hansard 5 November 1987, col. 713.

36. (1990) 90 Cr App R 107; [1990] Crim LR 62.

37. [1964] All ER 610 CA.

38. *R* v *McIKenny and Others* [1991] 93 CR AR 287.

39. The Royal Commission on Criminal Justice, *Report,* Cm 2263 (HMSO, 1993).

40. Ibid., p. 91 para 33.

41. *R v Ward* [1993] 2 All ER 577.

42. Ibid., at p. 599.

43. Ibid., at p. 601.

44. [1994] 2 All ER 478.

45. Unreported, December 20, 1993, as cited in D. Corker and S. Parkinson, *Disclosure in Criminal Proceedings* (Oxford: Oxford University Press, 2009) at p. 15.

46. *R v Keane* [1994] 2 All ER 478, 484.

47. The Royal Commission on Criminal Justice, *Report*, Cm 2263 (HMSO) 1993 at para 42.

48. D. Corker and S. Parkinson, *Disclosure in Criminal Proceedings* (Oxford: OUP, 2010) at p. 15.

49. The Royal Commission on Criminal Justice, *Report*, Cm 2263 (HMSO) 1993 at para 49.

50. Ibid., at para 59.

51. Ibid.

52. Ibid.

53. Ibid.

54. M. Zander and P. Henderson, "The Crown Court Study" [1993] Royal Commission on Criminal Justice Research Study No. 19 , 14–15.

55. R. Leng, *The Right to Silence in Police Interrogation*, Royal Commission on Criminal Justice Research Study No. 10 (1993) Ch. 5.

56. The Royal Commission on Criminal Justice, *Report*, Cm 2263 (HMSO) 1993 para 73.

57. Ibid., at p. 221 para 1.

58. Ibid., at p. 221 para 3.

59. M. Levi, *The Investigation, Prosecution and Trial of Serious Fraud*, Royal Commission on Criminal Justice Research Study No. 14, 1993.

60. The Royal Commission on Criminal Justice, *Report*, Cm 2263 (HMSO) 1993 p. 222.

61. Michael Zander's speech to the British Criminology Conference in July 1993 as cited in S. Field and P. Thomas, "Justice and Efficiency? The Royal Commission on Criminal Procedure" [1994] *The Journal of Law and Society*, Vol. 21(1), 1–19 at p. 9.

62. In relation to sentence canvassing, the need to improve efficiency of the system appeared to be afforded the greatest weight.

63. S. Field and P. Thomas, "Justice and Efficiency? The Royal Commission on Criminal Procedure," *The Journal of Law and Society*, Vol. 21(1), 1–19 at p. 9.

64. S. Field and P. Thomas, "Justice and Efficiency? The Royal Commission on Criminal Procedure" [1994] *The Journal of Law and Society*, Vol. 21(1), 1–19 at p. 14.

65. S. Greer, "The Right to Silence, Defense Disclosure and Confession Evidence" [1994] *The Journal of Law and Society*, Vol. 21(1), p. 102.

66. Ibid., at p. 102.

67. Please see Greer above, A. Owers, Runciman Reviewed" (1993), 90 L.S.G. 2, M. McConville, "An Error of Judgment," Legal Action, September 1993.

68. L. Bridges and M. McConville, "Keeping Faith with Their Own Convictions: The Royal Commission on Criminal Justice" [1994] *Modern Law Review* Vol. 57, 75 at 90. The authors also argue the presumption of guilt is reinforced by giving the police more powers to obtain evidence from suspects and by the accused continuing to suffer from poor quality legal advice in the court and police station.

69. Michael Howard speaking at the Conservative Party Conference, October 1993.

70. Some of the changes suggested by the then home secretary, such as the abolition of the right to silence, outright rejected the findings of the commission.

71. S. Field and P. Thomas, "Justice and Efficiency? The Royal Commission on Criminal Procedure" [1994] *The Journal of Law and Society*, Vol. 21(1), 1–19 at pp. 6–7.

72. P. Thornton, A. Mallaliey and A. Sceivener, *Justice on Trial: Report of an Independent Civil Liberty Panel on Criminal Justice* (Civil Liberties Trust: London, 1993). at p. 1.

73. Ibid., at Para 11.11 p. 55.

74. The Royal Commission on Criminal Justice, *Report*, Cm 2263 (HMSO) 1993 at para 11.10.

75. Disclosure: A Consultation Paper, May 1995 CM 2864.

76. Ibid., at , p. 4 para 13.

77. Ibid., at at paragraph 2.

78. Ibid., at p. 5 para 16–17.

79. Ibid., at , p. 15, para 48.

80. Ibid., at , p. 15, para 52.

81. Investigation and Prosecution of Criminal Offences in England and Wales: Law and Procedure (Command 8092-I) (HMSO: London), 1981.

82. See Inquiry into the Circumstances leading to the trial of three persons on charges arising from the death of Maxwell Confait (HCP 90) London HMSO 1977.

83. Ibid., at para 4.50.

84. The Police and Criminal Evidence Act 1984 was seen to be the high-water mark of offering due protections to those suspected of committing a criminal offence.

85. H. Quirk, *The Rise and Fall of the Right of Silence* (2017) Routledge: Oxon) at p. 36.

86. The Birmingham Six (*McIKenny and Others [*1992] Crim LR 117; Stefan Kiszko (Kiszko, 1992); The Cardiff Three (*Paris, Abdullahi and Miller* [1993] 97 Cr App Rep 99; and Judith Ward (*R v Ward* [1993] 1 WLR 619 96 Cr App Rep 1).

87. H. Quirk, *The Rise and Fall of the Right of Silence* ((Oxon: Routledge, 2017) at p. 40.

88. Ibid., at p. 43.

89. A. Travers (1993) "Right to Silence abolished in crackdown on crime," *Guardian* October 7, as cited in at p. 44.

90. See L. Bridges, "Normalising Injustice: The Royal Commission on Criminal Justice" [1994] *Journal of Law & Society* Vol. 21, 20–29 at p. 20.

91. Ibid., at p. 36.

92. The Royal Commission on Criminal Justice (HMSO: London 1994), Cm 2263 at para 5–10.

93. S. Field and P. A. Thomas, "Justice and Efficiency? The Royal Commission on Criminal Justice" [1994] *Journal of Law & Society* Vol. 21, 1–19 at p. 8.

94. Field and Thomas, "Justice and Efficiency?" [1994] *Journal of Law & Society* Vol. 21, 1–19 at pp. 13–14.

95. Greer, "The Right to Silence, Defense Disclosure and Confession Evidence," at p. 104.

96. The Royal Commission on Criminal Justice, *Report,* Cm 2263 (HMSO, 1993) p. 84 para 3.

97. R. Leng, "The Right to Silence in Police Interrogation: A Study of Some of the Issues Underlying the Debate" [1993] *RCCJ Research Study* Vol. 10, p. 58.

98. M. Levi, "The Investigation, Prosecution and Trial of Serious Fraud" [1993] *RCCJ Research Study* Vol. 14, pp. 104, 182.

99. The Royal Commission on Criminal Justice, *Report,* Cm 2263 (HMSO, 1993), Note of Dissent, M. Zander p. 222.

100. Greer, "The Right to Silence, Defense Disclosure and Confession," at p. 109.

101. Field and Thomas, "Justice and Efficiency?" p. 10.

102. The *Disappearing Trial* Report in the United States found that out of 149 successful appeals in 2015, 44 percent had entered a guilty plea. See, *The Disappearing Trial: Towards a Rights Based Approach to Trial Waiver Systems*, Fair Trials, 2017 available here: http://www.fairtrials.org/sites/default/files/publication_pdf/Report-The-Disappearing-Trial.pdf [last accessed December 2020].

103. The Royal Commission on Criminal Justice, *Report,* Cm 2263 (HMSO, 1993), p. 97.

104. Greer, "The Right to Silence, Defense Disclosure and Confession Evidence," at p. 106.

105. Criminal Procedure and Investigations Act 1996.

106. S.34 Criminal Justice and Public Order Act 1994.

107. S.35 Criminal Justice and Public Order Act 1994.

108. S.36 Criminal Justice and Public Order Act 1994.

109. S.37 Criminal Justice and Public Order Act 1994.

110. H. Quirk "Twenty Years On, the Right of Silence and Legal Advice: The Spiraling Costs of An Unfair Exchange" [2013] *NILQ* Vol. 64(4), 465–483 at p. 466.

111. S. Chakrabarti "A Thinning Blue Line? Police Independence and the Rule of Law" [2008] Vol. 2(3) Policing, 367–374 at 369.

112. s.3(1)(a) Criminal Procedure and Investigations Act 1996.

113. Ibid., at s.7(2)(a).

114. R. Leng and R. Taylor, *Blackstone's Guide to the Criminal Procedure and Investigations Act 1996* (London: Blackstone's Press, 1996) at p. 1.

115. Ibid., at p. 2.

116. s.1(2) Criminal Procedure and Investigations Act 1996.

117. Which is where almost 94 percent of criminal trials are held.

118. Richard Card and Richard Ward believe the section is unnecessary as it is always open to the accused to disclose facts about his defense. For further discussion please see R. Card and R. Ward, *The Criminal Procedure and Investigations Act 1996* (Bristol: Jordan's Publishing, 1996) at p. 37.

119. s.5(7)(a) CPIA 1996.

120. s.5(7)(b) CPIA 1996.

121. s.11 Criminal Justice Act 1967.

122. S.30 Criminal Justice Act 1988.

123. s.11(3)(a) CPIA 1996.

124. s.11(3)(b) CPIA 1996.

125. S.11(5) CPIA 1996.

126. Crown Prosecution Service Inspectorate, *The Inspectorates Report on The Thematic Review of the Disclosure of Unused Material*, Thematic Report 2/2000, March 2000 at p. 4 para 1.4.

127. Ibid., at p. 36 para 5.6.

128. Ibid., at p. 38 para 5.19.

129. Ibid., at p. 38 para 5.19.

130. Ibid., at p. 38 para 5.23.

131. Ibid., at p. 39 para 5.25.

132. J. Plotnikoff and R.Woolfson, "A Fair Balance? Evaluation and Operation of Disclosure Law," RDS Occasional Paper No 76, 2001 at p. ix.

133. Ibid., at p. 77 table 25.

134. Ibid., at p. 77.

135. Ibid., at p. 127.

136. Ibid., at p. 128.

137. Ibid., at p. 128.

138. Hannah Quirk discusses these issues at length in "The Significance of Culture in Criminal Procedure Reform: Why the Revised Disclosure Scheme Cannot Work," 10 Evidence and Proof (2006), 42.

139. C. Taylor, "Advance Disclosure: Reflections on the Criminal Procedure and Investigations Act 1996" [2001] *Howard Journal* Vol. 40(2), at pp. 114, 117.

140. However, in light of the Criminal Procedure Rules and the Overriding Objective, the Court explicitly prohibits ambush defenses. This point will be discussed later in this chapter.

141. H. Quirk, "Disclosure: Significance of Culture in Criminal Procedural Reform" [2006] 10 E&P 42–59 at 56.

142. An Ambush defense is one which surprises the prosecution at trial. The prosecution have no idea what evidence the defense will call and is therefore "ambushed" by their tactics.

143. R. Leng, "Losing Sight of the Defendant: The Government's Proposals on Pre-Trial Disclosure" [1995] *Criminal Law Review* Vol. 704, 706.

144. Ibid.

145. Ibid.

146. M. Zander and P. Henderson, "The Crown Court Study," Royal Commission Research Study No. 19 [1993], 14–15.

147. M. Zander"s Note of Dissent to the RCCJ report (CM2263) (HMSO: London, 1993) at p. 223.

148. The miscarriage of justice in *R v Ward* [1993] 1 W.L.R. 619 96 Cr.App.R.1 was the final example of a number of miscarriages of justice in the early 1990s. The day after the quashing of her conviction, the government announced the creation of the Runciman Commission.

149. A. Heaton-Armstrong, "The (Un)Workability of the Provisions in the Criminal Procedure and Investigations Act 1996—Disaster in the Criminal Law?" [1999] *Medicine, Science and Law* Vol 39(2), 93–98 at 94.

150. J. Sprack, "The Criminal Procedure and Investigations Act 1996: Part 1: The Duty to Disclose" [1997] *Criminal Law Review* 308–320 at 319.

151. M. Redmayne, "Process Gains and Values: The Criminal Procedure and Investigations Act 1996" [1997] *MLR* Vol. 60(1), 79–93 at 93.

152. J. Sprack, "Will Defense Disclosure Snap the Golden Thread?" [1998] *E&P* Vol. 2(4), 224–231 at 231.

153. R. Leng, "Losing Sight of the Defendant: The Government's Proposals on Pre-Trial Disclosure" [1995] *Criminal Law Review* Vol. 704, 711.

154. See E. McLaughlin, J. Muncie and G. Hughes, "The Permanent Revolution: New Labour, New Public Management and the Modernization of Criminal Justice" [2001] *Criminal Justice*, Vol. 1(3), 301–318 at 307.

155. Home Office, Criminal Justice System: Strategic Plan 1999–2002 (1999) para 1.3.

156. M. Zander, *Lord Justice Auld"s Review of the Criminal Courts: A Response* (2001) at p. 6, available here: https://www.lse.ac.uk/collections/law/staff%20publications%20full%20text/zander/auld_response_web.pdf [Last accessed December 2020].

157. Ibid., at p. 5.

158. Ibid.

159. R. Auld, *A Review of the Criminal Courts of England and Wales* (2001) chapter 1, Paragraph 1.

160. Ibid.

161. Ibid., at chapter 10 para 271.

162. Ibid., at , Ch. 10 para 163 p. 463.

163. Ibid., at p. 466 para 171.

164. Ibid.

165. Ibid.

166. Ibid.

167. Ibid., at p. 470 para 180.

168. JUSTICE: A Response to the Auld Review p. 30 para 75.

169. Ibid., at para 78.

170. Lord Chancellor and Attorney General Secretary of State for Home Department, *Justice for All*, Cmmd 5563 (2002) (Cm 5563).

171. JUSTICE: A Response to the Auld Review p. 11.

172. Criminal Justice Act s.32 amending s.3(1)(a) CPIA 1996.

173. M. Redmayne, "Criminal Justice Act 2003: (1) Disclosure and its Discontents," [2004] *Criminal Law Review* Vol. 441 at p. 443.

174. CPIA s.6A(2)(a) and (b) explains what details are required to disclose in the defense statement.

175. S. 34 Criminal Justice Act 2003 inserting s.6C CPIA 1996. This provision was not implemented until May 2010.

176. J. Plotnikoff and R. Wolfson "A Fair Balance? Evaluation and Operation of the disclosure law" RDS Occasional Paper no 76, 2001 at 446.

177. [2004] Crim LR 579.

178. As Per LJ Auld, [2004] 1 Cr. App. R. 29, para 36 cited from Auld Review, para. 154 of Ch. 10.

179. As Per LJ Auld, [2004] 1 Cr. App. R. 29 at para 35.

180. *The Review of the Criminal Courts of England and Wales* (2001), Para 184.

181. S.69(4)(a) and (b) Courts Act 2003.

182. P. Plowden, "Make Do and Mend, or a Cultural Evolution?" [2005] *The New Law Journal* 331 at 337.

183. Rule 1.2(2) Criminal Procedure Rules.

184. D. Atkinson and T. Moloney, *Blackstone's Guide to the Criminal Procedure Rules 2005* (Oxford: Oxford University Press, 2005) at p. 13 para 2.13.

185. Rule 3.2(1) Criminal Procedure Rules 2015.

186. [2004] EWCA Crim 696.

187. [2004] EWCA Crim 696 as per Judge LJ at 114.

188. S. 34 Criminal Justice Act 2003 inserting s.6C CPIA 1996.

189. The Law Society Practice Note, Defense Witness Notices, January 27, 2011.

190. [2007] EWHC 1836 (Admin); [2008] 1 W.L.R. 2001.

191. For a more detailed account of the threats, please see https://www.bbc.co.uk/news/uk-england-surrey-42665187 [Last accessed September 1, 2018].

192. H. Quirk, "The significance of Culture in Criminal Procedure Reform: Why the Revised Disclosure Scheme Cannot Work" [2006] *International Journal of Electrical Power* Vol. 10, 42, 46.

193. Ibid.

194. Ibid., at p. 48.

195. A. Owusu-Bempah, "Defense Participation through Pre-Trial Disclosure: Issues and Implications" [2013] *E&P* Vol. 17, 183–201 at p. 195.

Chapter 4

Theoretical Implications of the "New Regime"

As discussed in chapter 3, the changes to disclosure and then the creation of case management provisions of the CrimPR have led to the creation of a "new regime." Chapter 2 established that the defense lawyer has three core duties: to his client, the court, and the public.[1] Despite having no relative weighting attached to them, these duties establish the core elements of the obligations for the defense lawyer. This chapter will theoretically examine how the lawyer prioritizes these obligations. Chapter 2 concluded that the fact that although the defense lawyer is his client's mouthpiece does not absolve him of all moral responsibility and he has to consider his other obligations. It is with these core duties in mind that this chapter will examine the theoretical implication of the new regime of pretrial defense disclosure and case management.

THE OBLIGATIONS OF THE MODERN DEFENSE LAWYER

For the purpose of examining the theoretical impact of the obligations, it is important to reiterate what is expected of the "modern-day" defense lawyer. This modern-day picture will be examined through the lens of the legislative obligations placed on him. It is also important to clarify upon whom the obligations rest. Some obligations rest directly on the defense lawyer. Other obligations rest ostensibly on the accused but operate as an indirect obligation on the lawyer, as it is unrealistic to expect a layperson to understand complex legal directions and comprehend the ramifications of compliance.

As stated in chapter 2, from the genesis of the adversarial criminal trial in the mid-nineteenth century until 1967, neither the defense lawyer nor his client were under any obligation to disclose any facet of their case to the prosecution or the court in advance of trial.[2] The CPIA 1996 fundamentally altered this and imposed the most radical and onerous obligations on the accused. The Act required a defense statement to be disclosed in advance of trial.[3] The content of the defense statement was defined by s5(6) CPIA 1996. The statement had to set out "in general terms, the nature of the accused's defense."[4] This obligation was enhanced by the Criminal Justice Act 2003. The Act removed the "general terms" of the nature of the accused's defense and replaced it with something far more onerous. Now, the defense statement had to be far more detailed including an outline of what points of law and authority he will be relying on. The regime is enforced by the threat of adverse inferences being drawn should the defendant fail to disclose the statement in the prescribed time or if his defense deviates at trial from the disclosed case statement.[5] In May 2010,[6] a new obligation came into force, giving effect to s.35 of the Criminal Justice Act 2003.[7] The details of any witnesses the defense intends to call at trial, other than the accused, have to be disclosed. These details include the names, addresses, dates of birth, and any other information that may assist the prosecution in locating the witnesses. The prosecution is allowed to interview the witnesses, although during any witness interview the defense lawyer is permitted to be present.

As well as disclosure obligations imposed by the CPIA 1996, the CrimPR have imposed further obligations on the defense lawyer. The CrimPR have an overriding objective of "dealing with cases justly"[8] and the defense lawyer is required to contribute to fulfilling this overriding objective. Should any "significant failure" arise the court should be informed at once, regardless of whether or not that participant is responsible for the "significant failure."[9] Additionally, the CrimPR state that each party must actively assist the court in fulfilling its duty under rule 3.2,[10] "with or without a direction from the court." Rule 3.3(b) does allow a participant to apply for a direction, should that be necessary.

In a little over forty years, the legislative obligations have changed from the defense and his client having to disclose no information in advance of trial to a situation where detailed information must be provided. As well as having to fulfill many disclosure provisions, the CrimPR have imposed a duty on the defense lawyer to further the overriding objective; the lawyer has to help the court fulfil the requirement that "cases are dealt with justly." A pivotal aspect of this overriding objective is "dealing with cases efficiently and expeditiously."[11] This represents a fundamental shift caused by the CPIA 1996 and the CrimPR, the implications of which will be highlighted throughout this chapter.

The Conflicts with the Traditional Role of the Defense Lawyer

The pretrial disclosure requirements established by the CPIA 1996 and the CrimPR potentially conflict with the notion of zealous advocacy. Should the lawyer fail to comply with the provisions, his client faces the possibility of the court making "such comment as appears appropriate"[12] which may result in the "court or jury . . . [drawing] such inferences as appear proper in deciding whether the accused is guilty of the offence concerned."[13] This is problematic: first, the duty rests on the accused to fulfil the statutory provisions, not directly with the defense lawyer. However, it has to be questioned whether placing the obligation on the accused is realistic. If one assumes that it is an unrealistic obligation, it can be assumed that the defense lawyer completes the defense statement and therefore the obligation rests ostensibly on him.

The traditional conception established in chapter 1 shows the lawyer acting as the zealous advocate of the accused; he acts with vigor as the partisan defender of his client's rights and advances the interests of his client at any given opportunity. The problem with advancing the interests of the client is that it may lead to frustrating the administration of justice, thereby frustrating the duty to the court. It has been noted that the "win at all costs" mentality of lawyers means "[they are] running roughshod over witnesses, and with court procedures and the truth."[14] This poses a question of how does a lawyer "win"? Arguably, a win would mean that his client is acquitted at trial. If this is the only measure of success, it is arguable that defense lawyers are failing their clients. The reason for this is the fact that in 2017 and 2016, the guilty plea rates in the Crown Court remained at 67 percent.[15] So it is clear that the vast majority of cases are not "won" by the defense lawyer. However, the answer is not as simplistic as that. The lawyer may "win," even if a guilty plea is entered. For example, the lawyer may have reached a charge bargain with the prosecution which means his client enters a guilty plea to a lesser offence carrying a less severe sentence. In theory, the lawyer may wish to win at all costs, but the current practice illustrates that there is more than one way to "win" but also the lawyer simply cannot advance his client's best interest, to the exclusion of his other duties.

As an Officer of the Court, he has to pay a great deal of attention to his duty to the court and he is expected to facilitate justice in the courtroom by assisting the court to discover the truth which will enable the court to serve justice. Thereby, if the defense lawyer adopts this approach, he will satisfy his duty to the court and, should justice be served, his duty to the public. It is arguable that those two duties are satisfied at the expense of advancing the best interests of his client. This is an example of conflict that epitomizes the conflict role faced by defense lawyers. Justice Crampton in *R v O'Connell*[16] identified the goal of truth-seeking as the primary goal of all actors in the legal process when he said "we are all . . . concerned with the truth . . . that is primary and paramount."[17]

Although it is arguable that truth-seeking should be the primary goal of the lawyer, the classic conception established that the primary duty of the lawyer is to advance the best interests of his client but that does not necessarily satisfy the truth-seeking goals of the court. This conflict between two duties can be illuminated by examining the ambush defense. This is the classic example of two duties coming into conflict or tension with each other and the question remains, which duty should take precedence: the duty to the client or the duty to the court? By using the tactics of an "ambush," the late introduction of evidence may catch the prosecution off guard and may advance the interests of the client. However, it will certainly frustrate the duty to the court as the latter means resources are wasted. In an effort to combat the problem[18] of ambush defenses, the accused is now required to give a defense statement to the court; this has effectively eradicated the use of the ambush defense as a valid weapon of the defense lawyer.

Disclosure and the Impact on the Defense Lawyer

The requirements of the defense statement have already been outlined in chapter 4 and will not be repeated here. This section will concentrate on the conflicts the defense statement may cause for the defense lawyer. The CPIA 1996 provisions state that the defense statement must set out "the nature of the accused's defense including any particular defenses on which he intends to rely."[19] The admissions made in the defense statement will clearly have ramifications at trial. Despite the wording of the statutory provision and direct obligation on the accused, the defense statement has a theoretical impact on the classic conception of the defense lawyer, especially in terms of the lawyer-client relationship; the accused may not wish to divulge certain facts that the lawyer is compelled to reveal. How the lawyer tackles this problem will be addressed in the empirical study but theoretically, it could have a great impact on his role.

The completion and service of a defense statement is a statutory requirement and it has been held wholly unacceptable to attempt to circumvent this obligation, even if the accused has no positive case to answer. In *Essa*,[20] the court made it clear that it is professionally unacceptable for the lawyer to advise his client not to complete the defense statement. Lord Justice Hughes was "at a loss to understand how any lawyer can properly give the advice [not to file the defense statement] in the face of s.5(5) CPIA 1996, . . . its requirement is that the accused provide [a copy] of the defense statement to the court and prosecutor."[21] In the pre-CPIA era, if the defendant had no positive case to advance yet wanted to enter a plea of not guilty, the lawyer would simply put the prosecution to proof and ask them to discharge the burden of proof. However, the CPIA provisions have fundamentally altered the traditional conception of the adversarial defense lawyer and therefore his approach to advancing the best interests of his client. It is no longer acceptable for him to consider the duty to his client as his primary duty; the duty he owes to the court is reinforced with the weight of statutory authority. Following *Essa*,[22] it appears that the duty to the court could potentially override the lawyer's duty to the client. The overriding of the primary duty to the client with that of the court creates a seismic swing; the primary duty theoretically swings from being the zealous advocate of his client to an advocate that has a duty of cooperation with the prosecution which serves an overarching duty to the court.

By disclosing the nature of the accused's defense in the statement, the client will lose the strategic advantage of surprise. The defense case statement is effectively showing the hand of the defense to the prosecution and enhances this notion of cooperation between the defense and the prosecution. *Gleeson*[23] illustrates the erosion of the penalty shoot-out theory[24] of the criminal trial. The penalty shoot-out theory is based on the premise that traditionally the prosecution has one shot to secure a conviction against the defendant; much like a footballer in a penalty shoot-out, should the player miss his penalty, he does not get an opportunity to re-kick. However, post-*Gleeson*, it is clear that the prosecution may be permitted to amend its case should the defense be at fault for not identifying a law in the prosecution's case and reap the benefit of that flaw. Further, case law illustrates that the adversarial weapon has not only been blunted but completely prohibited from use. The courts have frowned upon on "ambush" attempts as can be seen from a number of judgments. In *Brett v DPP*, Leveson LJ reiterated the judgment from the *Chorley Justices*[25] case: "For defense advocates to seek to take advantage of such errors by deliberately delaying identification of an issue of fact or law in the case until the last possible moment is in our view no longer acceptable, given the legislative and procedural changes to our criminal justice process in recent years."[26]

The days of the defense being able to raise points at the last moment are clearly over. In *Malcolm v DPP*,[27] the Divisional Court explained that the defense has a duty to make the points they will raise and their defense clear to both the prosecution and the court at an early stage. In this case, the defense took a point in the closing speech that was not raised with any prosecution witness. As such, the court permitted the prosecution leave to call further evidence. The Divisional Court commended the justices for "refusing to succumb to this kind of forensic legerdemain"[28] and it is apparent that the tactics of the defense lawyer has begun to have stern restrictions placed upon them. Owusu-Bempah suggests that the defense disclosure regime, and the linked dilution of the ambush defense, indicates a move to a more inquisitorial model of criminal justice.[29] She goes onto argue that issues regarding prosecutorial nondisclosure represents a greater threat to truth-finding than defense nondisclosure. Ultimately, she concludes that the defense disclosure is not an inquisitorial trait as "inquisitorial jurisdictions do not require defense disclosure."[30] However, the regime has cultivated a culture of defendant participation whereby the defendant is co-opted into the process in seeking to ensure the criminal justice process runs smoothly. Ultimately, this means that should the defense lawyer attempt to advance the interests of his client by using ambush tactics, that behavior will be deemed wholly inappropriate. In ruling ambush tactics as inappropriate, the courts are effectively saying that whilst the duty to the client is of importance, the furthering of that duty must not come at the expense of the duty to the court. In essence, by ensuring that the defense lawyer will not spring a surprise at trial, that duty will be satisfied. Of course, by that ensuring the nature of the accused's defense is disclosed and prohibiting ambush defenses, these provisions have potentially altered the relationship between the defense lawyer and his client. Previously, the lawyer's position was based on "zealous advocacy." It can now be described as resting on the foundation of cooperation with the prosecution. Not only does this notion of cooperation hamper the lawyer in advancing the best interest of his client, it could also have ramifications for the lawyer-client relationship. For example, if the client knows that his lawyer has an obligation to cooperate with the prosecution, it could potentially lead to the client not trusting his lawyer or viewing them as a different side to the same coin. As a result, the notion that the lawyer is the "zealous advocate" of the accused is defeated, because he is unable to zealously protect his client owing to the other competing duties that the lawyer must recognize and comply with.

Witness Disclosure

As of May 2010, the accused had his disclosure obligations further enhanced. Section 34 Criminal Justice Act 2003 (hereafter, CJA 2003) inserted a new section 6C into the CPIA 1996. This new section created a requirement for the defendant to disclose in advance of trial the names, addresses, and dates of birth of any witnesses, other than himself, that he intends to call at trial.[31] Furthermore, any other information that may be of material assistance in identifying or finding the proposed witness is required to be disclosed. Previously, this obligation only existed in relation to a witness who was giving evidence to support an alibi defense or an expert witness.[32] Following the service of initial prosecution disclosure, the defendant has fourteen days in which to disclose which defense witnesses he intends to call. *R v Ensor*[33] concerned the late service of expert evidence; the court excluded the defense evidence as the defense did not alert the court to a significant failure. The Court of Appeal held that "it is incumbent upon both the prosecution and defense . . . to alert the court and the other side at the earliest practical moment" and the court were entitled to exclude the evidence. The Law Society issued a Practice Note concerning Defense Witness Notices and this suggests a similar interpretation is likely to apply to defense witness notifications.[34] Therefore, the defense will not be able to wait until the close of the prosecution's case before deciding the witnesses they will call. Should the defendant call a witness who was not disclosed, the court cannot prohibit him from giving evidence. Although the available sanctions to the court often hold little bite, *R (Tinnion) v Reading Crown Court*[35] stated that the court will not exclude the evidence of the witness being heard. The case was heard in the youth court and any disclosure of a defense statement was voluntary.[36] Furthermore, the court held that if the defendant was under an obligation to provide a defense statement, failure to do so does not render the evidence inadmissible. The "sanction against a defendant who fails to give such notice is not that the witness cannot be called, but that adverse comment can be conducted, and that the court or jury may draw such inference as is proper."[37]

Therefore, in a true adversarial process, the prosecution should not be able to access defense witnesses for fear of an inimical risk of adverse pressure being placed on the witnesses by the police. This risk might influence the witness to not testify or alter their accounts of events. Furthermore, a theoretical risk exists that if the lawyer is not present at the interview the police may assert undue influence on the suspect by bullying or intimidating them to change their statement or not to testify at trial. Fundamentally, the police are not neutral actors in the criminal justice process; they want to obtain as much evidence as possible that will lead to the conviction of the defendant.[38]

Potential Conflicts with the CrimPR

Theoretically, the disclosure provisions of the CPIA 1996 fundamentally alter the classic conception of the defense lawyer's role. By altering the role, the provisions place a number of obligations ostensibly on the lawyer, which create a number of conflicts or tensions that he will have to address. These conflicts and tensions are further heightened by the requirements of the CrimPR. Whereas previously the CPIA 1996 governed the pretrial disclosure obligations of the accused, or more indirectly, the lawyer, the CrimPR place obligations directly on the defense lawyer as well as a number of indirect obligations. The rules place obligations on both "parties" and "participants." The glossary of terms the CrimPR states that a party is a person or organization directly involved in a criminal case, either as a prosecutor or a defendant. It is important to note that the defense lawyer is not classed as a "party." The

CrimPR provide that "anyone involved in any way with a criminal case is a participant in its conduct for the purposes of this rule," which does include the defense lawyer.[39] This distinction is important as some obligations rest with a party, thereby not directly placed on the defense lawyer and some obligations are placed directly on a participant, which includes the defense lawyer. However, the question remains whether it is realistic to presume the defense lawyer will not take on an obligation, despite it being placed on the accused.

The overriding objective is succinctly outlined in Rule 1.1(1): The overriding objective of the CrimPR is that criminal cases be dealt with justly. The rules[40] state that each participant, in the conduct of each case, must prepare and conduct the case in accordance with the overriding objective. However, the efficiency drivers are abundantly clear through both the CrimPR and judicial tenor post-*Auld* Review.[41] It is Rule 1.2(2)(e)[42] that provides the core issue to this chapter; whilst dealing with the case efficiently and expeditiously is not to be derided; little thought appears to be given to the impact on the role of the defense lawyer. This notion of "efficiency" implicitly lays at the heart of the CrimPR and the courts have been clear to enforce the notion that time is not unlimited and a strict timetable is to be adhered to. In 2009, the then senior presiding judge for England and Wales, Lord Justice Leveson, published guidance on how courts should apply the CrimPR.[43] The guidance stated that "unnecessary hearings should be avoided by dealing with as many aspects of the case as possible at the same time."[44] This includes taking the plea of the defendant or if no plea can be taken, an indication as to what plea would be "likely."[45] This plea or indication of the plea needs to be taken either at the first hearing or as soon as possible after the first hearing.[46] Surprisingly, the guidance states that this obligation does not depend on the extent of advance information, service of evidence, disclosure of unused documents or the grant of legal aid.[47] A footnote to the guidance explicitly states that the rules are not mere guidelines. Compliance is compulsory.[48] The requirement for a plea at the earliest possible moment creates a professional conflict for the defense lawyer. On one hand, his duty to the court will be satisfied by compliance with this provision and advising his client to enter a plea. However, if the lawyer has insufficient information about the nature of the prosecution case, it may not be possible to give proper advice as to plea.[49] The lawyer or the accused should not be cajoled into entering a plea without proper thought and attention to what the consequences are.

This notion of efficiency is exemplified by the court's reluctance to grant adjournments. In *Balogun v DPP*,[50] Leveson LJ stated that any application to adjourn proceedings needed to be subjected to "rigorous scrutiny."[51] In suggesting this, Leveson LJ reiterated the judgment of Openshaw J in *Aravinthan Visarathnam v Brent Magistrates' Court*[52] where he said:

"An[y] improvement in timeliness and the achievement of a more effective and efficient system of criminal justice in the Magistrates' Court will bring about great benefits to victims and to witnesses and huge savings in time and money."[53] But clearly, the omission to mentioning the defendant is glaring.

This desire for efficiency and a reduction of adjournments, thereby saving both time and other resources, is assisted by the compliance with the Case Management powers of the court and the completion of the case management forms. These provisions are found in Part III of the CrimPR and the management of cases applies to both magistrates' court and Crown Court cases.[54] Rule 3.2(1) sets out the duty of the court: the court must further the overriding objective by actively managing the case. Interestingly, active case management is partly defined as "the early identification of the real issues"[55] and the "early identification of the needs of witnesses."[56] If the accused is entering a not guilty plea, the prosecution and defense must identify what the issues are at trial and what witnesses will be required to attend court. If the parties do not tell the court, the court must require them to do so. Any disputed issues will need to be explicitly identified so the court can ensure that the "live" evidence heard at trial is confined to these real issues.[57] Rule 3.10 of the CrimPR allows the court to "limit the examination or re-examination of a witness, and the duration of any stage of the hearing."[58] This provision alters the trial dynamic and the classic adversarial conception of the defense lawyer; the contemporary defense lawyer will have to justify how long he intends to cross-examine a witness. Whilst "fishing expeditions" are best avoided, some speculative questioning by the defense may be necessary to properly probe the evidence of a prosecution witness.[59] Again, this demonstrates a clear tension between the duty to the client and the duty to the court. The interests of the client will be best served by his lawyer vigorously probing the prosecution witness in order to discover inconsistencies with their version of events. However, the duty to the court is satisfied by the court's time being used in the most efficient fashion and the trial process being conducted in a more streamlined manner. The CrimPR makes this task of furthering the interests of the client even more difficult. Rule 3.10(b)(i) states that the court may require a party to indicate what witnesses they wish to give evidence in person. The court will then decide whether or not the attendance of the witness is justified or whether the witness statement could be read out under s.9 of the Criminal Justice Act 1967.[60] However, if a defense lawyer contests the s.9 admission, he could be liable for a Wasted Costs Order[61] if his client is found guilty. This presents an obvious tension for the lawyer; he could be penalized financially for trying to advance the interest of his client by exercising his duty to fully test the evidence of the prosecution by way of cross-examination.

Further Disclosure under the CrimPR

It was noted in chapter 3 that the requirements of the CPIA 1996 to provide a defense statement only apply to trials on indictment. Should the defendant wish to disclose a defense statement in the magistrates' court, he can do so but this is not a mandatory provision.[62] However, the overriding objective of the CrimPR increases the disclosure obligations. The objective requires cases to be dealt with efficiently[63] and this drive for efficiency includes completing a case management form.[64] The forms can be found in the Consolidated Criminal Practice Direction and the form is extensive. It consists of six pages, asking various questions about the offence including the defendant's plea[65] and what witnesses will be required.[66] Hungerford-Welch claims that the form is so extensive it effectively requires a defendant to provide much of the information that would be required in a s.6A CPIA defense statement. These provisions effectively undermine the exclusion of summary trial from the mandatory defense statement regime.[67] The provision places a duty to disclose elements of the defendant's defense prior to trial, regardless of whether the case is heard in a magistrates' court or the Crown Court.

The completion of the form has the potential to be inherently dangerous for the accused; as was illustrated by *Firth v Epping Magistrates' Court*.[68] As described in chapter 3, in this case the defense lawyer made an assertion in the Case Progression Form that the accused was acting in self-defense. At trial, the prosecution successfully relied upon this as an admission to prove presence at the scene. In *Gleeson*, Auld LJ stated that the trial was "a search for truth in accordance with the twin principles that the prosecution must prove its case and that a defendant is not obliged to inculpate himself."[69] However, in the *Firth* case, it is hard to argue that either of those principles have been satisfied. The defense tested the prosecution's point and quite properly took the point that identification could not be established.[70] However, the magistrates admitted the case management form as evidence of an admission by the defendant that she was present at the scene and struck the complainant. In the Divisional Court, Toulson LJ upheld the magistrates' court decision, explaining:

> It does not infringe against the principle that a defendant is not required to incriminate himself for the court to require that the nature of the defense is made plain well before the trial. Of course, any requirement for disclosure of the nature of the defense must be a fair requirement, in the sense that it must not be extracted from a defendant in circumstances where the prosecution has no case.[71]

In *R v Newell*,[72] the appellant appealed against a conviction for possession of cocaine with intent to supply. At the Plea and Case Management Hearing

(PCMH), the appellant did not serve a defense statement and when completing the case management form, the lawyer, who did not represent N at trial, stated "no possession." On the morning of the trial and under the instruction of new solicitors, a defense statement was served in which he accepted possession of cocaine but denied the intent to supply. The CPS sought to cross-examine him because there were inconsistencies with his Case Progression Form and the defense statement admission. The judge allowed the cross-examination and the defendant was subsequently convicted. The Court of Appeal allowed the appeal, holding that the judge should have excluded the Case Progression Form under s.78 Police and Criminal Evidence Act 1984, as the sanction of adverse inferences for the failure to serve the defense statement was sufficient.[73] This highlights just how careful the lawyer needs to be when completing the form in order to not incriminate his client.

Although, it is clear that the completion of the Case Progression Form is inescapable. Andrew Keogh believes that the forms are analogous to the defense statement in the Crown Court and uses the case of *Rochford*[74] to illustrate why. In this case, the court held:

> There is a statutory obligation to file a defense statement and in addition there are statutory consequences if one does not. . . . counsel, or for that matter a solicitor or other legal adviser, cannot properly advise a defendant to disobey the statutory duty imposed by section 5(5) [CPIA 1996]. He can of course advise the defendant what his obligation is, what he must put in his defense statement (which in turn depends upon how the trial is going to be conducted) and he must advise him of the consequences of not doing so.[75]

Rhodes suggests that as there are no adverse inferences for failure to complete the Case Progression Form, perhaps the lawyer should write on the form "the issue at trial is whether the prosecution can prove its case, I am not instructed to make any factual admissions until after the prosecution has complied with its duty of disclosure."[76] If the completion of the case management form is analogous with the defense statement then perhaps the detail required in the defense statement will also correspond to the case management form. In *R v Malcolm*,[77] a defense statement was said to be hopelessly inadequate in light of the requirements of s.6A CPIA. The statement involved an allegation of the theft of a number of items from a flat. Hooper LJ said:

> It was insufficient merely to say that the Defendant did not accept that he took all the items being claimed by the Complainant. The Appellant was required to identify what was taken by him from the flat and to identify those items said to be stolen which he had left in the flat. If he had taken, for example, the fridge freezer and dishwasher, what had he done with them? If, as alleged, he did

> not intend permanently to deprive the owner of the items, what was his intention particularly in relation to those items missing . . . To satisfy the statutory requirements, the Appellant ought also to have explained whether he accepted the value of some £15,000-£20,000 for the items taken and explained why, in his view, he was entitled to take the items which he did take.[78]

However, if the lawyer did adopt the approach to the Case Progression Form suggested by Rhodes, it is hard to believe that the courts would find that response adequate. They would undoubtedly argue that this type of response directly breaches the lawyer's duty to the court, as he will not be assisting the court to fulfill the overriding objective of dealing with cases justly, of which dealing with cases expeditiously and efficiently is a core element.[79]

Enforcement Mechanisms for Noncompliance with the New Regime

Inferences

For noncompliance with the disclosure provisions under the CPIA 1996, the court permitted make adverse comment and/or to draw adverse inferences. Section 39 CJA 2003 inserted an amended s.11 into the CPIA 1996. The statutory sanction available to the court for disclosure faults is that of drawing inferences. Should the accused fail to provide the defense statement,[80] provides one outside the prescribed time limits,[81] fails to give any updated version of the statement required by s.6B CPIA 1996,[82] gives the updated statement outside of the prescribed time period[83] or sets out inconsistent defenses in his statement, then the court will make such comment that appears appropriate,[84] or the court or jury may draw such inferences as appear proper in deciding whether the accused is guilty of the offence concerned.[85] Further to proper inferences being drawn in the above examples, should the accused fall into the below categories inferences can also be drawn:

(i) puts forward a defense which was not mentioned in his defense statement or is different from any defense set out in that statement,
(ii) relies on a matter (or any particular of any matter of fact) which, in breach of the requirements imposed by or under section 6A, was not mentioned in his defense statement,
(iii) adduces evidence in support of an alibi without having given particulars of the alibi in his defense statement, or
(iv) calls a witness to give evidence in support of an alibi without having complied with section 6A(2)(a) or (b) as regards the witness in his defense statement.

These failures may also result in inferences being drawn by the court or jury.[86] The final examples of when inferences can be drawn concerns when the accused provides a witness notice but then at trial he calls witnesses who are not adequately identified in the witness notice.[87]

Costs

Despite not carrying any statutory weighting, the case management forms are akin to the defense statement. However, failure to comply with any CrimPR provision carries no express sanction. The CrimPR is an administrative rule rather than a statutory provision; as such, it cannot carry a sanction of adverse comment. Although the rules do not contain an adverse inference sanction, there are a number of other enforcement mechanisms designed to ensure all parties comply with the provisions. Auld LJ noted the problem of creating an enforcement mechanism for compliance with case management orders or other procedural orders. Auld stated that "[He had] anxiously searched here [in England and Wales] and abroad for just and efficient sanctions and incentives to encourage better preparation for trial . . . we are not alone in this search and that, as to sanctions at any rate, it is largely in vain."[88]

Rule 3.5(2) states that should a party fail to comply with a rule of direction, the court may fix, postpone, bring forward, extend, cancel, or adjourn a hearing.[89] The court has the power to make a costs order[90] or the court can impose any sanction as may be appropriate.[91] The final provision appears to give the court a great deal of latitude in administering and ensuring an effective enforcement mechanism. However, with no statutory weight behind the rules, it is difficult to envisage anything other than the court administering a financial penalty in respect of costs being ordered. Although costs seem the most likely enforcement mechanism for breaching the rules, Auld LJ did highlight the difficulty of using such tools. He believed that orders of costs, wasted costs orders, the drawing of adverse inferences or depriving one side or the other of the opportunity of advancing an aspect or all of their case, are not "apt ways of encouraging and enforcing compliance with criminal pre-trial procedures."[92] Furthermore, orders against defendants are rarely an option owing to their lack of means and the difficulty in apportioning blame between them and their lawyer. The wasted costs order against a defense or prosecution lawyer is possible but again, there is difficulty in identifying where the fault lies.[93] Costs against a defendant are governed by s.18 Prosecution of Offences Act 1985 (hereafter, POA 1985). In the case of any person convicted of an offence before the Crown Court, the court can make such an order as to the costs to be paid by the accused to prosecution as it considers just and reasonable. The amount shall be specified in the order,[94] which potentially means any order can be uncapped. Both the POA 1985 and the

CrimPR state that the payment of costs from a defendant to the prosecution requires him to have been convicted.[95] This is applicable to both convictions in the magistrates' and the Crown Court.

The *Wasted Costs Order* is governed by S.19A POA 1985; the Act allows the Crown Court to order the legal representative concerned to meet the whole of any wasted costs or such part of them.[96] A legal representative is further defined as "a person who is exercising a right of audience or a right to conduct litigation on behalf of any party to proceedings.[97] It is clear that the defense lawyer will fall within this category. A "wasted cost" means any costs incurred by a party "as a result of any improper, unreasonable or negligent act or omission on the part of any representative."[98]

Guidance for the court can be found in the Practice Direction (Costs) Criminal Proceedings.[99] Judges contemplating a wasted costs order should bear in mind the guidance given by the Court of Appeal in *Re P(A Barrister)*.[100] This case outlined a three-stage approach when a wasted costs order was being contemplated. First, has there been any improper, unreasonable, or negligent act or omission? Secondly, as a result have any costs been incurred by the party? Thirdly, if the answers to the first two questions are "yes," the court could exercise its discretion to order the representative to meet the whole or part of the relevant costs. Paragraph 1.5 of the guidance illustrates that the Court of Appeal has given further guidance in the case of *Re P (A Barrister)*.[101] It was held that the primary purpose was to compensate rather than punish and because of the penal element to the sanction, a mere mistake is not sufficient to justify an order, there must be a serious error.

The case of *R v SVS Solicitors*[102] concerns wasted costs order against a firm of solicitors. The court ordered the firm to pay £3,402.50 in respect of wasted costs incurred by the prosecution for flying a witness from Australia. The court reminded the appellant law firm that it had to balance its duty to the court with its duty to the client. In this instance, the defendant was manifestly seeking to manipulate the court's process by insisting on Mr. Amako's [the Australian witness] appearance at trial without disclosing the defense case that would be put to the witness. In the court's view, "the appellant firm made itself complicit in the manipulation being practiced by their client . . . and the appellant's conduct was improper, unreasonable and negligent."[103] Once again the court can be seen to further strengthen the notion that the lawyer's duty to his client has either been superseded by the duty to the court or, at best, is now on a level footing. Furthermore, theoretically, if the defense lawyer partakes in any behavior that is contrary to the overriding objective, he could be potentially levied with a wasted costs order. Could this could have ramifications when a defense lawyer is deciding whether or not to cross-examine a prosecution witness or allow the evidence to be admitted under s.9 Criminal Justice Act 1967. This section means that witnesses should not have to attend court unless it is unavoidable. The CPS believe there are a number of benefits to this, including the savings of costs, as trials can be shortened and the criminal justice system as a whole can run more effectively.[104]

The Refusal of an Application or Adjournment

Should an application to adduce new evidence or introduce a witness be made outside of prescribed time limits, the court can refuse an application to hear the evidence. In *Musone*,[105] at a late stage in a murder trial, the appellant attempted to introduce hearsay evidence without any prior notice. This evidence was highly damaging to the co-accused. The trial judge refused leave and the decision was upheld. Moses LJ said: "The Act thus gives power to the judge to prevent that which, in the judge's assessment, might cause incurable unfairness either to the prosecution or to a fellow defendant. Plainly, the procedural rules should not be used to discipline one who has failed to comply with them in circumstances where unfairness to others may be cured and where the interests of justice would otherwise require the evidence to be admitted."[106]

Both defendants were blaming the other for the murder. Moses LJ thought it was not possible to see how the overriding objective could be achieved if the court has no power to prevent deliberate abuse of the trial process. The codefendant would have no opportunity of dealing with the allegation properly. As such the court had the power to exclude the evidence. Furthermore, to combat an ambush defense, the court could allow the prosecution to introduce further evidence even though the prosecution had closed its case. A similar approach was adopted in *Writtle v DPP*.[107] Here, the defense sought to introduce an expert report after the close of the prosecution case. The magistrates rejected the application, as it was not relevant to the issues outlined in the Case Progression Form. The defense lawyer was effectively seeking to introduce wholly new evidence. The Court of Appeal held that if the expert evidence was disclosed at a very early stage and the late application to adduce further evidence would undoubtedly cause delay then this approach was to be "deplored."[108] In this case, the court held that the defense lawyer either knew the nature of the defense but failed to raise it appropriately, or the defense was contrived at the close of the prosecution's case.[109] The court believed that the efficient administration of justice would be delayed as the prosecution would need adequate time to consider how to refute the "new" evidence and reiterated the point that the issues in the case "are identified well before a hearing."[110] This is a demonstrative example of the efficiency of the process being prioritized over anything else.

Professional Censure

Andrew Keogh believes that this is the most "nuclear option, but this initiative may require a scalp before the message hits home."[111] Keogh's statement indicates that currently there are no examples of this sanction being used for breaching the CrimPR. However, by examining the court's reaction to other examples of "bad behavior," it is clear the court will not tolerate such an attitude. In the *Three Rivers*[112] case, Tomlinson J openly criticized the behavior of the defendant's lawyer. The lawyer was infrequently rude to the judge, which the judge ignored. However, the sustained rudeness to his opponent "was of an altogether different order. It was behavior not in the usual tradition of the Bar and it was inappropriate and distracting."[113] In 2009, the Law Society Gazette reported a case where a judge "slams solicitor-advocates for incompetence."[114] The judge felt that the defendant was represented so poorly that he almost discharged the jury owing to the incompetence of his lawyers. The lawyers were accused of not understanding the rules of reexamination and the jury were misled about the bad character of one of the defendants. The judge added that the basic rules of both law and procedure had been regularly broken.[115] Although these examples are vastly different from a breach of the CrimPR, they give a flavor of the expectations of the court. Theoretically, the court will be willing to use this sanction should a lawyer fail to comply with the overriding objective of the rules.

Furthermore, the lawyer's professional body could potentially censure the lawyer. The Solicitor's Regulation Authority Handbook contains a number of disciplinary measures for lawyers. The lawyer can be given a written rebuke,[116] he can be made to pay a penalty[117] or/and have details of the rebuke or penalty published.[118] Furthermore, he can be disqualified from acting as a head of legal practice, a head of finance and administration or being a manager/employee of a licensed body.[119] The final opportunity is for an application to the Solicitors Disciplinary Tribunal. Because of the severity of the sanctions, it is perhaps unrealistic that the final three sanctions will be used to punish a breach of the rules. Theoretically, it is entirely plausible that the first two sanctions *could* be used to punish lawyers who do not comply with the CrimPR. To give a written rebuke, three conditions need to be met. Firstly, the act or omission needs to be deliberate or reckless,[120] caused or had the potential to cause loss or significant inconvenience to any other person.[121] Furthermore, the act or omission could have occurred because the lawyer failed to recognized the obligations given by the court.[122] If the lawyer continued acting in this manner for a period of time,[123] or persisted once he knew it was improper,[124] he has the potential to mislead clients or the courts.[125] The second condition is that a proportionate outcome in the public interest is either a written rebuke or a direction to pay a penalty.[126] The final condition is that the act or omission was neither trivial nor justifiably inadvertent.[127]

A barrister may also be sanctioned should his conduct be called into question. The Professional Conduct Handbook[128] states there are seven potential sanctions if charges of professional misconduct are proved. Section 6.12 states that the barrister could be disbarred,[129] suspended,[130] ordered to pay a fine,[131] order to forgo/repay fees,[132] reprimanded,[133] permanently or temporarily excluded from undertaking publicly funded work,[134] or finally advised to his or her future conduct.[135] Again, as with the SRA, the more severe sanctions are likely to be unsuitable for breaches of the rules, but the less severe, such as the reprimand or the warning over future conduct, could potentially incur a sanction from the Bar Standards Council.

Sanctions: Conclusion

As this section has illustrated, there are a number of enforcement mechanisms that are available to the court. However, their application is fraught with difficulty. A direction to draw adverse comment for breaching the disclosure provisions only affects the defendant and at times the defense lawyer may have difficulty in obtaining instructions from his client. Furthermore, Denyer indicates that courts are unlikely to allow adverse comment for late disclosure unless it was "very very late indeed."[136] Furthermore, it is not appropriate to draw inferences should the fault lie with the lawyer. Costs orders against the defendant are unlikely: firstly, owing to his lack of means; secondly, as Auld LJ stated, it is difficult to establish who was at fault. Wasted costs could be imposed on the lawyer, but again the difficulty is found in establishing who was at fault. The courts could refuse to grant an adjournment or allow certain evidence to be adduced. These provisions would surely undermine the overriding objective of dealing with cases justly. After an analysis of the available sanctions, it appears there is not one "fix-all" sanction that the court can apply and therein lies the difficulty faced by the courts.

The Law Society's Code for Advocacy states that "advocates have an overriding duty to the court to ensure in the public interest that the proper and efficient administration of justice is achieved: they must assist the court in the administration of justice."[137] Paragraph 2.3 acknowledges that the lawyer has a duty to the client but again, this acknowledgment comes after the duty to the court is acknowledged. The paragraph states that advocates must "promote and fearlessly protect and by all proper and lawful means the client's best interests and will (should) do so without any regard to their own interests."[138] But again there is no guidance on how to act should one or more of the duties conflict. The Bar Standards Council almost mirrors the aforementioned pieces of professional guidance. Rule 302 states that "a barrister has an overriding duty to the Court to act with independence in the administration of justice; he must assist the court."[139] Rule 303 then outlines the duty to the client: "He must promote and protect fearlessly and by all proper and lawful means the lay client's best interests and do so without regard to his own interests."[140]

It is clear by analyzing the professional guidance that the professional and disciplinary bodies regard the duty to the court as being primary and having paramount importance. However, there is very little guidance on what to do should the duty to the court come into conflict with the duty to the client. The Law Society's Practice Note[141] also offers very little guidance, although the note does use the cite of *Arthur J.S. Hall and Co v Simmons*[142] to illustrate that the duty to the court: "[does] not just that he must not mislead the court, that he must ensure that the facts are presented fairly and he must draw attention of the court to the relevant authorities even if they are against him. It extends to the whole way in which the client's case is able to focus on the issues as efficiently and economically as possible."[143]

The practice note takes the time to reiterate what was stated in the SRA handbook. It lists the duty to uphold the proper administration of justice as the lawyer's primary duty. The duty to advance the best interests of the client is only the fourth duty of the lawyer, coming after acting with integrity and independence. It would seem that the legal professions, in the post-CPIA/CrimPR era, have accepted that the primary duty of the modern defense lawyer is explicitly to the court and to the administration of justice. Three different sets of professional guidance state this, as does case law and a Law Society Practice Note. However, no guidance is given as to how the lawyer should deal with any conflict, save for a brief explanation that at times the client will have to be informed that a duty to the court outweighs his own duty. This is significant departure from the classic conception of the defense lawyer that established in chapter 2.

The Implications of the CPIA and CrimPR for the Defense Lawyer

As this chapter has illustrated, the obligations that Lord Reid highlighted in *Rondel v Worsley*[144] have been fundamentally altered. The duty to the client appears to have been superseded by the duty to the court; this usurping of duties can be seen through the enhanced obligations the defense lawyer now has to comply with under the CPIA 1996 and CrimPR regimes. These obligations include furthering the overriding objective of dealing with cases justly, which incorporates an obligation to deal with the case efficiently and expeditiously[145] and complying with case management provisions, which include assisting the court in fulfilling the overriding objective. A key component of the overriding objective is the early identification of the real issues;[146] he must inform the court and the other side of any significant failures, even if he is not responsible for the failures;[147] he must advise his client to cooperate and comply with the disclosure obligations and subject to the instructions of his client, he must draft and serve both the defense case statement[148] and/or the Case Progression Form; the identity and details of the witnesses the defense intends to call is required to be disclosed to the prosecution and a Case Progression Officer has to be appointed.[149] It is important to remember that not all of these obligations rest directly on the defense lawyer. However, it is arguable that it is unrealistic to assume the accused is capable of fulfilling such onerous duties, with no legal training to identify the ramifications of the obligations. As such, it is clear that the obligations rest indirectly on the defense lawyer.

It is arguable that the fulfilment of some of these duties does not further the best interest of the client, for example, the completion of the defense statement. By submitting the statement, the defendant might lose any strategic advantage that he held. *Gleeson*[150] illustrates that the prosecution no longer has a sole attempt to secure a conviction; the prosecution might be permitted to amend their indictment should the defense attempt to "ambush" the prosecution at a late stage. As Thomas LJ stated, this type of behavior is "no longer acceptable, given the legislative and procedural changes that have taken place."[151] This notion of cooperation with the prosecution holds potential implications for the lawyer-client relationship. It might lead to the client becoming untrusting of his lawyer, as he is aware that furthering his best interests is not his lawyer's primary obligation. The CPIA 1996 disclosure regime is a statutory obligation and the defense lawyer cannot advise the client not to comply with the regime, as this would be professionally improper. In *Essa*,[152] the court made it clear that the lawyer can advise the client that it is his choice whether or not to file the defense statement and he can outline the merits of either approach, but it is for the client to decide if he will submit the statement. The lawyer cannot advise him to simply not complete the statement.

Although the defense case statement is only required for trials on indictment, the Case Progression Form in the magistrates' court is effectively a mirror to the defense statement.[153] This effectively extends the compulsory disclosure regime to magistrates' courts. The completion of the Case Progression Form could potentially lead to breaching the privilege against self-incrimination or, at the very least, not be in the best interests of the client. For example, in the *Firth* case the prosecution established the identity of the defendant as the assailant by using an admission on the Case Progression Form. The court allowed the admission and held that "it does not infringe against the principle that a defendant is not required to incriminate himself for the court to require that the nature of the defense is made plain well before the trial."[154] However, theoretically, one could argue that the completion has led to a breach of the privilege, as without the completed form, it would be unlikely that the prosecution could place Ms. Firth at the scene and ultimately, be unable to discharge the burden of proof. Further to not being in the client's interest, it could be argued that the Case Progression Form, whilst furthering the overriding objective, effectively extends the compulsory disclosure regime into the magistrates' court. Whilst it may not be as comprehensive as the defense statement, the Case Progression Form clearly contains elements analogous to the s.5 CPIA 1996 defense statement. The impact of this statement forces the defense lawyer to disclose key facts concerning the case. This provides a clear conflict of duties for the defense lawyer. In order to combat the potential breach of self-incrimination, Rhodes suggests that the content of the Case Progression Form should not contain vast amounts of detail.[155] Edwards also suggests that the form should be completed with the word "privileged."[156] Whilst the approaches suggested by Rhodes and Edwards appear sound in a theoretical context, the court may well view the approaches as inadequate.

The enforcement mechanisms available to the court are, on the whole, relatively weak and the stronger sanctions available to the court relate to the accused rather than the lawyer. The sanction of adverse inferences only applies in limited cases, where the accused fails to comply with the compulsory disclosure regime in the Crown Court cases. There is no statutory sanction for failing to complete a Case Progression Form, although the accused might be punished because the court may allow the prosecution to amend their indictment or reopen their case. As mentioned above, should the accused not wish to complete the case management form, this potentially could be a "significant failure." The ramification of this might be seen as a further dilution of the lawyer-client relationship. The Case Progression Form potentially turns the lawyer into a witness against his client and should the accused not wish to complete the form, the lawyer must report him to the court and "tell tales" regarding his lack of cooperation. This could further strain the relationship between lawyer and client to the point where the client does not feel he is acting in his best interests.

The implications of the CPIA 1996 and CrimPR appear to suggest that the duty to the court is the paramount obligation for the defense lawyer to satisfy. However, both the courts and Law Society are guilty of advancing mixed messages. In *Medcalf v Mardell*,[157] Lord Hobhouse stated: "at times . . . duties to the client will be liable to bring him into conflict with the duty to the court . . . this may require more courage to represent a client in the face of a hostile court but the advocate must be prepared to act fearlessly."[158] The statement espouses that the defense lawyer is still the zealous advocate of the accused, but the reminder from Lord Hobhouse does not provide any practical guidance to address any conflict or tension the changing legislation has created. The professional guidance somewhat contradicts the statement by Lord Hobhouse and appears to give precedence to the duty to the court being the paramount obligation of the lawyer—"The CrimPR stipulates that solicitors must assist the court in the management of the case. This can come into conflict with their duty to act in the best interests of their client where the client wishes to exercise their right to put the prosecution to proof and offers little by way of assistance to the court."[159]

Although the professional guidance offers no assistance in how a lawyer should deal with between his duty to his client and the court, one can assume that the expected approach would be to advance the duty to the court as the paramount duty. Should the lawyer only advance the interests of his client and adopt an uncooperative approach to his duty to the court, it is clear that the court will be frustrated. This will leave the overriding objective of dealing with cases justly unsatisfied. In the modern era, it appears that this approach will be deemed wholly unacceptable. The lawyer is required to assist in the satisfaction of the overriding objective by identifying the real issues in dispute, even if this means losing his client any tactical advantage.[160] By identifying the real issues, the trial can be conducted in a very efficient fashion. The courts have fully endorsed this approach, such as in *Jisil*[161]where the court held that it was not a concomitant of a right to fair trial that each side could take as much time as they like.[162]Judge LJ reiterated the same point in *Chaaban*[163] when he said "time is not unlimited. No one should assume that trials can continue to take as long or use as much time as both sides may wish."[164] This shift of duty, by way of increased obligations in order to deal with cases in the most efficient manner, has potentially come at the cost of advancing the client's interests. Whilst the drive for a more efficient trial process should be applauded, speed must not be achieved at the expense of the accused's fair trial rights. This includes allowing his lawyer sufficient time to prepare the case and the right to present that fully.[165] The consequence of this shift in duty is threefold:

1. Role Confusion: The lawyer is the "zealous advocate" of his client and the furthering of his best interests is the paramount obligation. If the duty to the court has superseded this obligation, this could cause confusion as to what the role of the defense lawyer should be.
2. Tensions for Lawyer: Following on from the above point, the confusion illustrated above may lead to the various tensions for the defense lawyer. When the two duties clash, what is the best course of action? The professional guidance is unhelpful in this instance and by examining the *Firth* case it appears the duty to the court takes precedence and the case management form must be completed. This comes at the cost of furthering the

best interests of the client. Does the modern-day defense lawyer consider advancing the client's best interests or have they been operationalized to the extent that the duty to the court is accepted as the paramount obligation they have to satisfy?

3. Implications for the lawyer-client relationship: Does the paramount duty to the court diminish or impact upon the relationship between the defense lawyer and his client? This will be elucidated more in the empirical chapter as no work, thus far, has highlighted this concern. Theoretically, it could be argued that compliance with the CrimPR may lead to a lack of cooperation between the lawyer and his client. The client may not wish to divulge information that he feels may incriminate him in the pursuit of the overriding objective. The notion of cooperation may leave the client feeling untrusting of his lawyer, because he does not hold advancing his interests as the paramount obligation he has to satisfy.

Furthermore, the requirement for the defense lawyer to cooperate with the prosecution potentially weakens the privilege against self-incrimination. The lawyer is being compelled to assist in building a case against his client. The watering down of principle appears to suggest that the building of a case against the accused no longer rests solely with the prosecution but it is in fact a shared burden. To return to the *Firth* example, the accused assists in the fulfilling the overriding objective by completing the case management form yet he also incriminates herself; the Crown uses the admission on the form to establish her presence at the scene. However, the judiciary does not believe this example will cause any conflict or problem. In the *Review of Disclosure in Criminal Proceedings*, Lord Justice Gross stated: "A constructive defense approach to disclosure issues should be seen and encouraged as professional 'best practice'. It involves no sacrifice of the defendant's legitimate interests; in large and complex cases it is difficult to see how the system can otherwise remain affordable."[166]

This illustrates the complexity regarding the shift in duties and further emphasizes the role confusion and the ramifications of such role confusion. On one hand, we have very drastic changes to both the role of the defense lawyer and the obligations they have to undertake. On the other, the judiciary claims the legitimate interests of the client are not sacrificed; although it is difficult to fathom how Ms. Firth's interests were not sacrificed by completing the Case Progression Form, and effectively breaching her privilege against self-incrimination. This is even more difficult to understand as a magistrates' court case would not fall into Gross's category of "large and complex." The privilege against self-incrimination is enshrined in the European Convention of Human Rights. Whilst the Article 6 right is not absolute, it is a "strong right."[167] Owusu-Bempah suggests that the notion of the defendant providing the prosecution with information that could be used against him is deeply non-adversarial. Such changes are at best, diluting, or at worst, ignoring these fundamental defense rights that have been established to both protect the defendant and ensure that the process is fair. By forcing the lawyer to cooperate with the prosecution in order to achieve maximum efficiency, it is arguable that the role of the defense lawyer has been implicitly diluted. Cape suggests that there has been "a growing antipathy towards adversarial principles and the adversarial role of defense lawyers."[168] The empirical study in the next chapter will ascertain if these theoretical concerns manifest in reality.

NOTES

1. As stated by Lord Reid in *Rondell v Worsley* [1969] 1A.C. 191.
2. Save for S.11 Criminal Justice Act 1967 and s.2(3) Criminal Justice Act 1987.
3. The first disclosure obligation was placed on the prosecutor; the defense lawyer would fulfill the second aspect by submitting the defense statement. The prosecutor would then be responsible for a second stage of prosecutorial disclosure.
4. s.5(6)(a) Criminal Procedure and Investigations Act 1996.
5. S.11 Criminal Procedure and Investigations Act 1996.
6. By virtue of Criminal Justice Act 2003 (Commencement no.24 and Transitional Provisions) Order 2010, SI 2010/1183
7. This section inserted a new s.6C Criminal Procedure and Investigations Act 1996.
8. Rule 1.1 Criminal Procedure Rules 2016.
9. Rule 1.2(c) defines a significant failure as one "[that] might hinder the court in furthering the overriding objective," as such it takes a very wide approach to what may constitute a failure. Effectively, it could be argued that the defense lawyer should point out flaws in the case of this opponent, thereby ensuring the overriding objective has been satisfied.
10. Rule 3.2(1) states "The court must further the overriding objective by actively managing the case." Examples of active case management are then provided. These have been discussed in chapter 3 and the impact of the rules will be critically examined in this chapter. As such, the examples will not be repeated here.
11. Rule 1.1(e).
12. Section 11(5) Criminal Produce and Investigations Act 1996.
13. *Ibid.*
14. A. Smith and W. Montross (1998) "The Calling of Criminal Defense," 50 Mercer L.R., 523.
15. Criminal court statistics quarterly, England and Wales, January to March 2018 (annual 2017), published June 2018 available here: https://assets.publishing.service.gov.uk/government/uploads/system/uploads/attachment_data/file/72002 6/ccsq-bulletin-jan-mar-2018.pdf [last accessed August 28, 2018].
16. (1844) 7 I.L.R. 261.
17. (1844) 7 I.L.R. 261 at 312.

18. Although, as illustrated by the RCCJ, ambush defenses were only run in 5 percent of trials and provided little obstacle to the conviction of the defendant.

19. S.5(6)(a) Criminal Procedure and Investigations Act 1996.

20. [2009] EWCA Crim 43.

21. Ibid., at para 18.

22. [2009] EWCA Crim 43.

23. [2004] 1. Cr. App. R. 29

24. R. Spencer, "Acquitting the Innocent and Convicting the Guilty—Whatever will they think of next!," [2007] *Calcutta Law Journal* Vol. 66(1), 27–30 at 27. By this Spencer means the prosecution gets one shot at goal and should their striker miss, he does not get another shot, no matter how unlucky the shot.

25. *R (on the application of the DPP)* v *Chorley Justices* [2006] EWHC 1795.

26. Ibid., per Thomas LJ at para 35.

27. [2007] EWHC 363.

28. Ibid., at para 44.

29. A. Owusu-Bempah, "Defense Participation through pre-trial disclosure" (2013) 17 E&P 283-201 at 200.

30. Ibid.

31. S.6C(1)(a) Criminal Procedure and Investigations Act 1996.

32. S.6A(2) Criminal Procedure and Investigations Act 1996.

33. [2009] EWCA Crim 2519 at para 30.

34. The Law Society's Practice Note on Defense Witness Notices, January 27, 2011, at para 2.4.1.

35. [2009] EWHC 2930 (Admin).

36. [2009] EWHC 2930 (Admin) per Clarke J at para 8.

37. 2009] EWHC 2930 (Admin) per Clarke J at para 8.

38. Baldwin suggests that police interviews are crucial to the investigation of crime as they may obviate the need for further enquiries. This notion can be transferred from interviewing the suspect to interviewing defense witnesses. See J. Baldwin "Police Interview Techniques: Establishing Truth or Proof?" [1993] *The British Journal of Criminology* Vol 33(3), 325–352.

39. Rule 1.2(2) Criminal Procedure Rules 2011.

40. Rule 1.2(1)(a) Criminal Procedure Rules 2011.

41. See *Gleeson* [2004] Crim LR 579; *R v Essa* [2009] EWCA Crim 43; *Malcolm v DPP* [2007] EWCA 363 and *Firth* [2011] EWHC 388 (Admin).

42. Rule 1.2(2) Criminal Procedure Rules dealing with the case efficiently and expeditiously.

43. Lord Justice Leveson, *Essential Case Management: Applying the Criminal Procedure Rules*, Judiciary of England and Wales, 2009. Available here: https://www.judiciary.gov.uk/publications/applying-criminal- procedure-rules/ [Last Accessed May 17, 2017].

44. *Ibid.*, Point A.

45. Rule 3.8(2)(b) Criminal Procedure Rules 2010.

46. Rule 3.8(1) Criminal Procedure Rules 2010.

47. Point A, Lord Justice Leveson, *Essential Case Management: Applying the Criminal Procedure Rules* (Judiciary of England and Wales, 2009).

48. Ibid.

49. P. Hungerford-Welch, *Summary Trial—Too Summary?* in Criminal Justice Matters, No. 84 June 2011 10–11, 10.

50. [2010] EWHC 799 (Admin).

51. Ibid., para 8.

52. *Aravinthan Visarathnam v Brent Magistrates' Court* [2009] EWHC 3017 (Admin)

53. Ibid., as per Openshaw J at para 19.

54. Rule 3.1 Criminal Procedure Rules 2011.

55. Rule 3.2(1)(a) Criminal Procedure Rules 2011.

56. Rule 3.2(1)(b) Criminal Procedure Rules 2011.

57. *Ibid.*

58. Rule 3.10(d)(i) Criminal Procedure Rules 2011.

59. P. Hungerford-Welch, *Summary Trial—Too Summary?*, 11.

60. Written statements are admissible as evidence to the extent of oral evidence.

61. The ramifications of which will be discussed in a later section; however, it is important to highlight the potential tension faced by the defense lawyer.

62. S.6 Criminal Procedure and Investigations Act 1996.

63. Rule 1(2)(e) Criminal Procedure Rules 2011.

64. Rule 3.11(1) Criminal Procedure Rules 2011.

65. Magistrates' Court, Preparation for Trial, question 7, page 2.

66. Ibid., question 10, page 4.

67. P. Hungerford-Welch, *Summary Trial—Too Summary?*11.

68. [2011] EWHC 388 (Admin).

69. *R v John Vincent Gleeson* [2004] 1 Cr App R 29, per Auld LJ at para 36.

70. D. Rhodes, "Life in Crime: The Truth Is Out There," *Solicitors' Journal*, Vol. 156, no 19, May 16, 2011.

71. *Firth v Epping Magistrates' Court* [2011] EWHC 388 (Admin), per Toulson LJ at para 22.

72. [2012] EWCA Crim 650.

73. Ibid., at para 36.

74. [2010] EWCA Crim 1928.

75. Ibid., per Hughes LJ at para 23.

76. D. Rhodes, "Life in Crime: The Truth Is Out There" [2011] *Solicitor's Journal*, Vol. 156, 19.

77. [2011] EWCA 2069.

78. Ibid., per Hooper LJ at para. 76.

79. Rule 1.2(e) Criminal Procedure Rules 2011.

80. S.11(2)(a) Criminal Procedure and Investigations Act 1996.

81. S.11(2)(b) Criminal Procedure and Investigations Act 1996.

82. S.11(2)(c) Criminal Procedure and Investigations Act 1996.

83. S.11(2)(d) Criminal Procedure and Investigations Act 1996

84. S.11(5)(a) Criminal Procedure and Investigations Act 1996. [566]S.11(5)(b) Criminal Procedure and Investigations Act 1996.

85. S.11(5)(b) Criminal Procedure and Investigations Act 1996.

86. S11(2)(f)(i-iv) Criminal Procedure and Investigations Act 1996.

87. S.11(4)(b) Criminal Procedure and Investigations Act 1996.

88. Auld LJ, *The Review of the Criminal Courts* (2001) at para 231.

89. Rule 3.5(6)(a) Criminal Procedure Rules 2011.

90. Rule 3.5(6)(b) Criminal Procedure Rules 2011.

91. Rule 3.5(6)(c) Criminal Procedure Rules 2011.

92. *Review of the Criminal Courts of England and Wales,* 2001, Para 229.

93. Ibid., para 230.

94. S.18(1)(3) Prosecution of Offences Act 1985.

95. Criminal Procedure Rules 2010 Rule 76.5(1)(a).

96. S. 19A(1)(b) Prosecution of Offences Act 1985.

97. S.19(3) Prosecution of Offences Act 1985.

98. S.19(3)(a) Prosecution of Offences Act 1985.

99. [2004] 2 Crim R 26.

100. (No 1 of 1991) [1993] QB 293.

101. [2001] EWCA Crim 1728; [2002] 1 Cr App R 207.

102. [2012] EWCA Crim 319.

103. Ibid., as per Field J at para 24.

104. Please see Evidence: Admitting evidence under s.9 and s.10 Criminal Justice Act 1967. http://www.cps.gov.uk/legal/d_to_g/evidence_admiting_evidence_under_the_cja/#a03 [Last accessed December 2020].

105. [2007] EWCA Crim 1237.

106. Ibid., per Moses LJ at para 37.

107. [2009] EWCA 236 (Admin).

108. Ibid., at paragraph 14.

109. Ibid.

110. Ibid.

111. A. Keogh, speaking at the Eldon Lecture Series 2011 at Northumbria University School of Law. November 24, 2011. http://www.youtube.com/watch?v=2bhMweYNF24 [Last Accessed April 16, 2012].

112. [2006] EWHC 816 (Comm).

113. Ibid., per Tomlinson J at para 135.

114. C. Baksi, "Fraud Case Judge Slams Solicitor-Advocates for Incompetence," *Law Society Gazette*, April 23, 2009.

115. Please see http://www.lawgazette.co.uk/news/fraud-case-judge-slams-solicitor-advocates-incompetence [Last accessed June 9, 2012].

116. *Solicitors Regulation Authority Handbook* (3rd Edition, 2012),para 2.1(a), http://www.sra.org.uk/solicitors/handbook/discproc/part1/content.page [Last accessed May 9, 2017].

117. Ibid., at para 2.1(b).

118. Ibid., atpara 2.1(c).

119. Ibid., at 2.1(d).

120. Ibid., at 3.1(a),(I).
121. Ibid., at para 3.1(a),(ii).
122. Ibid., at para 3.1(a),(iii).
123. Ibid., at para 3.1(a),(iv).
124. Ibid., at para 3.1(a),(v).
125. Ibid., at para 3.1(a),(vi).
126. Ibid., at para 3.2(a),(i)–(ii).
127. Ibid., at para 3.1(c).
128. Professional Misconduct 2006/07, Inns of Court School of Law, City University, London (Oxford University Press: Oxford, 2006).
129. Ibid., at s.6.12(a).
130. Ibid., ats.6.12(b).
131. Ibid., at s.6.12(c).
132. Ibid., at s.6.12(d).
133. Ibid., at s.6.12(e).
134. Ibid., at s.6.12(f).
135. Ibid., at s.6.12(g).
136. R. Denyer, "The Defense Statement" [2009] *Criminal Law Review* Vol. 340, 343.
137. The Law Society's Code for Advocacy, para 2.2.
138. Ibid., at para 2.3.
139. Bar Standards Council, Part III, Fundamental Principles (2004) Rule 302, http://www.barstandardsboard.org.uk/regulatory-requirements/the-code-of-conduct/the-code-of-conduct/part- iii-fundamental-principles/#appall [last accessed December 2020].
140. Ibid., Rule 303.
141. Law Society, Practice Note, Criminal Procedure Rules: Impact on Solicitors Duty to the Client (2009).
142. [2000] UKHL 38, [2002] 1 AC 615.
143. Ibid., Per Lord Hope at 715.
144. [1969] 1A.C. 191. The three duties identified were the duty to the client, the duty to the court and the duty to the public.
145. Rule 1.1(2)(e) Criminal Procedure Rules 2010.
146. Rule 3.2(2)(a) Criminal Procedure Rules 2010.
147. Rule 1.2(1)(c) Criminal Procedure Rules 2010. A significant failure is one that is likely to hinder the court in furthering the overriding objective.
148. Where applicable in Crown Court cases.
149. Rule 3.4 Criminal Procedure Rules 2010.
150. [2004] 1. Cr. App. R 29.
151. *R (on the application of the DPP) v Chorley Justices* [2006] EWHC 1795 per Thomas LJ at para 35.
152. *R v Essa* [2009] EWCA Crim 43.
153. A. Keogh, speaking at the Eldon Lecture Series 2011 at Northumbria University School of Law. November 24, 2011. http://www.youtube.com/watch?v=2bhMweYNF24 [Last Accessed July 2, 2012].

154. *Firth v Epping Magistrates' Court* [2011] EWHC 388 (Admin), per Toulson LJ at para 22.

155. D. Rhodes "Life in Crime: The Truth is Out There," *Solicitor's Journal*, Vol. 156, no. 19 May 19, 2011.

156. A. Edwards, "Case Management Forms" [2011] *Criminal Law Review* Vol. 546 at 548.

157. *Medcalf v Mardell* [2003] 1 AC 120 (HL).

158. Ibid., per Lord Hobhouse at para 142.

159. Legal Policy Directorate, *Criminal Procedure Rules: Impact on Solicitor's Duties to the Client* (London, The Law Society, 2009) at p. 9.

160. Legal Policy Directorate, *Criminal Procedure Rules: Impact on Solicitor's Duties to the Client* (London, The Law Society, 2009) at p. 10.

161. [2004] EWCA Crim 696.

162. Ibid., per Judge LJ at para114.

163. *R v Chaaban* [2003] EWCA Crim 1012.

164. Ibid., per Judge LJ at para 37.

165. Hungerford-Welch, *Summary Trial—Too Summary?*, 11.

166. Gross L. J., *Review of Disclosure in Criminal Proceedings*, Judiciary of England and Wales, at p. 8.

167. A. Owusu-Bempah, "Defense Participation through Pre-Trial Disclosure" [2013] *E&P* Vol. 17, 283–201 at 193.

168. E. Cape, *The Rise (And Fall?) of a Criminal Defense Profession*, Criminal Law Review Vol. 415 at p. 421.

Chapter 5

The Defense Lawyer in the Modern Era

Perceptions from Practice

This chapter is drawn from an empirical study, which held the classic conception of the lawyer at its foundation; the classic conception was established in chapter 1. The conception is used as the starting point and, using interviews with defense lawyers, an assessment is made of whether it provides an accurate depiction of the modern-day practice of the defense lawyer. That conception suggested that the primary duty of the lawyer was to the client, despite the fact there were other duties that competed for priority. This empirical study sought to ascertain the duty which was prioritized and the implications of this prioritization for the defense lawyer's role. The interviews were designed to garner the lawyer's views on the potential implications of the "new regime." The empirical study was split into three distinct sections. First, a general obligations section would explain the obligations encountered by a defense lawyer. The second section would highlight the tension faced by the lawyer. This examined how the aforementioned obligations influence the daily practice and routine of the lawyer. Third, a conflict section would elucidate how the lawyer tackles any conflict arising from the obligations and the impact they hold for the lawyer-client relationship. Smith and Montrose suggest that defense lawyers have a "win-at-all-costs" mentality.[1] This clearly intimates that the only duty that should exist is that to the client. From the responses from the lawyers interviewed, a clear picture emerged that suggests that different lawyers take different approaches to prioritizing their respective duties. It will be argued that the responses of the lawyers in the interviews indicate that there are three distinct types of lawyer:

- *The Classic Adversarial Lawyer*—The lawyer identifies their role as being to advance the best interest of the client. This comes at the cost of any other objectives.

- *The Conflicted Adversarial Lawyer*—The lawyer maintains that their primary obligation is to the client but recognizes that, in a culture of cooperation, they have to satisfy more than one duty. Frequently, but not exclusively, the lawyer resolves the conflict by prioritizing the duty to the court, despite the earlier proclamation that the primary or main obligation is to the client.
- *The Procedural Adversarial Lawyer*—Generally, the lawyer sees no conflict between their existing pretrial obligations. Should any conflict be encountered, the lawyer simply views it as an occupational hazard that requires careful navigation but will generally be settled by prioritizing the obligation to the court. As an officer of the court, nobody is more suited to this careful navigation than a skilled procedural adversarial lawyer.

The three categories of lawyer take different approaches to their obligations. Whilst the categories have been influenced by the existing literature[2] in this field, they differ because they examine the drivers and goals of individual lawyers rather than that of criminal defense firms. Furthermore, this monograph sought to understand the lawyers' priorities rather than the culture of firms as a whole. The implications of this typology of lawyers will be examined to discover whether this has consequence for the notion of adversarialism in England and Wales; in particular, whether there are any repercussions for fundamental fair trial rights such as the presumption of innocence[3] and the privilege against self-incrimination.[4]

ROLE CONFUSION

Confuse: n. throw into distortion, disconcert, perplex, fail to distinguish, make indistinct[5]

The defense lawyer has to balance the interests of their client with the duty that is owed to the court. This presents the lawyer with an ethical dilemma. The classic conception developed in chapter 1 stated the primary duty of the lawyer was to the client. It was suggested in chapter 5 that by creating a climate of cooperation between the prosecution and defense, a "growing antipathy toward adversarial principles and the adversarial role of the defense lawyer has been created."[6] The interviewees did not always recognize such antipathy. In fact, the notion that lawyers have a duty to fearlessly raise every issue, advance every argument, and ask every question appeared to be alive and well.

Some lawyers were extremely forthright in their view that the duty to the client was their absolute, paramount duty. However, many lawyers were acutely aware that this duty was tempered by other existing duties and thus created an interesting dynamic.

The Hierarchy of Duties

As previously discussed, the three interwoven duties Lord Reid spoke of in *Rondell v Worsley*[7] were not accompanied by any form of weighting or priority. Rather unhelpfully, the duties were merely listed and explained. However, it is clear that the interwoven duties cannot be equally treated; as such, their individual goals may conflict. A question remains whether the lawyers recognized that there is a conflict, and, if they do, whether they are confused by it.

It is clear that some scholars believe the duty to the client is the only obligation owed by the lawyer. Fried takes this point a step further by arguing the lawyer should be permitted to lie in defense of the client's interests[8] However, this approach would defeat the objective of dealing with cases "justly" and ultimately render the criminal justice process unsafe. Should the lawyer lie to advance the best interests of his client, the truth-seeking goals of the trial process will also be defeated. The lawyer should not be allowed to break the rules or cheat the system in order to satisfy any of his competing obligations. Furthermore, it should be made explicitly clear, none of the lawyers interviewed for this study ever intimated they would lie or have lied in order to advance their client's interests.[9] The monograph accepts that this may represent a methodological flaw and perhaps the lawyers are telling the researcher what they think he wants to hear. Smith and Montross suggest that devotion and faithfulness are more important than serving the truth.[10] The importance of truth-seeking is a common theme and will be addressed fully later in the chapter. Any limitations on zealous advocacy[11] are articulated by the other obligations faced by lawyers.

Legal authors have long wrestled with the question of how to balance the roles of zealous advocate and officer of the court charged with the pursuit of justice.[12] Wendell suggests that a defense lawyer has a number of different titles he can use: "hired guns, mouthpieces, instruments or tools [of the accused]."[13] He states that in legal terms, the lawyers are "agents" and that agent acts on behalf of another, the principal, who in this context is the client. He goes on to state that the agent is an extension of the principle, who acts to effectuate the principle's instructions.[14] As the lawyer acts as an extension of the principle, it is unsurprising that some lawyers may prioritize the interests of the client above all others. What might be surprising is the fact this approach is not universally adopted by defense lawyers. Boon and Levin suggest that describing lawyers as "hired guns" or "mouthpieces" is too simplistic and poses two problems. Firstly, such descriptions require the lawyer to abandon any moral evaluation of the client's objectives or how they will achieve these goals. Secondly, this description suggests that the lawyer should not show any concern for the requirements of both law and the professional conduct codes. The characterization of the lawyer as a "hired gun" is not consistent with the lawyer's obligation to take into account the public interest, the interests of justice and their duty to the court.[15] This comment highlights an enormous ethical conflict for the lawyer. Simply put, the classic adversarial lawyer and the win-at-all-costs mentality[16] cannot coexist with the other pretrial obligations of the modern era and the subsequent rise of the new regime of criminal justice. The notion of advancing the best interests of the client, as a paramount duty, should be extinct since a duty of cooperation is thrust upon both defense lawyers and prosecution. Both are expected to work together in order to satisfy the overriding objective of the CrimPR.

A number of interviewees highlighted that cooperation is permeating the criminal justice process.[17] Advancing the best interest of the client was almost universally[18] viewed as the primary obligation. However, some lawyers were quick to accept that the duty is qualified by other conflicting obligations: "The first and prime duty is to act at all times in your client's best interests because you are there as guidance for him and his mouthpiece. Running alongside that are the duties to the court. As an officer of the court, you uphold the principles of justice and perhaps nowadays you do things quickly and do not waste money basically" (003 solicitor, seven years' experience).

"I feel the duty to my client is paramount. It is coloured by my professional obligations to the court. I do things in a lawyer-like way in line with my professional standards; I will not mislead the court and at the very tail end, follow the CrimPR as closely as possible" (009 senior partner, twenty-nine years' experience). The aforementioned comments of the lawyers are interesting. They both espouse terms such as "prime" and "paramount." The *Oxford English Dictionary* defines prime as "the best, choicest, most attractive, or desirable part of something."[19] Paramount is defined as "to rise to the highest position."[20]As well as recognizing the prime or paramount duty, the lawyers were quick to illustrate that this duty is qualified by the duty to the court. Daniel Newman found that "lawyers talk the talk but do not walk the walk."[21] Newman conducted an ethnographic study investigating the everyday reality of legally aided criminal defense work. The present study consisted purely of interviews and did not contain any ethnographic observations. However, Newman argues that lawyers need to be taught to care about their clients and take responsibility for providing those accused and suspected of crime with the service they deserve.[22] Lawyer 006 advocated that having a primary duty to the court "fudges" the duty to the client and as such viewed it as "unhelpful" to treat the duties as equal. In fact, he stated that he does not view the duty to the court as the primary duty. Lawyer 007 was equally as zealous concerning the primacy of the duty to the client: "I'll ignore what it says in the procedure rules; we are there to protect the legal interest of the client" (007 partner, twenty-one years' experience). The most fervent example of a lawyer advancing the duty to the client above all other duties was espoused by Lawyer 019. He went as far as to say: "If the client tells me he's done it, I'm not going to tell the court that. I cannot call him to give evidence at trial but I can still put the prosecution to proof" (019, senior partner, thirty years' experience).

Arguably, this approach compromises the obligations under the Code of Conduct for Solicitors. Outcome 5.1[23] of the Code states that the solicitor should not attempt to deceive or knowingly or recklessly mislead the court and the solicitor must not be complicit in another person knowingly or recklessly misleading the court. Misleading of the court will qualify as a "significant failure" of which the court has to be made aware.[24] A significant failure is defined as a failure that might hinder the court in furthering the overriding objective.[25] Such hindrances would include undue delay, the need for an adjournment, or a client not providing instructions. Lawyer 020 (senior partner, eighteen years' experience) strenuously disagreed with the approach taken by Lawyer 019 (senior partner, thirty years' experience). When questioned about professional duties, the response was clear: "Duty number one is an overriding duty to the court and number two is to the client. Nobody else needs to be considered." Lawyer 020 was the sole advocate from the study to explicitly suggest that the duty to the court takes precedence over that owed to the client. It is noteworthy that the lawyer ended the answer to the question by saying, "it's a tricky position to be in." This reflects the taut difficulty faced by the lawyers in reconciling their obligations.

Interestingly, some lawyers did not share the idea that the duties should not be treated as equal. Lawyers often placed the duty to the client first, although not with the fervor illustrated by Lawyers 006 (senior partner, forty years' experience) and 007 (partner, twenty-one years' experience), both of whom were members of the same firm, which might point to the particular culture of that firm. Lawyer 019 also shared a similar stance but came from a separate firm. With the exception of Lawyer 020, all participants accepted the duty to the client came first. However, a number of lawyers suggested that their duty to the client was severely hamstrung by conflicting obligations to the court. There were differing levels of impact regarding how the duty might be tempered. Lawyer 018 (solicitor, four years' experience) said: "[the duties] are numerous, I have loads of duties. The main one is to further the best interests of the client. Although, that has to be considered in light of duty to never mislead [the court]. That's the most important ethical obligation I have. That said, the one I think of the most is the best interest of the client." This is an example of clear conflict between the obligations the lawyer faces and the duties they owe to differing parties. Lawyer 018 is saying that the main duty is to their client but that there are other obligations that need to be considered.

Other lawyers were also well aware of the conflicting duties, and that perhaps the duty to the client was less of a priority:

> The duties to the client are paramount but there are ever-increasing duties to the court, especially in the criminal procedure rules. The obligations are very straightforward: you should always act in the best interest of your client and give them the best advice possible. To the court we have a duty to be open and we need to comply with our professional obligations. [010, solicitor, twelve years' experience].

"[My duty is to] advance the cause of the client commensurate with my professional duties to not mislead the court and abide by the court rules and procedures" [012, solicitor, seven years' experience]. Lawyer 011 (partner, nineteen years' experience) opened with a statement that represented their approach to the various duties: "[It is] to represent your client conscientiously without fear of reprisals." However, the impact of their statement was diluted as the lawyer was quick to add: "You also have a parallel duty to the court; your higher duty is to them. Their duty is to convict the guilty and acquit the innocent. My duty to my client is to represent them fairly, properly, without prejudice" [011].

The conflict between the duty to the court and client was one that was readily identified by Lawyer 024 (solicitor, nine years' experience). Like the lawyers above, there is a clear and identifiable conflict between the duty to the court and to the client. Lawyer 024 identifies his duties as: "to protect and advance my client's interests through openness and fearless presentation . . . the court's interests are not entirely chiming with the client's and that is where the conflict enters the fray. You have to balance the two obligations."

However, some were keen to express their ability to balance the conflicting duties. Some lawyers saw it as a balance and not a conflict. The balance was described as an "occupational hazard" but one that a skilled, confident, and trained advocate could handle. Lawyer 022 (solicitor, six years' experience) identified this "occupational hazard." He said, "the duties to the court and client exist together—you have got to operate with both of those in mind at all times." When further pressed, he gave no indication that the two duties are theoretically incompatible. He gave the impression that the potential conflict is a minefield that a skilled advocate can navigate successfully. This suggests that lawyers have the extraordinary power to overcome conflicting obligations with neither side losing out. The notion that those working in the legal profession can somehow see things differently to ordinary people is nothing new. The judiciary dislikes the imposition of minimum sentences because they impose fetters on discretion and ultimately hamper the notion of doing justice. Ashworth argues that they believe that they possess a particular talent in regard to sentencing and only they have the capability to decide what sentence should be handed down.[26] Lawyer 021 (solicitor, twelve years' experience) shares the view of Lawyer 022 (solicitor, six years' experience) that there should not be any conflict: "If you apply it properly and you are being honest then the two should not conflict." However, the lawyer recognized that in practice it is sometimes out of the hands of the advocate. If a client does not want to give instructions, this raises a conflict with the duty to the client, because the lawyer will have to tell the court.

Lawyer 023 (solicitor, seven years' experience) painted the picture that the "protection of the clients" was of primary importance. The drive for cooperation and efficiency permeated into how the lawyer would describe their duties. The lawyer claimed that he needed to ensure "proceedings are conducted against the client both fairly and efficiently." Furthermore, lawyers ought to be mindful of their "ethical behavior" toward all other participants. These participants would also include "victims." Kirchengast argues that the victim in the modern criminal trial is an "significantly determinative and constitutive agent of justice."[27] Whilst crime victims have always been substantially connected to the process of policing, prosecution, evidence, and sentencing, they have also taken an increasingly active role in the criminal trial process.[28] For example, in the mid-1990s, many common law jurisdictions allowed the victim to prepare a statement which would "provide them an opportunity to explain in their own words how a crime has affected them"[29] at the sentencing stage. Many other victim-focused procedural and evidential reforms have followed. With the ever-growing presence of the victim, is the criminal trial "losing sight of the defendant?"[30] Furthermore, the Victims' Right to Review scheme allows the victim to seek a review of a CPS decision not to bring charges or to terminate all proceedings. The upshot of things detracts from the finality of the criminal justice process, as discussed in chapter 1. Should the accused go through the process and find the CPS decides not to charge, the rise of victim-focused reforms such as the review scheme may mean that the matter is not fully disposed of and the life of the suspect will continue to be disrupted. Whilst it is important to correct errors, the promptness of the overriding objective may mean that decisions are made too quickly, mistakes are made and then victims appeal against this hastily made decision. As such, there is untold delay for courts, witnesses, and the suspect, who at no juncture appears to be considered in this process. Indeed, the suspect is not permitted to make representations as part of the Victim Right to Review Scheme. Lawyer 023 highlighted whilst that he has never encountered any decisions to review CPS decision and in reality, the decisions are very rare. In the period from April 2016 to March 2017, there were 1988 appeals received and only 137 of them were upheld. Out of the 103,113 CPS decisions made in this period, the percentage of appeals that were upheld was 0.13 percent and ultimately paints a picture that is not as great a concern in reality, as it is in theory.[31] Despite this worry, the lawyer stated that the "obligation to the court has to come first." This lawyer, who may be characterized as a *Conflicted Adversarial Lawyer*, appeared to want to hold on to the notion of being the defendant's "white knight" and fearless representative, but the era in which he operates would not allow him to do so. The notion of efficiency, and the interwoven notion of cooperation, has clouded the mindset of some defense lawyers. The goals have become firmly established in how he rationalizes the conflicting duties before him. Stating that his duty was to the "court and his opponent" is somewhat surprising. No other lawyer even hinted that this conflict existed. All other conflicts of duties identified by the lawyers centered on that between the best interests of the client and the interests of the court. The lawyer was further asked why he felt that the duty to the prosecution and the court took precedence. He explained that "the Rules [the CrimPR] state we have to help the court fulfil the overriding objective. With that in mind, it is impossible to advance the duty to the client above those two duties. The Rules come first." Whilst a number of lawyers indicated there was a conflict as to what should be prioritized, Lawyer 023 was the only interviewee who explicitly believed that the managerialist aims of the CrimPR should trump the classic adversarial position that the duty to the client should be prioritized. Whilst Lawyer 022 (solicitor, six years' experience) sensed there was absolutely no conflict between the obligations, Lawyer 023 (solicitor, seven years' experience) takes that a step further. He begins to incorporate the principles of the CrimPR, the notions of efficiency and cooperation. Lawyer 015 (solicitor, thirteen years' experience) also illustrated how the "sea change"[32] impacts their view on their duties. The lawyer stated that their "primary duty is to the client, I also have a duty to the court and tied in with that is a duty to my opponents." The lawyer reiterated that the duty to the client takes "primacy," but this was clearly tempered by other competing obligations. The duty to their opponents was intriguing. Here, the lawyer mentioned the notion of cooperation. He said, "I cannot mislead nor ambush them; I have to inform them [and the court] if there is any significant failure." Whilst the notion of cooperation has been elicited from the aforementioned lawyers, Lawyer 016 (solicitor, eighteen years' experience) was the only participant to suggest there is a duty to the prosecution. The importance of clarifying the lawyer's role was highlighted by Newman and Ugwudike. They suggested that the defense lawyer's role is of vital importance as he is considered to be one of the closest allies of the client.[33] However, none of the respondents used the term "ally" or even intimated that they were allies or even resembled members of the same team. To return to Lord Broughman's quote, "[A]n advocate, in the discharge of his duty, knows but one person in the all the world and that person is their client."[34]

Lord Reid attributed no weight to the three individual duties in *Rondel.*[35] However, what this section has identified is that the lawyers interviewed prioritized differing approaches to their duties. The chart below highlights the prioritization of duties (figure 5.1):

The majority of the established work in this field has looked at the culture of the law firm rather than the individual lawyer, and different themes operating in the same arena is nothing new.[36] Newman talks of "Radical" and "Sausage Factory" firms to illustrate the different lawyers' attitudes, behaviors, and approach to the lawyer-client relationship.[37] Newman also highlighted a number of themes that emerged in studies by Max Travers[38] and Hilary Sommerlad.[39] These themes were:

- *Social Agenda*—lawyer's virtuous reasons for being engaged in this area,
- *Facilitators*—how lawyers saw their role with clients; and,
- *Satisfaction*—the fulfilment derived from helping clients.

The themes derived from my own empirical work do not look at personal factors as above. But the lawyers who were interviewed from the same firms prioritized the same duty. For example, both 001 and 003 were from the same firm in the South East of England. Both of these lawyers espoused the same view. Lawyer 001 stated that "my duty is to try and get the best result for my client within the bounds of the law," whereas Lawyer 003 stated, "first and foremost [the primary duty is] to act in the best interests of your client . . . but running alongside that is the duty to the court." Both readily identify the primary duty is to the client but that it is quickly tempered to acknowledge

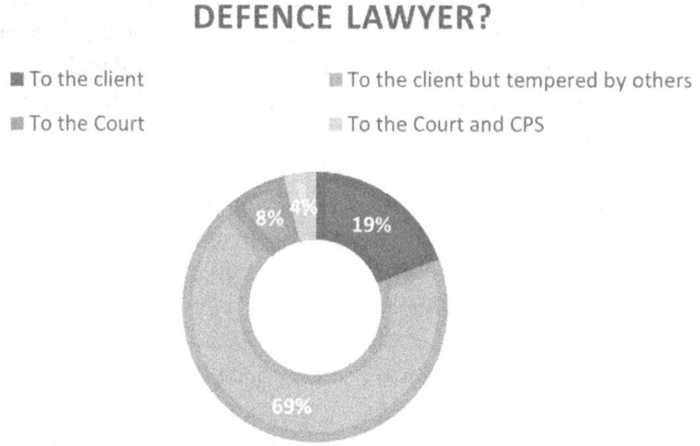

Figure 5.1 Data Compiled by Author Survey.

other duties that have to be satisfied in the pursuit of advancing the client's best interest. Lawyers 006 (senior partner, forty years' experience), 007 (partner, twenty-one years' experience) and 008 (solicitor, six years' experience) were the only other lawyers who worked for the same firm as one another. Lawyer 006 stated, "the professional codes say the duty is to the court and the client, I do not look it at that way. The duty is to the client alone." Lawyer 007 was more explicit, stating "I'll ignore what it says in the procedure rules; we are there to protect the legal interests of the client and get the best possible sentence." The above two examples are the only ones in the study where more than one interviewee worked in the same firm. This means that no firm conclusions can be drawn as to whether the culture of the firm has any bearing on how the lawyer prioritizes their duty.

The Overriding Objective

The overriding objective of the CrimPR underpins the aspirations of the criminal justice system[40] and has been influenced by the *Auld Review* in which Auld LJ explicitly stated that the "criminal trial is not a game where guilty defendant should be given a sporting chance."[41] In order to eliminate this "sporting chance," the overriding objective of the CrimPR was created. This objective is to "deal with cases justly."[42] The objective consists of a number of component parts to ensure the aspirations of the criminal justice systems were met. One such part is "to acquit the innocent and convict the guilty"[43] and it is this part that appeared to garner the most attention from the participants. Rule 1.1(2)(a) appeared to have induced a fundamental misunderstanding of the overriding objective. A number of the participants were extremely forthright that the overriding objective is to convict the guilty and acquit the innocent, rather than the correct answer to deal with cases justly:[44] "The overriding objective is to convict the guilty and acquit the innocent. They forget all about dealing with the D which is fundamental . . . we have circumvented the basics of our CJ practice by a set of arbitrary rules . . . the purpose [of which] is to get more convictions" [002] (senior partner, thirty-two years' experience). "The official word is to convict the guilty and acquit the innocent . . . it's a managerialist system which assumes guilt and this is all about processing guilty cases. That's my cynical view" [007] (partner, twenty-one years' experience). "The system is striving to acquit the innocent and convict the guilty. It's as simple as that"[010] (solicitor, twelve years' experience). "It's effectively to convict the guilty and acquit the innocent and you have to assist the court to promote this overriding objective" [011] (partner, nineteen years' experience). "To ensure we have a smooth-running system in which we convict the guilty and acquit the innocent" [012] (solicitor, seven years' experience).

These lawyers made no mention of the other component parts of the objective, not even those that arguably enhance defendant rights. Those rights include dealing with the prosecution and defense fairly[45] or recognizing the rights of the defendant, particularly those under Article 6 of the ECHR.[46] However, the requirement to deal with cases efficiently and expeditiously[47] did elicit some cause for concern. "[The rules are] painted by policy that is not statute and based [on] speedy justice"[003] (solicitor, seven years' experience) "my understanding is that it's a money-saving exercise . . . the courts are insistent on a plea at the first hearing despite only seeing the client for 20 minutes and there are plenty of outstanding issues such as witnesses etc.. . . sometimes clients are shoehorned into pleading guilty when they should plead not guilty" [004] (solicitor, eight years' experience). "The Rules are designed to be as speedy as possible and not be wasteful of either time or money" [003] (solicitor, seven years' experience).

The notion of efficiency is an explicit goal of the CrimPR. Lord Justice Leveson explained that, pursuant to Rule 3.8(2)(b) of the CrimPR, the court must take the plea of the defendant at the first hearing. The obligation does not rest on the extent of advance information, service of evidence, disclosure of unused material, or the grant of legal aid. Leveson continued that exceptions to the rule are rare and must strictly be justified but that if a plea cannot be entered, the court must ascertain what the plea is "likely" to be.[48] Lawyer 004 (solicitor, eight years' experience) illustrated the concerns they held about advising a defendant on a plea within twenty minutes of meeting them for the first time. Lawyer 024 shared the concerns about advising clients without full disclosure from the prosecution: "It is an unrealistic demand on the defense to be in a position [to adequately advise] without knowing what the issues are. The CPS is at a distinct advantage here."

The notion of dealing with the case efficiently and expeditiously is explicitly outlined in Rule 1.1(2)(e). However, it appears the notion of efficiency obfuscates the role of the defense lawyer. He has to balance the duty to the client alongside that of the court and fulfil those duties as expeditiously as possible. To ensure the efficiency goal is met, the era of Active Case Management has been ushered in. The requirement that trials become more efficient and expeditious can be traced back prior to the genesis of the CrimPR. In the wake of the *Auld Review*, the criminal courts acted swiftly to adopt the notion of efficiency; illustrated by the cases of *Chabaan*[49] and *Jisl*,[50] he explicitly outlined that the starting point of a criminal case is simple: "Justice must be done. The defendant is entitled to a fair trial: and which is sometimes overlooked, the prosecution is equally entitled to a reasonable opportunity to present the evidence against the defendant. It is not however a concomitant of the entitlement to a fair trial that either or both sides are further entitled to take as much time as they like."[51]

In order to provide effective representation at trial, it is necessary to know all the facts of the case. Fuller and Randall suggest that lawyers should employ a "devil's advocate" approach to their role.[52] However, Luban suggests that for financial reasons defense lawyers do not employ a devil's advocate approach.[53] Furthermore, in the era of expedited hearings, such an approach would be nearly impossible because of the strict time constraints. Defendants may not immediately trust their lawyer. They might believe they will "rat them out and disclose incriminating facts to the prosecutor or judge."[54] As such, they may not wish to be fully open with the lawyer and withhold certain key facts. Freedman provides an example of an American lawyer who represented a woman charged with killing her husband.[55] First, the client said she was with her sister at the time of the killing but upon investigation the alibi could not be confirmed. It was only with the promise of strict confidentiality that the client indicated she had suffered years of physical and emotional abuse.[56] This represents a danger in the current climate; the client would put these facts in her defense case statement, enter a guilty plea on the face of the fact she killed her husband. It would only be much later (if ever) would the admission of the mitigating circumstances come to light. This potentially has an extremely adverse impact on the defense case and an innocent person might be imprisoned because of a perceived lack of trust in the first instance.

The case management forms[57] are analogous with the defense case statement provisions of the CPIA 1996.[58] However, defense case statements were only voluntary in the magistrates' courts but with the implementation of the case management forms, especially "identifying the real issues," there is a danger that the voluntary disclosure regime has been supplanted by a mandatory disclosure regime that masquerades as Active Case Management:[59] "What they require you to do is provide a defense case statement in the magistrates' court, which is only voluntary under the CPIA 1996. They are subverting statute through the back door by using the Rules, rather than statute" [011] (solicitor, nineteen years' experience). The completion of the form posed great concern for the participants, especially when given that such a duty is combined with the obligation to deal with the case in an efficient and expeditious manner, as the lawyer has not had the requisite time to adequately consider the charge against their client and identify the best course of action to take. "They are dangerous—you're being forced into completing a form with only a partial picture. That's my major objection" [001] (senior partner, sixteen years' experience).

> I do not have a problem with the form itself but the management of the form. I'm told to name the witnesses I intend to call. This is wrong. Because I don't name a witness I intend to call until such a time that I've decided to call the

> witness. The courts cough and splutter but it's important to remember there is one issue: can the prosecution prove the case against the D. That is the true issue. Mags say "well your client knows if he has done it." That's wrong. It shows a fundamental misunderstanding of the law and it's a deliberate manipulation. [002] (senior partner, thirty-two years' experience)

"The problem you have is that at the first hearing you are expected to put down your defense, agree witnesses, all without full disclosure. Case Management forces your hand at an early stage and it becomes a rod because you cannot divert from it. The pendulum has swung back toward the victim rather than the D" [003] (solicitor, seven years' experience). "We are filling out forms yet do not hold all the information. You have to be very careful with what you put on these forms" [011] (partner, nineteen years' experience).

Although a number of lawyers were concerned about the impact the completion of the case management forms had for the defendant, one lawyer in particular took no issue with the forms.

> The forms create an environment and culture where you are expected to do more . . . but I don't personally believe they add any further obligations than what is strictly in the rules" [022] (solicitor, six years' experience). Lawyer 023 (solicitor, seven years' experience) shared the view that the rules do not add any further obligations to their role. He emphasized the requirements to identify the real issues were effectively unproblematic: "The identification of real issues basically means the lawyer is doing a mini-plan script, frankly that is ridiculous . . . most summary cases are simple and it's just a couple of words that's needed." [022] (solicitor, 6 years' experience)

Surprisingly, Lawyer 024 (solicitor, nine years' experience) had no objection to the CrimPR. Earlier in the interview, the lawyer claimed that the CrimPR placed the defense at a distinct disadvantage because frequently the lawyer is advising the defendant without a full picture. However, when questioned about the overriding objective, the lawyer claimed it was just a matter of "terminology" and that there is nothing wrong with it in practice despite the earlier claim of the CrimPR being "unrealistic." The lawyer thought that the overriding objective would be better suited if it were explained as "convicting the legally guilty" rather than "convicting the guilty." The lawyer explained that if the client states that "he is probably guilty but he wants to test the prosecution's case," he would have no issue putting the prosecution to proof. In the main, the advocates displayed an element of confusion and disagreement concerning both the prioritization of duties and the overriding objective. Those interviewed focused on a singular component part of the objective rather than the objective as a whole. The overriding objective is to "deal with cases justly"; this perhaps points to a culture of attempting to increase the number of convictions which was alluded to by Lawyer 002 (senior partner, thirty-two years' experience). The advocate believed that we have "circumvented our criminal justice practice by a set of arbitrary rules [with] the purpose of getting more convictions." Whilst not all lawyers shared this view, it was clear participants did feel the traditional adversarial justice system was changing to become more efficient and a by-product of this efficiency drive might be increased numbers of convictions at trial.

Under the "new regime," it is perhaps not surprising that defense lawyers might appear confused when focusing on the overriding objective. With many defense tactics diluted, the ability of the lawyers to zealously defend their client has potentially been impinged; it is perhaps easy for the lawyers to adopt a cynical view that the overriding objective is yet another attack on defense practice. Ultimately, some lawyers in the study believe that the overriding objective is to "acquit the innocent and convict the guilty" and not to deal with cases "justly." In order to combat this, the lawyers adopt differing approaches to satisfy and discharge their obligations. The differing approaches allow for the lawyers in the study to be placed in one of three categories; arguably, the differing approaches mean that the overriding objective is not met.[60] The Classic Adversarial Lawyer is akin to Lord Broughman's lawyer; the only duty is to the client and the client alone. The Conflicted Adversarial Lawyer wants to project an image of Broughman's zealous lawyer but this projection is merely a veneer of zealous advocacy. This lawyer had the duty to their client tempered by the other obligations. Finally, we have the Procedural Lawyer; this lawyer sees no confusion at all. He is an officer of the court first and foremost. He complies with the rules even at the expense of the potential interests of the client. However, by adhering to the rules and satisfying multiple duties,[61] there could be severe ramifications for the defendant. Lawyer 019 (senior partner, thirty years' experience) gave an example of the defendant being penalized in this era of efficiency. He had a client who had been previously convicted three times and was currently accused of nine burglaries. At the initial hearing, the lawyer argued that the client was not fit to plead. This potentially contravenes the guidance given by Lord Justice Leveson as he suggested the plea must be taken at the first hearing,[62] indicating that exceptions to this rule will be rare. In this case, the court adjourned for eight weeks to allow the defendant to be assessed by medical professionals to ascertain his ability to plead. The client was deemed fit to plead and returned to court eight weeks later with his lawyer. The defendant was convicted, and the court stated that he would not receive the full one-third sentence discount[63] because he did not enter a guilty plea at the preliminary hearing. The lawyer thought this absurd and felt aggrieved. He thought he was doing the right thing: "I was being perfectly diligent and specifically not taking instructions from somebody who might have been mad." So, by acting in the client's interest, to seek a medical evaluation, the court decided that it was not the most expeditious way to deal with the case and therefore did not allow the full sentence discount. This illustrates that there is pressure to prioritize the duty to the court when any duties conflict. With this in mind, it is not surprising there is an element of role confusion as under pressure from the courts, by virtue of the CrimPR, the lawyer acts in the best interest of the client by seeking a medical evaluation but this ultimately has a detrimental impact on the client as he lost any discount for an early guilty plea. Ultimately, this presents the lawyer with a conundrum and one which highlights their role confusion. How can lawyers act as the zealous advocate, if advancing the client's best interests ultimately has a detrimental impact on that client.

TENSION IN THE ERA OF COOPERATION

Tension: n. effect produced by forces pulling against each other.[64]

The post CrimPR era of cooperation has highlighted the importance of both efficiency and economy. The courts have outlined that delay is inimical to the interests of justice.[65] Furthermore, it is self-evident that proceedings in magistrates' courts ought to be simple, speedy, and summary.[66] However, the quest for simple, speedy, and summary justice is not necessarily compatible with fairness and compliance with this implicit goal.[67] Arguably, the notion of cooperation and satisfying the overriding objective might be adverse to the best interests of the client. This section will examine whether the lawyer perceives any tension between the competing duties. The theoretical conception of the defense lawyer highlighted that these requirements might be problematic for the lawyer as the duty to the client and the court competes for priority; chapter 5 concluded it would be impossible for both duties to receive equal weighting. As such, this causes a tension; either the lawyer has to dilute the duty to the client in order to satisfy their obligation to the court; or the court would be left frustrated as the lawyer prioritizes the best interests of the client. This section examines these issues and where the lawyers recognized a tension, how they said they would deal with it.

The Case Management Form

The rules dictate that the advocates must assist the court with their active case management responsibilities,[68] and the courts' quest for cooperation and increased efficiency. In the *Chorley Justices*[69] case, Thomas LJ indicated that if the "defendant refuses to identify what the issues are . . . he can derive no advantage from that or seek . . . to attempt an ambush at trial. The days of ambushing and taking last minute technical defenses are gone." In order to assist the court with their active case management, both sides have to complete a case management form, which includes, inter alia, the identification of the real issues, monitoring and progressing the case, discouraging delay and encouraging participants to cooperate in the progression of the case.[70] A number of theoretical issues with the case management form were highlighted in chapter 1; the lack of time between meeting the client and the expectation to identify the real issues, which theoretically is incompatible with the presumption of innocence.[71] Finally, the empirical study examined how the lawyers deal with failures to disclose from the prosecution and what tactics and strategies are adopted to advance the client's best interest.

Identifying the Real Issues and a Lack of Time

Some lawyers expressed great dismay about the duty of cooperation as they had to disclose the real issues at the earliest opportunity whilst not necessarily knowing what evidence is in the possession of the prosecution.[72] Some prosecutors want you to outline your cross-examination plan at the very first hearing; these are points for the trial, the testing of evidence not for now. The CPS effectively wants everything. Identify the issues should not be a script of how the trial will go. Some want that [022] (solicitor, six years' experience). Other lawyers were concerned about having to disclose the relevant issues when they were only dealing with a partial picture of the facts. Often the lawyers would only be meeting their client on the morning of trial and they sometimes have to complete the case management forms within twenty or thirty minutes of meeting the client. A difficulty emerges because of the potential loss of sentence discount for a guilty plea. McEwan states that prosecution evidence is frequently not available at the first instance:[73] "The only difficulty is an unrealistic demand on the defense to be in a position to know what the issues are. Once charged, the prosecution should be ready to go to trial. The CPS is at a distinct advantage, as they are trial ready. The defense is not anywhere near that position" [024] (solicitor, nine years' experience).

> A fundamental problem with these forms is that you are expected to fill them in on the first occasion which is often when you have been given the evidence for the first time and had an opportunity to speak to the client for the first time. You are in court; it is not the appropriate environment so solicitors should be saying "I want an adjournment; I don't want to deal with case management issues today" but the courts don't really allow that. So, the solicitor then has to decide—am I going to push ahead anyway notwithstanding and make sure I get it right or am I going to advise the client that I don't feel in a position to properly

represent you today and withdraw from the case. [021] (solicitor, twelve years' experience)

The drive for efficiency creates tensions for the lawyers. The above-mentioned lawyers stated that they feel it is difficult to provide adequate legal advice as a plea has to be entered and the case fully managed at the first hearing, irrespective of prosecution disclosure or access to legal advice.[74] As Lawyer 003 (solicitor, seven years' experience) stated, "[the speed creates great difficulty] you're making decisions with only a partial picture [of facts]." Lawyer 019 (senior partner, thirty years' experience) gave an example that highlighted the inherent dangers of advising a client without a full picture of the facts. The lawyer highlighted that the culture change is not just about the notion of cooperation; there has been a change in culture from the judiciary and magistrates as well. When complaining to a judge that he could not adequately advise their client owing to a lack of information, the judge retorted quickly, "well, your client knows if he's done it." What muddies the water further is the fact the defendant might not know he is guilty; a view that was not always accepted by magistrates. Four lawyers commented that they had heard magistrates proclaim words to the effect of "your client knows if he's done it or not."[75] Lawyer 006 (senior partner, forty years' experience) intimated that this approach is "pretty much universal" in their region. Edwards commented on the aggressive judicial behavior, as regards the completion of statements; the judges and magistrates have evolved a long way from their original purpose of assisting in the identification of relevant material for further prosecution evidence.[76]

Traditional theory holds that the truth emerges where two sides present their own version of events and are pitted against each other on equal terms.[77] Langbein was critical of such a process when he argued that truth-finding is flawed because each side tailors their case to suit their own self-interest.[78] The courts have been quick to adopt the mantra of efficiency in the post-*Auld Review* era at the expense of adversarial justice. The courts have suggested that meeting the Overriding Objective will require both efficiency and expedition[79] and embracing the notion of cooperation would lead to greater efficiency and the truth.[80] Lawyer 007 (partner, twenty-one years' experience) revealed that he witnessed a magistrate depart from their traditional adversarial stance of passivity[81] when he effectively "bullied" two young advocates to agree to the summary of police interviews being admitted without actually hearing the tapes. Whilst the lawyer admitted that he did not believe it was the intention of the magistrate to bully the advocates, the net effect of the changing judicial demeanor meant the advocates felt they did not have the courage to do anything other than to agree to the summaries. This is to the obvious detriment of their client's best interests as the advocate had not heard the tape and thereby should not agree to its contents. This presents a very worrying example, which may well be an isolated incident but nonetheless represents a concerning attitude pervading the magistracy in the quest for efficiency. Whilst the notion of efficient and expedited trials should not be derided, it is disconcerting to see even an isolated case of the magistracy flexing their muscles in order to meet such objectives.

McEwan states that the defense might find it difficult to marshal an accurate picture of facts in the time limits set. She notes there are many problems in arranging meetings with clients and the court generally fails to take account of these failings.[82] Some lawyers in this study indicated that there is a "local arrangement" with the CPS and in places, the court, not to "grass" on each other. For example, to avoid sanctions for noncompliance with particular orders, some lawyers have struck up good working relationships with the CPS and they operate on quid pro quo basis; if you do not meet a deadline, we will not tell on you if you do not tell on us. "To be honest we have a reasonable working relationship with the majority of CPS lawyers, and it is sort of a quid pro quo, we don't make a fuss about them failing to meet deadlines to the extent that we could and it works both ways" [004] (solicitor, eight years' experience) "The rules are informally enforced instead of any hard and rigid sticking to the rules" [001] (senior partner, sixteen years' experience).

A number of lawyer's believed the sanctions to be one-sided and geared toward the defense, whereas the prosecution receives no sanction for breaches. Furthermore, some lawyers suggested: "the disclosure obligations are very much crime control . . . let's get quicker and convict earlier. But forget about receiving disclosure so you can advise your client. The prosecution can fail with their obligations. We cannot" [002] (senior partner thirty-two years' experience). This sentiment was echoed by 007 (partner twenty-one years' experience) who said: "We have to advise on a partial picture of evidence . . . the real risk of defeating the overriding objective [of dealing with cases justly] comes from CPS failings not from us." The notion that the regime allows for a conveyor belt[83] like process that is punished for failures was mentioned by 014 (partner, twenty-four years' experience). He believed that the carrot and the stick approach was being used by the courts routinely ignored CPS failings. Whilst it is outside the scope of this monograph, the failings in terms of police and prosecution disclosure are worth briefly raising. In *R v Allan*, which concerned the offence of rape, one police officer had 57,000 lines of message data and whilst there is no indication that the potential exculpatory evidence was purposively withheld from the defense, the defense were not given access to the material. However, the CPS placed pressure on the police, and this led to the phone records being disclosed to both sides. This disclosure yielded vital evidence that suggested "the complainant at best was giving a misleading impression as to her sexual relationship with Allan or at worst, maliciously lying."[84] And whilst there is no suggestion that the police withheld the information with any poor intentions; it does point to a flaw in a reciprocal disclosure regime. Simply put, the police are looking for evidence to convict the suspect and are not too concerned with finding exculpatory evidence. As suggested, an adversarial culture does not readily accept the notion that the police will find exculpatory evidence. However, this is at odds with the general approach to managerialism and the desire for a cooperative criminal justice system. In the wake of the Allan case, the metropolitan police and the CPS quickly made a list of recommendations concerning disclosure. Much like Plotnikoff and Wolfson and the other inquiries into disclosure, the report focused on the issue of training of officers.[85] However, this simplistic answer neglects to address the issue of funding. The drive for efficiency can arguably be described as the drive to become more economic. The early guilty plea scheme embodies this; by offering a reduction in sentence for a guilty plea, the system is saving money. Should the defendant wish to have his day in court and is found guilty, he is likely to receive a harsher sentence than if he copped to an early plea. If the system is looking to become more efficient, and effective, the composite bodies need adequate funding. The metropolitan police and CPS suggested better training is required but the question remains if the police have the necessary personnel[86] and time to undertake the vital work with disclosure,[87] especially in the light of the extensive digital material the police may now hold. As such, the Justice Committee welcomed the formation of a technology group to deal with this problem.[88] The joint review of disclosure by the HMCPSI and the HMIC found that policing schedules for disclosure were routinely poor and contained inadequate descriptors.[89]

Strategies and Tactics: Advancing the Client's Best Interest

Defense lawyers are placed in an unenviable position of having to provide advice to clients without a full picture of the facts. The impact of the advice at this early stage might have massive ramifications at the later sentencing stage and this was explained by Lawyer 019.[90] Here, he did not enter a plea at the first hearing and as such he paid a penalty by not receiving the full sentence discount. By advising with only a partial picture, the situation is akin to a surgeon having to operate on a patient without the full knowledge of his condition. This situation is clearly undesirable and yet lawyers are expected to offer advice on the basis of the "client knows if he's done it."[91] To combat this issue, some defense lawyers employ a somewhat tactical approach to completing the form. Andrew Keogh has said that the "clever technical lawyer is now officially dead."[92] However, that position appears rather extreme; although it is impossible to refute that the courts have adopted a new approach to hearing criminal cases.[93] However, to say the clever technical lawyer is dead might not necessarily be the case. It was clear from the interviews that some lawyers have reinvented themselves and adopted a technical approach to fulfilling their case management responsibilities: "I try to be as vague as possible and supply as little detail as possible to satisfy the court" [008] (solicitor, six years' experience). "I complete the form with as little detail, but sufficient detail, to satisfy my obligation to the court. I will not go chapter and verse into my client's defense" [010] (solicitor, ten years' experience). "I won't disclose his defense . . . the form is completed in minimal detail. But completing the form causes difficulties because we are working from a skeleton. The response is very basic, not very detailed" [011] (partner, nineteen years' experience).

The approach of submitting minimum detail in the case management form is a problem the courts have faced since the inception of the CPIA 1996.[94] Plotnikoff and Wolfson found that 52 percent of defense case statements contained a bare denial of guilt or did not meet the requirements of S.5 CPIA 1996.[95] Furthermore, they highlighted that nearly 90 percent of judges and barristers "rarely or never adduce evidence of the contents of the defense statement at trial, other than to rebut alibi evidence."[96] The defense statement was designed to narrow the issues at trial, and the case management forms were designed to "identify the real issues" and make the trial process more efficient and expeditious. However, Quirk found that the defense case statements were "merely an administrative requirement rather than anything of any practical utility."[97] A number of lawyers interviewed had established a more cooperative attitude toward their obligations and they did not feel the need to strategically withhold information in order to protect their client. In fact, some said there was little point in doing so because the culture of the court has now changed and they would be criticized for taking such an approach. "I flag all issues as there is no point springing the issues later as you will be criticized by the court . . . it's difficult because, I know it's not a listed penalty, but you don't want your client receiving a heftier sentence but it does have that effect sometime. But we will not write paragraphs; we will just say what the 'nature' is" [004] (solicitor, eight years' experience). "The CrimPR [are] generally a positive tool, although it faces a risk of falling into disrepair because of courts' failure to sanction those who don't comply. The CPS cannot keep up with the pace [of the Rules]. They know if they breach it, there's no sanction" [024] (solicitor, nine years' experience).

Ultimately, these lawyers have embraced the era of cooperation and do not necessarily adopt a technical approach to completing the case management forms. They think the forms are a positive tool and those who do not reply should be sanctioned. This is an example of the non-adversarial defense lawyer at work. The adversarial defense lawyer would not go "chapter and verse" into the form. The lawyers I interviewed did not really fear any judicial sanction, save for costs orders, and as such, thought the best approach for the client was to set out a little more than a skeleton outline of the issues at hand. However, other lawyers disagreed with this approach and thought it to be pointless, with one lawyer, unrealistically (Lawyer 007) fearing, unofficially, that his client may get a "rougher ride" with the magistrate, if the lawyer did not comply with the CrimPR.

The minority of lawyers who were positive about the CrimPR are in contrast to Garland and McEwan's findings, who found that failure of the defense to file defense case statements was "a perennial problem."[98] Furthermore, the court had to press the defense lawyer on what the issues were because they only provided one or two word answers.[99] "I do not think it's unreasonable to say to a D we need you to identify what your defense is. These are public funds. Because of *Newell*,[100] we do not have to be as cautious as one once was" [006] (senior partner, forty years' experience). Lawyer 019 (senior partner, thirty years' experience) held the opinion that the protection afforded in *Newell* was robust enough to withstand any tactical use by the prosecution. Nonetheless, the lawyer adopted a very cautious approach to completing the forms: "I complete the forms with great care. Although, the higher courts have said the forms would not be used against a defendant[101] . . . but someone will always raise it in my view . . . We basically need a full picture [of evidence]. That is not happening. We have to make progress, but we have 1/3 of evidence yet have to advise the client. If he is pleading not guilty, we have to complete the case management form. It has to be done very carefully; it could undermine his position at trial."

It appears the lawyers face a number of tensions or concerns when completing the case management requirements. Some were very concerned with the implications of what might happen with the information contained within the form, whilst a minority were happy to comply with the rules, because to them, they provide a good framework in order to operate efficiently. However, the existing literature suggests that there are high levels of noncompliance with the new regime disclosure requirements. The defense fraternity have been accused of failing to produce a defense case statement.[102] Furthermore, some defense lawyers produce statements which omit details of their defense,[103] or serve them out of the time limits.[104]

The lawyers who expressed concern with the *Newell*[105] protections were correct in their caution. A review of the sanctions for failures relating to disclosure made an interesting point. Lord Justice Gross and Lord Justice Treacy stated: "We see no reason why a defense statement should not be capable of forming part of the prosecution's case . . . since the statement is deemed to be made with the defendant's authority it is thus akin to comments he makes in an interview."[106] Whilst this point concerns the defense statement, if the case management form has been deemed to be "analogous to the defense case statement"[107] any repercussions may present a similar danger to lawyers. *Rochford*[108] suggests it is not a contempt of court to fail to file a defense statement and Edwards indicates that the defendant is entitled to hold back the information provided the defendant is prepared to take the risk an inference being drawn.[109] However, a basic completion of the form is now viewed rather dimly by the courts; it is expected to be completed fully, containing extensive detail.[110] This provides a difficulty for the lawyer. On one hand, the courts are pressing them to ensure the form is completed adequately and on the other, the D will not be in contempt should he not file one; he can hold information back and face the sanctions available to the court.

If this is the case, it is arguable that the defense lawyers were acting in the best interests of their client by adopting a tactical approach to the case management forms. Sir John Thomas stated, "statements should be made without the risk they would be used at trial [against the defendant], provided the advocate follows the letter and spirit of the CrimPR."[111] Currently, there have only been a small number of reported cases where the case management forms were used by the prosecution.[112] Despite the protection afforded by *Newall*,[113] the case management forms appear to "maximize the opportunities for the prosecution to obtain knowledge helpful to its case."[114]

The desire to have the defense reveal its hand in advance of trial supports the argument that the CrimPR represent a departure from classic adversarialism. The pretrial disclosure of salient facts indicates a move toward a more truth-orientated model of criminal procedure.[115] As discussed in chapter 1, the original rationale for prosecution disclosure was to level the playing field as the prosecution had a far greater arsenal of resources than the defense. So much so, that until 1996, the defense only had to disclose alibi witnesses and expert evidence. Owusu-Bempah[116] and McEwan[117] suggest that the current disclosure regime represents a shift to a managerial model of criminal procedure that prioritizes efficiency at the expense of justice and due process. If the piecemeal changes to disclosure have ultimately shifted the legal landscape in which the lawyer operates, recognition ought to be given to this to fully explain the implications of such a shift.

Despite the apparent managerial elements permeating the adversarial process, evidence from the interviews conducted suggests that the "clever, technical lawyer" has not officially died;[118] he is very much alive and functioning within the criminal justice system, albeit as a minority in this study. He submits enough detail to satisfy the court but insufficient detail to fully reveal the composition of his case to the CPS. McEwan and Garland suggest that the "most significant influence on whether or not a lawyer will comply with the provisions is down to their own perception of their professional obligations."[119] This could go some way to explain why there is not a uniformed approach to the case management provisions. McEwan and Garland also argue that there is a conflict between the efficiency drivers of the CrimPR and how to advance the client's best interest. This point was reiterated by Lawyer 002 (partner, thirty-two years' experience), who stated, "the system is about getting convictions, ideally via a guilty plea, as quickly as possible. We need to convict, convict, convict. Despite this, I'll still put the client's interest before any crime control conveyor belt." Whilst the goals of efficiency are clear, he will still advance the best interest of the client. He was adamant that complying with the CrimPR could be seen to benefit the CPS rather than his client and he took measures to counter this impact. He would complete the case management forms with minimal detail but still satisfy the court. He stated that occasionally this attracts comment from the magistrate, who is frustrated with the lack of detail. But here is where his years of experience benefit him; he was neither intimidated nor flustered by the court's response. Lawyer 007 (partner, thirty-two years' experience) also stated that he can withstand challenge from the magistrates but has seen less experienced advocates crumble under such pressure. Here the experience and perhaps "thick skin" of the advocate allows him to withstand an annoyed or frustrated magistrate. The implication being that the experienced lawyer advances his client's best interest by standing by their approach of minimal detail. If the less experienced advocate crumbles when faced with "your client knows if he's done it—why is there a lack of detail?," this may paint the client in a bad light in the eyes of the magistrates and the client may lose confidence in his lawyer.

However, some lawyers do not take the technical route and are happy to embrace the CrimPR to identify the real issues without resorting to such tactics and they do not view the obligation as onerous. However, this is somewhat surprising. McEwan and Garland found that it was "difficult to see how defendants can be persuaded that they have an interest in the smooth running of the CJS . . . and they may want to put things off for as long as possible."[120] The lawyers interviewed stated this is unproblematic and it is a matter of managing the expectations of the client. Lawyer 016 (solicitor, sixteen years' experience) stated that all the obligations and manner of handling things are highlighted in the client care letter: "Here we outline what is expected of us and of the court. Frankly, the client probably does not read the letter." As such, the change in the rules likely makes little difference to the client as they may not actually recognize that there has been any change to the law.

Advance Disclosure of Witnesses

The advance witness disclosure regime was another potential tension that was highlighted in chapter 5. Section 34 of the Criminal Justice Act 2003 introduced s.6C into the CPIA 1996. Under this provision, the accused must give the court and prosecution a notice which indicates whether he intends to call any other witnesses other than himself at trial. An immediate problem occurs here; the responsibility falls on the accused to give this notification. However, it is not realistic for the defendant to make such a disclosure; as a result, the responsibility falls on the defense lawyer. Theoretically, there were a number of potential problems concerning the advance disclosure of defense witnesses.

- The principle of requiring advance disclosure is one that is distinctly non-adversarial.[121]
- Whether the police or prosecution have the resources to contact and interview witnesses.
- Whether the courts prevent lawyers from calling witnesses in respect of whom prior notification has not been given?

Hungerford-Welch suggests that the concern expressed by the lawyers is not unfounded. He stated that revealing defense witnesses to the prosecution was a cause for concern as it was likely the police would want to speak to witnesses, who may be put off from testifying.[122] However, to combat this potential threat, a Code of Practice was issued under s.21A CPIA 1996.[123] This code introduced a number of safeguards including a requirement that witnesses be asked whether they consent to be interviewed, that they be informed that they are not obliged to attend the interview, and that they are entitled to be accompanied by a solicitor.[124]

Anthony Edwards suggested that the effect of the new rule would mean that "careful tactical decisions [would] need to be made in each case."[125] However, a lack of available resources has effectively rendered the provision unproblematic and in practice the rule appears to have had little effect, despite the initial concern resulting from the implementation of the rule. The initial panic[126] rested on the fear that the prosecution or police might dissuade the defense witness from testifying. However, these theoretical tensions are yet to manifest themselves in practice. In fact, there was a distinct lack of concern among the lawyers interviewed with the advance notice of witnesses and this response was somewhat surprising. The lack of concern stems from a pragmatic response that the police and prosecution generally do not have the resources to interview potential defense witnesses. However, a small number of participants expressed a level of disappointment with the rule because of the adverse implications the regime might hold for the best interest of the client:

> It does tip them off and allows them to go away and check whether they have any previous convictions themselves. It allows them to go away and speak to them but obviously they would have to notify that they are going to . . . But

> it just seems to be, it is becoming more weighted against the defendant really because the police and the CPS have a substantial amount of weight behind them whereas a defense solicitor does not. [004] (solicitor, eight years' experience)

> I can only recollect [in my practice] the prosecution only ever speaking to one defense witness in a case where my firm has been involved, so it is not really an issue for us. [005] (solicitor, four years' experience)

However, some lawyers have experienced this problem: "I don't agree with what we have to disclose to them, they go and see the witness. The last time I disclosed, the police went round without my knowledge, it's irritating as I would have liked to listen how they would do it. Witness was put off and CPS dropped it on day of trial" [018] (solicitor, four years' experience). Despite the experience of Lawyer 018, it is clear that the theoretical concerns did not manifest in practice: "I cannot give you a single example of a trial that I have conducted where we have not told the prosecution witness contact details and the court have not let them give evidence. The fact of the matter is the CPS (at the moment) has no people working for them, no budget, and no time to chase up witnesses even if we did supply the contact details. I think it is almost becoming a moot point. It seems to have slid out the window as far as I can tell" [003] (solicitor, seven years' experience). In the main, this viewpoint was echoed by each of the participants. "The defense community got in a bit of flap about it when it came in but in reality, it doesn't matter" [006] (senior partner, forty years' experience). The reality of the matter, as Edwards intimated,[127] is that it is not practical for the police or prosecution to interview the majority of defense witnesses in the current economic climate. "We need to divorce the theory from the practice—the theory that the Crown can interview defense witnesses was worrying. In many cases, they might already have spoken to the law enforcements or be known to the police. The dissuading of giving evidence was a real concern. Reality is resources are scarce that I've not had a case where the prosecution interviews the witness. Practical implications are not outweighed by the theoretical concerns" [014] (partner, twenty-four years' experience).

Since the genesis of the disclosure regime, courts have been hampered by the lack of an effective sanction for failing to comply with the disclosure requirements. This lack of sanction means that the provision effectively loses its teeth and compliance with the regime slips. Lawyer 020 indicated that the court does not really mind if they call witnesses that have not been disclosed. The lack of sanction was recognized in *R (on the Application of Kelly) v Warley Magistrates*,[128] where it was held that the imposition of an effective sanction, such as a prohibition on relying on the evidence of a witness not previously identified, would require primary legislation.[129] However, the courts have explicitly expressed a desire to comply with the advance notification of defense witnesses; it has been held that "the defendant's interests are best served by early identification of witnesses and obtaining statements from them."[130]

Currently, it appears that the potential tension caused by the implementation of the rule has yet to come to fruition and it may not be realistic to think that the S.6C provisions will lead to routine interviewing of defense witnesses.[131] The participants noted the current economic climate which meant the prosecution and police are not fully equipped with the resources to take advantage of the benefits of interviewing defense witnesses. What this section has found is rather surprising. A number of the projected tensions outlined in chapter 5 have not become problematic in practice. It appears that in places, the defense community has embraced the concept of a case progression officer and acted in a pragmatic fashion by allowing the individual lawyer to become responsible for the individual progression of the case. An issue arises where failures occur with the prosecution's progression officer and the ramifications of this will be dealt with in the next section.

CONCLUSIONS

The defense lawyer is facing immense pressure to complete the case management forms shortly after meeting his client for the very first time. Often the lawyers feel that they are not operating with a full set of facts and as such, find it extremely difficult to adequately advise their client. As a result, a client might be advised to enter a not guilty plea where a plea of guilty might be more appropriate.[132] The result of such inadequate advice would be a more severe sentence for the defendant. The rule regarding Advance Disclosure of witnesses is generally viewed as unproblematic. That is not to say that when the economic climate changes the theoretical concerns may indeed become manifest when resources to interview defense witnesses are available. However, the case management forms and the obligation to identify the real issues present problems for some lawyers. According to Gordon, lawyers are expected and even encouraged to exploit every loophole in the rules, "take advantage of every one of their opponents' tactical mistakes or oversights . . . to favor their client."[133] However, with the focus on case management and the overriding objective, that is simply impossible to do. The rules simply will not allow it and the courts will not tolerate such an approach. If a defense case statement is lacking in detail, the lawyer encounters a difficult line of questioning from the magistrate. Lawyers often hear "[when explaining the lack of detail in the forms] well your client knows if he has done it. That's wrong. It shows a fundamental misunderstanding of the law and it's a deliberate manipulation"[134] of the law to deal with cases more efficiently. The desire for more efficiency neglects to consider that the overriding objective is to deal with cases "justly,"[135] not merely speedily.

The Implications for the Lawyer-Client Relationship

Relationship: n. a state of being related; what one person or thing has to do with another; kinship.[136]

The final section of the empirical study sought to examine whether the effect of the changed obligations for the defense lawyer had any detrimental impact on the notion of the lawyer-client relationship. For example, does the requirement of cooperation between the defense and prosecution undermine trust between the lawyer and the client? Theoretically, the client is being asked to divulge information that has the potential to incriminate him and assist the prosecution in convicting him. If the client believes the lawyer has to disclose information that might be adverse to their position, the client might lose all confidence in their ability to confide in their lawyer, which ultimately means there is difficulty in establishing a basis for a fair trial. McConville and Marsh suggest that the role of the defense is to now cooperate with the prosecution, with the goal of satisfying the case management provisions of the court[137] and these formal duties may be diametrically opposed to the wishes of the client.[138]

The Obligation to Inform the Court of Significant Failures

In the wake of *Gleeson*[139] and *Chorley Justices*,[140] it became clear the defendant will not be permitted to benefit from errors made by the prosecution. He certainly will not be allowed to ambush the prosecution in order to reap a benefit. As such, should the defense spot a flaw in the case of the prosecution, they are expected to flag this flaw to give the prosecution time to remedy the issue. Prior to *Gleeson*, the defense could sit back and take advantage of the flaw to the benefit of their client. However, Rule 1.2 of the CrimPR outlines the duty of the participants in a criminal case and states that "each participant must at once inform the court and all parties of any significant failure (whether or not that participant is responsible for the failure)." The rule goes on to define a significant failure as something that "might hinder the court in furthering the overriding objective." Despite the requirement to disclose anything that might hinder the overriding objective, one of the lawyers interviewed indicated that he adopts a very technical approach to such disclosure: "If I do not have instructions from my client I have to, under the rules, inform the court. However, I have to phrase this carefully—something neutral like 'I still await detailed instruction' or something like that" [002] (senior partner, thirty-two years' experience). At times, the majority of lawyers indicated that they may have to "snitch" on their client because he is yet to provide instructions to the lawyer and the case requires progression.[141] In that instance, the lawyer pleads with their client to instruct him and clearly outlines the consequence of continued non-instruction, but the rules require cases to progress, so the lawyers have to take action: "We try everything before dobbing them in. It is often in a difficult situation in terms of ethics, the SRA helpline is also consulted. It covers your back" [018] (solicitor, four years' experience).

It is examples like this that Wendell alluded to. He intimated that the client worries that their lawyer would "rat them out."[142] However, in this instance, it is not because of something incriminating the client has told the lawyer, it is their own failure to act. Some lawyers intimated that without "grassing" on their client, the case would not progress. "The aim is to ensure that progress is not derailed and that the overriding objectives are satisfied throughout proceedings. It does feel somewhat uncomfortable exposing a client or a defense witness but the rules are there to be complied with. The best way around this issue is to manage your client's expectations from the start with a warning of the duty on all parties to report all failures" [016] (solicitor, sixteen years' experience). "You write to your client, you give them several opportunities and you warn your client before you actually ultimately have to do that. So yes, I suppose it is a conflict because you are telling on your client, aren't you?" [021] (solicitor, twelve years' experience).

Lawyer 020 was quick to point out that the reason for noncompliance was a genuine one: "Because of the chaotic nature of a defendant's life; moving home etc., it can be difficult to get them to give instruction. However, the threat of grassing them up works and they pick up the phone. At times it can be difficult to forge a relationship" [020] (senior partner, twelve years' experience).

However, realism and the overriding objective soon became apparent for Lawyer 023 (solicitor, seven years' experience) and he thought that informing the court was "sometimes . . . the only way to make progress with a case." Here, the pressures of cooperation come to the fore. Lord Broughman's lawyer only has a duty to the client and the client alone[143] but it is clear these competing interests might cause strain on the lawyer-client relationship. By reporting him to the court or the prosecution, the lawyer has discharged their duty to the court; however, this might be at the expense of the duty to the client. In general, this appeared to have no adverse impact on the lawyer-client relationship; the lawyers said that they went to great lengths to explain both their obligations to the court and what would be expected from them as a client. The majority of lawyers[144] commented that they provided a client care letter at the first consultation which explained the obligations that they have to meet and what conduct is expected of the client.

If the client was not adhering to advice and refusing to give instructions, this poses a conflict for the lawyer. The duty to the court will be become frustrated as the lack of instruction will not allow for an efficient and expedited trial. As such, the remedy will be simple: "Quite simply, if the conflict was such that I felt that continuing to rep[resent] him means I couldn't properly represent him, I would just withdraw and say, I can no longer represent him for professional reasons" [002] (senior partner, thirty-two years' experience). "I would speak to my client about any conflict, it can usually be resolved prior to trial but if it couldn't be resolved with my client then I would cease to act" [005] (solicitor, four years' experience). "I have had clients asking me to mislead the court or telling me one thing but saying they will say something different in the hearing itself and the way to deal with it is that I explain my obligations to the court, my obligations to the client. I explain to them that they can go in there and tell them the truth or if they insist on saying something different I will have to withdraw as their solicitor" [008] (solicitor, six years' experience). "I'll use the SRA helpline and partners (at the firm). At trial, the real reason could be that she hasn't been speaking to me. You're in a position where I don't want to 'dob' the client in but it's not really fair that the judge thinks I didn't do something. There isn't a right answer to this; this is incredibly tough . . . my personal career is conflicting with the duty to the client. Constantly put things in that compromise our integrity. You cannot always do what's best for the client" [018] (solicitor, four years' experience).

Lawyer's looking to protect their own careers is nothing new. Quirk found that "some solicitors appear more concerned with protecting their own positions than acting solely in their client's interest."[145] She found that lawyers were fearful of suggesting a client remain silent in the police station interview, one lawyer said, "I don't want to get the blame . . . I'm fearful of that . . . it's rare you advise them to remain silent . . . you always think "I may have to take the stand about this one day."[146] As such, in order to protect themselves from any liability they draft disclaimers that their clients have to sign in which the client accepts the consequences of a "no-comment" interview.[147] Again, this reaffirms McConville's findings that completely adversarial defense lawyers may not actually exist in England and Wales. From my own study, Lawyer 016 (solicitor, sixteen years' experience) stated that in order to inform the client of their obligations, some of which may be defeating the client's best interest, for example, case management disclosure, they draft a client care letter that highlights everything the lawyer does. As such, this absolves the lawyer of facing any conflict when the client turns around to say, "I don't like that you told the CPS that." The lawyer can then point to the letter and say, "we told you we had to do this." Whilst this satisfies the obligations to the court under the new regime, it does seem difficult to suggest that the client would see this as furthering their best interests; however, no lawyers suggested the client had an issue with this type of approach. This could mean that the client simply does not recognize there has been a cultural change in terms of cooperation. The client may not even care, Lawyer 012 (solicitor twelve years' experience) intimated that whilst client care letters are detailed, he thought the clients just "signs them without really digesting them, as they do not understand the nuances of criminal defense; they only want to avoid punishment."

The lawyer-client relationship might be further diluted by the erosion of the presumption of innocence. In adversarial theory, the accused is armed with the protection of the presumption of innocence. The presumption is enshrined in the European Convention on Human Rights.[148] This right is closely linked to the right not to incriminate oneself, which means that if a defendant elects to remain silent during the criminal process, he can do so without fear of adverse consequences. "The presumption of innocence in the magistrates' [court]? Yes. You have a number of clients who wish to put the prosecution to proof. The CrimPR does cause some difficulties in relation to that because you're being forced at a very early stage to declare your side—were you there, did you hit her etc. The CrimPR here can cause some difficulties in terms of the privilege against self-incrimination because you will be sometimes forced to admit something that it later turns out to be that the prosecution couldn't prove" [001] (senior partner, sixteen years' experience). "The privilege against self-incrimination is more problematic. A lot of politics becomes involved in this. If you go back to rule one [the overriding objective] it is to convict the guilt and acquit the innocent" [007] (senior partner, twenty-one years' experience). "It's moving too far in obligating the Ds to identify Crown failings. It doesn't contravene the presumption of innocence; it's the burden of proof it encroaches upon. The crown must prove it beyond reasonable doubt. I am not sure that principle is enforced by the CrimPR. The Crown proving the case as D now identifies their failures. They are assisted in proving the case. It goes beyond the adversarial system" [014] (senior partner, twenty-four years' experience).

It is clear that the defense participants believe there has been a great dilution of the presumption of innocence and the privilege against self-incrimination.

> Certainly, the privilege against self-incrimination, obviously you are being asked to disclose at an early stage in the proceedings what your defense is, I mean, ultimately I am not sure that they have any really because you are always going to have self-incrimination. Then the [Case Management] forms are potentially incriminating if you do not comply with the spirit of the rules. [004] (solicitor, eight years' experience)

"The presumption of innocence and privilege against self-incrimination are on the wane. I don't know how many times I have heard this year 'well your client knows whether he has done it or not' " [003] (solicitor, seven years' experience). The client effectively has to cooperate with the prosecution who is attempting to convict him. This notion is the complete opposite to traditional adversarial theory where the accused is fully protected from self-incrimination.

> I think [the CrimPR] completely undermines both [the presumption of innocence and the privilege against self-incrimination]. The whole ethos of the modern trial is "your client knew whether or not he did the act." You have got to tell us what your case is just in case we made a mistake . . . presumption of innocence is just not a presumption that is valid in the magistrate's court . . . so they have not levelled the playing field, they have tilted it on the side of a mountain. [002] (senior partner, thirty-two years' experience)

(In)Effective Sanctions for Failing to Comply with the Rules

Establishing an available sanction that would encourage better preparation and a more efficient trial has proven difficult. Chapter 5 examined the issue of a lack of effective sanctions. Should the defense lawyer not comply by raising a significant failure he runs the risk of receiving a sanction for failing to comply with the CrimPR.[149] Subsection (c) effectively means that any sanction can be handed down by the court providing it is deemed to be appropriate. However, the sanctions examined by the empirical study were Wasted Costs Orders,[150] refusal of an application, professional censure, and inferences drawn at trial.[151]

The danger of a Wasted Costs Order (WCO) being made against a defense lawyer for a breach of the CrimPR was highlighted in *SVS Solicitors*;[152] it was this sanction that provided the greatest concern for the lawyers. The lawyer in *SVS* had a very un-cooperative client and the firm failed to give appropriate reasons for opposing a hearsay notice after the defendant had failed to give timely instructions. The lawyer was deemed to have acted incompetently and the judge believed that this amounted to a deliberate and serious breach of the rules. The lawyers interviewed indicated that the potential threat of a WCO influences the way that they deal with a case: "For a start you very carefully advise your client of failing to identify witnesses, the need to identify issues that might cause a problem. So to that extent, yes it does. It also makes you watch case preparation a bit more defensively, defensive in terms of protecting yourself from wasted costs" [002] (senior partner, thirty-two years' experience). "The threat of wasted costs hangs over everything. Just very much the fact that if you get something wrong at the early stage and your client says, why can't that evidence go in and it is because you have cocked up early on, I think the worry that you are going to have to apply for an adjournment and might be refused or an application might be refused does play on my mind actually at the case management stage" [003] (solicitor, seven years' experience). "You are always very aware of Wasted Costs Orders and we are far more vulnerable to them than the CPS, so it is a real issue, particularly in a complex case" [004] (solicitor, eight years' experience).

Despite the fact that the WCOs provide the court with an effective sanction should the lawyers not comply with the rules, it appears not all lawyers are keen to advance the duty to the court above that of their own client. In terms of informing the court of a significant failure, the majority of lawyers interviewed were prepared to give their client every conceivable opportunity before they informed the court and prosecution of any defense failure. However, there exists a problem with the culture of prosecution disclosure and this poses a failing to meet the overriding objective. There appears to be no suitable sanction for the prosecution, so a cultural shift maybe required where the police and CPS turn all evidence over to the defense. However, this is not without difficulty, as an already overworked and underfunded defense fraternity may find it difficult to sift through vast amounts of evidence. What is clear is the fact it is not only the defense who solely needed to be whipped into shape to fulfil the overriding objective. The prosecution also requires the stick to ensure they comply with the rules.

Evidence suggests that the prosecution are more responsible for disclosure failings in criminal trials than the defense. This goes against the tone of the courts, where the defense lawyer is painted as someone who is trying to "game the system" to ensure a guilty client walks free. Yet, the below table indicates that the prosecution are responsible for more failures than their counterparts (figure 5.2).[153]

For the first time, it appears that these failings might lead to change. It is debatable whether the defense lawyer will continue to be painted as a schemer or a game-player but faults with prosecution disclosure have begun to be recognized. In December 2020, HMCPSI published a report, *Disclosure of Unused Material in the Crown Court.*[154] In the report, the HMCPSI acknowledge that although prosecutors compliance continues to improve in respect of the disclosure process, there is "still some way to go to deliver casework that could be as assessed as of the appropriate quality."[155] The blame for the failures have been "exacerbated by too few legal staff being spread too thinly over a volume of work of ever-increasing complexity."[156] As such, the report acknowledged that "prosecutors should be held accountable to this regime."[157] Whether this improves the disclosure regime is difficult to say but the acknowledgement that failures within the process do not rest solely with the defense lawyer is pleasing. Hopefully, having a fully functioning disclosure regime will allow the lawyer-client relationship to thrive as they

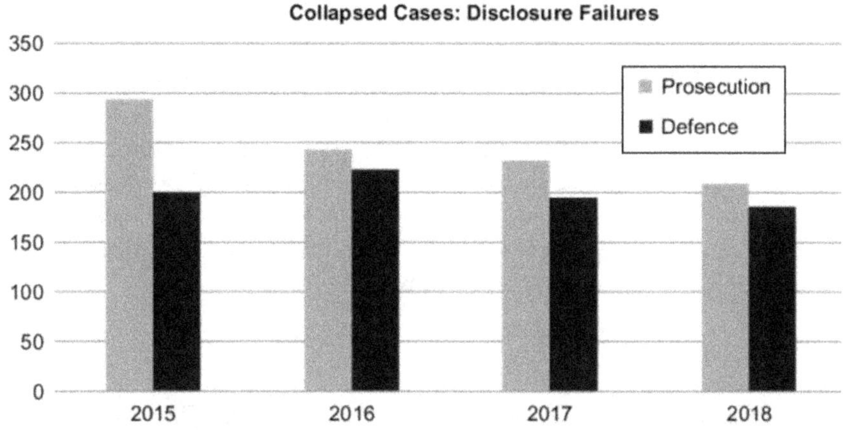

Figure 5.2 Data taken from "Trial Effectiveness Tool," *Criminal Justice Quarterly Statistics*, January to March 2019.

will see that blame game does not purely fall at their door and go some way to reasserting traditional adversarial values of the criminal justice process.

The Implications of the CrimPR for the Lawyer-Client Relationship

As suggested in the introduction, the obligations imposed on defense lawyers by the CrimPR potentially interfere with the lawyer-client relationship. Arguably, the environment of cooperation is not one that is compatible with advancing the best interests of the client in particular, or adversarialism in general. As such the client may not want to disclose certain elements of their defense as it gives the prosecution an upper hand or advantage. Furthermore, if the lawyer has to assist the court by flagging up any of the client's significant failures, the client may believe the lawyer to be untrustworthy or a "snitch." James Richardson suggests that preparing and conducting the case in accordance with the overriding objective is incompatible with an adversarial system of justice. However, the interview data suggested that this theoretical fear did not frequently arise in practice. The theoretical chapter indicated that having to inform the court of any significant failings on the interview data suggests the lawyers take a very pragmatic approach to adhering to this rule. Lawyers often outline their expectations of client behavior at the first meeting; this highlights the importance of providing instructions and keeping to a timetable. Lawyer 008 suggested that the benefit of such an approach was twofold; first, it shows the client he has a proactive lawyer and, second, it shows the lawyer is not wasting public money. However, it appears that a minority of lawyers thought the lawyer-client relationship was impacted by the rules. If the client wants to do something unethical or does not provide instructions, the lawyer will not jeopardize their personal career by risking professional embarrassment by the court. The strict timetable-based nature of the modern-day criminal trial has left lawyers no choice but to move on from cases where the lack of instruction might be prolonged. Lawyer 018 (solicitor, four years' experience) suggested that their first thought is "can I make this case profitable?" The lawyer intimated that this kind of thinking clouds their own integrity and believes the efficiency drivers are attempting to make the criminal justice system reflect a conveyor belt process.

The Role(s) of the Defense Lawyer

The interviewees illustrated an element of role confusion. There is difficulty in establishing which of the three duties espoused by Lord Reid should take priority. This difficulty led to different lawyers advancing different approaches to resolving the competing priorities. The data suggests that there are three distinct "types" of criminal defense lawyer.

First, there is the *Classic Adversarial Lawyer*. He is a lawyer who is fundamentally clear on which obligations compete for priority. He is single-minded and believes that the duty to the client is prioritized over any other duty. In this empirical study, only four of the twenty-four interviewed lawyers could be described as coming within this category. Lawyer 007 (senior partner, twenty-one years' experience) was an example of the *Classic* category and was steadfast in explaining his duties: "I'll ignore what it says in the Procedure Rules, we are there to protect the legal interest of the client." The lawyer effectively excludes all other duties in order to advance the best interests of his client. Lawyer 006 (senior partner, forty years' experience) was another who explicitly prioritized the duty to the client. The lawyer suggested that having competing duties "fudged" the issue; the single duty taking priority is to the client. The four *Classic Adversarial Lawyers* had a combined 123 years of criminal defense experience. They all qualified and practiced in the pre-CPIA 1996 era and therefore had experience of working in a time before the defense had to disclose any information, save for alibi and expert evidence. They had the adversarial weapon of an ambush defense and they could put the prosecution to proof without making an affirmative defense. The very notion of cooperation between the opposing sides would be shunned; prosecution and defense lawyers were adversaries, battling to advance the best interest of their respective clients. It is perhaps unsurprising to discover that the category most akin to the classic conception of the adversarial lawyer contains the fewest number of participants.

McConville and Marsh argue that lawyers have misread the extent to which their duty to the client has been overridden in the cause of efficient court administration.[158] This misreading has led to a fundamental departure from adversarial values and has given rise to lawyers who either (a) claim to be adversarial but illustrate elements of conflict, or (b) prioritize the managerial goals of the CrimPR ahead of their client's interest (figure 5.3).

As illustrated by the above table, the vast majority of the lawyers in the present study fell into the second category, the *Conflicted Adversarial Lawyer*. Fifteen of the twenty-four participants could be placed in this category. They are "conflicted" because they want to prioritize their duty to the client but, for a number of reasons, the impact of doing so is greatly diluted. The lawyers use terms such as "paramount," "prime," or "main." These terms suggest that the duty to the client takes priority, but it is quickly given a caveat that other obligations also exist that requires a great deal of attention. Lawyer 008 (solicitor, six years' experience) provides an illustration of the *Conflicted Lawyer*. The lawyer suggested that their duty was "mainly" to the client; this was not as explicit the *Classic Lawyers* as it recognized the existence, and importance, of other duties. Lawyer 009 (senior partner, twenty-five years' experience) felt that the duty to the client was "paramount" but accepted it was "colored" by the professional obligations to the court. These lawyers gave the impression that they are zealous advocates who are the shield of the accused, but, unfortunately, their other obligations dilute the impact of this shield. Lawyers in this category have a vast amount of experience; the most experienced lawyer qualified thirty-two years ago whereas the most recently qualified lawyer has four years' experience. The experience range of this group makes for some very interesting results when compared with the *Procedural* category.

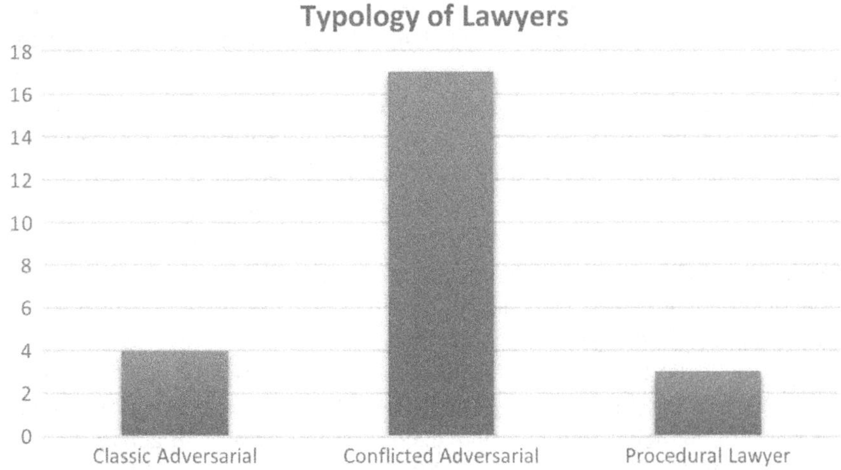

Figure 5.3 Data Compiled by Author Survey.

The final category is the *Procedural Lawyer* who ultimately sees no issue or conflict with the obligations placed upon the defense lawyer by the CPIA and the CrimPR. Lawyer 022 (solicitor, six years' experience) illustrated this point by explaining the obligations were merely an "occupational hazard." These lawyers placed a heavy emphasis on the notion of cooperation; Lawyer 023 (solicitor, seven years' experience) admitted they had an explicit duty to "their opponents." Perhaps, unsurprisingly, two of the three lawyers in this category had less than ten years' experience; therefore, they have only practiced in an era when the CPIA and the CrimPR have been in operation. What was surprising was the remaining two lawyers who had thirteen and eighteen years' experience respectively. These advocates did not think the CrimPR or CPIA 1996 held many ramifications for the role of the defense lawyer. What is interesting is that the most recently qualified lawyers who took part in the study, both of whom had four years' experience, provided responses that put them in the "Conflicted" category. A number of *Procedural* lawyers have less than ten years' experience and because they have been socialized into an era that prioritizes efficiency and cooperation, it might be expected that the most recently qualified lawyers would also occupy a space in the *Procedural* category.

Tension in the Modern Era

Although the CrimPR has "an upside in that they consolidated many procedural rules, they also have a sinister downside by putting the acquittal of the innocent and conviction of the guilty at the heart of the Rules."[159] The rules ultimately confuse procedure with outcome and fundamentally undermine adversarial criminal process. The sole objective of the process should be to provide a fair means to trying a criminal charge.[160] This provides a great tension for the lawyer: how does one balance the duty to the client against the duty to the court.

Andrew Keogh intimated that the "clever, technical lawyer had died."[161] However, the empirical interviews suggest that is not necessarily the case. The clever technical lawyer, who would zealously defend their client and be a white knight, is alive and well; although only a minority of the research sample are in the category of the *Classic Adversarial Lawyer*. The tension created by the managerial agenda from the CrimPR is clear. Within the new managerial agenda, the lawyer is required to positively contribute to the efficiency of the system; this is clearly identifiable by having to enter a guilty plea at the first hearing.[162] This aspect was a key indicator that led to the creation of the different categories. Those in the *Classic* category thought the rule was an aberration and that zealous advocacy and an active defense cannot be undertaken adequately within a short period of time. Lawyer 002 (senior partner, thirty-two years' experience) suggested that the courts were "asking you to nail your colours to the mast without operating with the full facts"; it is in this example where the technical lawyer is allowed to showcase their talents, he offers up enough information to satisfy the courts but not at the expense of the client's rights. The *Conflicted* lawyers did not go as far as this. They wanted to highlight the importance of the duty to the client but were quick to intimate that they had other duties such as fulfilling the overriding objective. The *Conflicted* lawyers wanted to illustrate that they were zealous advocates but their answers to the questions indicated that they prioritized other obligations over that of the client. The *Procedural* lawyer saw no problem with the rules and often thought they benefited the system, albeit not necessarily their client.

Some aspects of the CrimPR did not lead to different responses from the lawyers; the responses were almost universal across the three categories. Most notably, the issue concerning the advance disclosure of witnesses.[163] Although, only one of the twenty-four respondents had actually experienced the police interviewing any of the witnesses that they had identified, but this might alter if police or prosecution resources improve. It appears that in the age of austerity, the CPS does not have the resources to undertake such an investigation of defense witnesses. Lawyer 006 (senior partner, forty years' experience) remarked that a number of defense practitioners "got into a bit of a flap when the rule came in"[164] but in reality, the rule is not utilized in such a manner. That is not to say that the rule will not cause an issue in the future but as of today, the theoretical concerns are yet to manifest. In places the CrimPR were ineffective, this was most notably in respect of failures by the CPS. Whilst the view that prosecution was to blame for disclosure failures is not necessarily unrealistic,[165] it must be taken with appropriate care as only defense lawyers were interviewed for the purposes of the study, and not prosecution lawyers.

The *Classic* lawyer was not necessarily concerned by the threat of sanctions and would employ a tactical approach to ensure he avoided such a risk. The *Conflicted* and *Procedural* lawyers, on the other hand, were very concerned about potential sanctions even though, as the study has shown, the enforcement mechanisms for the CrimPR are limited. Recent reviews have identified this problem yet have not proposed any alternative.[166] Furthermore, Redmayne suggests that the American enforcement mechanism of exclusion of evidence is "hardly palatable."[167] However, the courts have routinely excluded evidence as a sanction for an inefficient use of time, especially when it is the defense who have been found at fault.[168] Arguably, with the growth of managerialism, the courts are more likely to enforce this sanction as they are permitted to enforce the CrimPR.[169]

The Lawyer-Client Relationship

It was argued in the Introduction that the lawyer-client relationship has potentially been diluted by the enhanced pretrial obligations of the defense lawyer since, especially, the lawyer has an enhanced duty to the court. What the empirical research discovered was somewhat mixed. In order to deal with cases justly,[170] the case needs to be dealt with efficiently and expeditiously.[171] As such, it was argued in chapter 1 that the lawyer might have to report to the court and prosecution any significant failures by the client. The client may potentially view this as the lawyer disclosing confidential information, which might have an adverse impact on the trust between the two. As Wendell said, the biggest fear of the client is their lawyer "ratting him out."[172] Although Wendell was referring to the lawyer informing the court or prosecution of something incriminating told to him by the client, the client's fear can be translated to telling tales for failure to comply with procedure. However, the study demonstrated that the lawyers gave their clients every possible opportunity to assist in satisfying the overriding objective.

The lawyer might be more inclined to "tell tales" on the client in order to avoid one of the numerous sanctions for failing to comply. However, despite the concerns caused by *SVS*,[173] which centered on a client who would not cooperate, the lawyers interviewed did not appear to have clients who did not comply. However, lawyers intimated that the threat of a WCO is a very real threat and looms large over their heads.[174] To circumvent this, they employed tactics to ensure they are not subjected to such an order. Lawyer 002 carefully advised the client of the failures of compliance, and across the board the lawyers carefully managed expectations to ensure the client was aware of their own obligations.

The majority of lawyers interviewed believed that the obligations imposed by the CrimPR represent an erosion of the presumption of innocence. Edwards suggests that adversarial justice only works if there is an effective defense and that there is no better way to discover facts.[175] Furthermore, the defense lawyer's role must be based upon a clear adversarial model, since nothing less will test the quality of the investigation.[176] The decision in *Firth*[177] represented an inherent danger of making an incriminating admission on the case management form. *Newell*[178] has gone some way to rectifying this problem but with the caveat that ensures the "spirit"[179] of the CrimPR is complied with. Some lawyers did not fully trust that caveat, as the notion of "spirit" was relatively loose and not explicitly defined. Surprisingly, as far as the lawyers interviewed were concerned, none of this appears to have an adverse impact on the lawyer-client relationship. The theoretical chapter was concerned with the lawyer having to "tell tales" on the client and the Case Progression Form potentially turning the lawyer into a witness against their client. Should the accused not wish to complete the form, the lawyer will report him to the court and "tell tales" regarding his lack of cooperation. This could further strain the relationship between lawyer and client to the point where the client does not feel the lawyer is acting in their best interests. However, the interview data suggests that this was not the case. Those interviewed explained to their client what their own individual obligations were under the CrimPR and what they had to do, as lawyers, to comply with the rules. Surprisingly, that did not appear to cause any conflicts between the lawyer and client. Conflict arose where the client wanted the lawyer to mislead the court; the lawyers said this was something that would be unpalatable. They said they would withdraw from the case and no longer act for the client should they wish to mislead the court. It is somewhat surprising that the obligation to inform the prosecution of various elements of the defense case did not provoke any response by interviewees along the lines of "why are you telling them that?! I do not want them to know that." This could be because the lawyers outline at the start of what their obligations are or it could be, as Quirk states, the fact that suspects do not recognize the changes.[180] Although Quirk was analyzing the impact of the right to silence, the same rationale could be transplanted to this study. Quirk states that the police interview and the trial should be a viewed as a "benign *continuum*"[181] but this is something that the suspect is unlikely to notice. As such, the suspect appears to have the protections of the burden of proof and legal advice, but these provisions "are devalued by the quandary in which the lawyer is now placed."[182]

The same approach applied with the possible dilution of the presumption of innocence and the privilege against self-incrimination. Chapter 5 argued that a client might not engage with obligations if they thought they were disclosing incriminating material to the prosecution. However, the study found that of the twenty-four lawyers interviewed, none of them said that any of their clients adopted this approach. Again, this comes down to managing the expectations of the client and informing them of what it is the lawyer is obligated to do. Lawyer 018 (solicitor, four years' experience), a *Conflicted Adversarial Lawyer*, explicitly said this, but no other lawyers indicated this was a problematic issue. Generally, the lawyers said they had the trust of their clients and they followed what the lawyer needed to do. Interwoven with this point is the dilution of the privilege against self-incrimination and the presumption of innocence. The client may not notice this dilution. The lawyers did and were explicitly clear; all suggested that the privilege against self-incrimination has been compromised; the majority thought there was also a dilution of the presumption of innocence.[183] Lawyer 002 even suggested that the presumption of innocence does not exist in the magistrates' court. The court takes the approach that "your client knows if he's done it, so tell me. They almost disregard any notion of the CPS having to prove their case." The dilution of these classic adversarial values[184] will have a wider implication for adversarialism in England and Wales.

Quirk suggests that there is a "danger of mission creep in these crime control policies" and gives the example of radical change becoming the accepted norm.[185] Arguably, this is the case with the new regime. In the mid-1990s, it was likely to be unimaginable that the silence provisions would open the floodgates for a radical overhaul of the criminal justice process in England and Wales. Yet, this is where we find ourselves. The notion of traditional adversarialism has been greatly diluted and with that, the client's valuable shield is rendered to be almost a cog in the process wheel, as such we moving toward a crime control model that prioritizes the efficiency of the process above the rights of the defendant. As this book has discussed, it is arguable just how "adversarial" defense lawyers actually are in practice but from the interviews for this study, it is clear that a number of defense lawyers view themselves as either the classic adversarial lawyer or one who holds adversarial traits but is conflicted in this approach. Nevertheless, the changes made to ensure the suspect is co-opted into participation should shake the foundations of the lawyer-client relationship, yet it does not. Perhaps the suspect does not recognize that these adversarial protections have been diluted or the fact the burden of proof appears easier to discharge because the suspect is co-opted into the process from a very early stage. Whilst the suspect *may* "know if he's done it" that should not weaken the burden of proof or require participation in pursuit of his own conviction.

The implementation of non-adversarial values aims to increase the efficiency and efficacy of the criminal trial and act as a mechanism to ascertain the truth.[186] It might be argued that the dual goal of active case management by the judiciary and magistracy combined with the desire for expeditious and efficient trials have the effect of returning the trial to the "accused speaks" format.[187] This modern-day "accused speaks" trial has the notable difference that the accused is speaking through written case management disclosures as opposed to oral disclosures. The final chapter of this monograph will examine if the adversarial process has reverted to an "accused speaks" type process.

NOTES

1. A. Smith and W. Montross, "The Calling of Criminal Defense" [1998–1999] *Mercer Law Review* Vol. 50, 523. However, other work suggests that, in practice, this characterization is somewhat of misnomer and does not exist in reality. For a detailed account of this, see p. 228.

2. Please see the aforementioned texts by Mike McConville et al and Daniel Newman.

3. Article 6(2) European Convention on Human Rights defines the presumption as "Everyone charged with a criminal offence shall be presumed innocent until proved guilty according to law."

4. *Blunt v Park Lane Hotel Ltd* [1942] 2 KB 253 as being "the rule . . . that no one is bound to answer any question if the answer thereto would, in the opinion of the judge, have a tendency to expose [him] to any criminal charge or penalty, or forfeiture which the judge regards as reasonably likely to be referred or sued for."

5. *The Oxford Dictionary of Current English* (Oxford University Press: Oxford, 1990) at p. 150.

6. E. Cape, "The Rise (And Fall?) of a Criminal Defense Profession," [2004], *Criminal Law Review* Vol. 415, 72.

7. [1967] 3 WLR 166.

8. C. Fried, "The Lawyer as a Friend: The Moral Foundations of the Lawyer-Client Relation," [1975-76] *Yale Law Journal* Vol. 85 .

9. Solicitors Regulation Authority, *Code of Conduct Handbook* [2011], Chapter 1 Outcome 5.1 states that it is an offence for a lawyer to attempt to deceive or knowingly or recklessly mislead the court. http://www.sra.org.uk/solicitors/handbook/code /part2/content.page [Last Accessed November 1, 2015].

10. Smith and Montross, "The Calling of Criminal Defense," 523.

11. Freedman defines zealous advocacy as distinguished from over-zealous—advocacy has always meant advocacy within the law and the disciplinary rules, in the same way that "at the edge" does not mean "over the edge." See M. Freedman, "Henry Lord Brougham and Zeal," [2006]. *Hofstra Law Review* Vol. 34 1319, 1320, 1323 at p. 312.

12. R. Goel, "Can I call Kimura Crazy? Ethical Tensions in the Cultural Defense," [2004] *Seattle Journal of Society Justice* Vol. 3, 450.

13. W. Bradley Wendell, *Ethics and Law: An Introduction* (Cambridge: Cambridge University Press, 2014), at p. 7.

14. Ibid.

15. A. Boon and J. Levin, *The Ethics and Conduct of Lawyers in England and Wales* (Oxford University Press: Oxford, 1999) at p. 188.

16. Smith and Montross, *The Calling of Criminal* 523.

17. 15/24 participants explicitly highlighted this concern.

18. 22/24 lawyers spoke of advancing the client's best interest prior to any other obligation

19. http://www.oed.com/view/Entry/151292 [last accessed December 2020].

20. http://www.oed.com/view/Entry/137536?rskey=LqtH4l&result=2&isAdvanced=false#eid [last accessed December 2020]

21. D. Newman "Still Standing Accused: Addressing the Gap between Work and Talk in Firms of Criminal Defense Lawyers," [2012] *International Journal of the Legal Profession* Vol. 19(1), 3–27 at p. 8.

22. Ibid., at p. 27.

23. Solicitors RegulationAuthority, Code of Conduct Handbook, (2011), Chapter 1 http://www.sra.org.uk/solicitors/handbook/code/part2/content.page [Last Accessed December 2020].

24. Rule 1(2)(1)(c).

25. Rule 1(2)(1)(c).

26. See A. Ashworth "The Techniques of Sentencing" (1984) Crim LR 519; see also J. N. Ferdico, H. Frandella and C. Totten, *Criminal Procedure for the Criminal Justice Professional* (California: Cengage Learning, 2012) at p. 589. The authors argue that the judiciary dislikes minimum sentences because "they do not have the ability to fashion a sentence appropriate to the facts of a particular case."

27. T. Kirchengast, *Victims and the Criminal Trial* (London: Palgrave, 2016) at p. 1.

28. Ibid., at p. 2.

29. Code of Practice for Victims of Crime, Ministry of Justice (2015) HMSO: London Chapter 2, Part A, paragraph.

1.12 available here: https://www.cps.gov.uk/sites/default/files/documents/legal_guidance/OD_000049.pdf [Last Accessed 9th September 2018].

30. R. Leng, "Losing Sight of the Defendant: The Government's Proposals on Pre-Trial Disclosure," [1995] *Criminal Law Review* Vol. 704, at 711.

31. Victims Right to Review, April 2016–March 2017 available here: https://www.cps.gov.uk/sites/default/files/documents/victims_witnesses/vrr_data_2016_2017.pdf[last accessed September 3, 2018].

32. *R (on the application of the DPP) v Chorley Justices and Anor* [2006] EWHC 1795 per Thomas LJ at para. 24.

33. D. C. Newman and P. Ugwudike, "Defense Lawyers and Probation Officers: Offenders" Allies or Adversaries? [2014], *International Journal of the Legal Profession* 183–207.

34. The Trial at large of Her Majesty, Caroline Emelia Elizabeth, Queen of Great Britain; in the House of Lords on Charges of Adulterous Intercourse 3 (London 18210 as cited in M.H. Freedman, "Henry Lord Brougham – Advocating at the Edge for Human Rights," [2007] *Hofstra Law Review* Vol. 36, 311, at p. 311.

35. [1969] 1 A.C. 191

36. The arena of criminal defense work.

37. D. Newman, *Legal Aid Lawyers and the Quest for Justice* (Oxford: Hart Publishing, 2013) at pp. 143–169.

38. See M. Travers, *The Reality of Law* (Aldershot: Ashgate Publishing, 1997).

39. H. Sommerlad, *Legally Aided Clients and their Solicitors* (London: Law Society Press, 2000).

40. D. Atkinson and T. Maloney, *Blackstone's Guide to the Criminal Procedure Rules* (2nd Edition, Oxford: OUP, 2011) at p. 2.

41. Auld Rt Hon R, *A Review of the Criminal Courts of England and Wales* (2001) http://webarchive.nationalarchives.gov.uk/+/http://www.criminal-courts-review.org.uk [Last accessed: December 2020].

42. Rule 1.1 Criminal Procedure Rules 2015.

43. Rule 1.1(2)(a) Criminal Procedure Rules 2015.

44. 21/24 gave this interpretation of the Overriding Objective.

45. Rule 1.1(2)(b).

46. Rule 1.1(2)(c).

47. Rule 1.1(2)(e).

48. Leveson LJ "Essential Case Management: Applying the Criminal Procedure Rules" Home Office, December 2009.

49. [2003] EWCA 1012.

50. [2004] EWCA Crim 696. Both of these cases are discussed at length in Chapter Three. Please see pp. 103–121.

51. Ibid., per Auld LJ at para 114.

52. L. L Fuller and J. D. Randall, "Professional Responsibility: Report of the Joint Conference," [1958] *American Bar Association Journal* Vol. 44, 1159–1162 at 1160. A Devil's Advocate was an approach employed by the Roman Catholic Church who, in canonization proceedings, would convey every possible argument against sainthood.

53. D. Luban, "The Adversary System Excuse" in D. Luban (Ed), *The Good Lawyer, Lawyer's Roles and Lawyer's Ethics* (Totowa, NJ: Rowman and Allanheld, 1983) at p. 96.

54. W. Bradley Wendell, *Ethics and Law: An Introduction* (Cambridge: Cambridge University Press, 2014), at p. 9.

55. See. M. Freedman and A. Smith, *Understanding Lawyers Ethics* (4th Edition, New Providence: NJ, 2010) at p. 152.

56. The abuse suffered constituted a full defense to the charge of murder.

57. The forms can be found here: http://www.justice.gov.uk/courts/procedure -rules/criminal/docs/october- 2015/cm001england-eng.pdf Preparation for effective trial: Criminal Procedure Rules Parts 1 and 3. [last accessed December 10, 2015].

58. Section 6 Criminal Procedure and Investigations Act 1996.

59. Please see pp. 76–121.

60. The Typology of Lawyers is available unabridged in the appendix.

61. Such as advancing the client's best interests and advancing the duty to court.

62. Lord Justice Leveson Essential Case Management: Applying the Criminal Procedure Rules which endorses Rule 3.8(2)(b).

63. In *R v Buffrey*14.Cr. App R (S) 511 the Court of Appeal indicated that whilst there was no absolute rule as to what the discount should be, as general guidance one-third would be appropriate. This is in line with guidance provided by the Sentencing Guidelines Council (2007) that recommends: one-third for a guilty plea at the first opportunity, one-fourth for a guilty plea once the trial date is set and one-tenth for guilty plea at the door of the court.

64. *The Oxford Dictionary of Current English*, 1990 at p. 775.

65. Per Sir John Thomas in *R (On the Application of Drinkwater) v Solihull Magistrates' Court* [2012] EWCA 765 at para 46.

66. Ibid., at para 47.

67. For further examples of this mantra pervading the criminal justice process please see: Ministry of Justice, *Swift and Sure Justice: The Government's Plans for Reform of the Criminal Justice System* Cm 8388, (London: TSO, 2012).

https://www.gov.uk/government/uploads/system/uploads/attachment_data/file /217328/swift-and-sure- justice.pdf [Last Accessed December 2020]; see also The

Stop Delaying Justice! Initiative which looked at eradicating adjournments and establishing best practice for active case management

68. CrimPR Rule 3.2.

69. [2006] EWHC 1795 (Admin).

70. Rule 3.2(2)(a)-(h).

71. The European Court of Human Rights, *Guide on Article 6: Right to a Fair Trial*, Council of Europe, 2014 at p. 34—Article 6(2) The principle of the presumption of innocence requires, inter alia, that when carrying out their duties, the members of a court should not start with the preconceived idea that the accused has committed the offence charged; the burden of proof is on the prosecution, and any doubt should benefit the accused. It is for the prosecution to inform the accused of the case that will be made against him, so that he may prepare and present his defense accordingly, and to adduce evidence sufficient to convict him http://www.echr.coe.int/Documents/Guide_Art_6_criminal_ENG.pdf [last accessed October 23, 2014].

72. This was not universal but 20/24 interview participants highlighted this as a concern

73. J. McEwan, "Truth Efficiency and Co-operation in modern Criminal Justice," [2013], *Current Legal Problems*, Vol. 66, 216.

74. See attorney general's guidelines on disclosure for investigators, prosecutors and defense practitioners, 2013.

75. Although this was not an explicit question on the *pro forma* four lawyers, from three different firms, in three different regions of England and Wales suggested that they have either encountered such a question of a magistrate.

76. A. Edwards "Case Management Forms," [2011] *CLR* 54.

77. J. Jackson "Towards a Dialectic Theory of Proof for Legal Procedure," [1991] *Journal of the Royal Statistical Society* Vol. 154, 107.

78. See generally J. Langbein, *The Origins of the Adversary Criminal Trial* (Oxford University Press: Oxford, 2005).

79. *D and Others* [2007] EWCA Crim 2485.

80. J. McEwan. "From Adversarialism to Managerialism: Criminal Justice in Transition," [2011], *Law of Studies*, 519.

81. The judiciary were traditionally expected to remain passive because if he "descends into the arena and is liable to have his vision clouded by the dust of conflict" Per Green MR, in *Yuill v Yuill* [1945] 1 All ER 183 at 189.

82. J. McEwan "Truth Efficiency and Co-operation in modern Criminal Justice," [2013] *Current Legal Problems* Vol. 66, 209.

83. The notion of a shift to a more crime control approach is covered in section 8.7 pp. 271–274.

84. T. Smith, "The "Near Miss" of Liam Allan: Critical Problems in Police Disclosure, Investigation Culture, and the Resourcing of Criminal Justice," [2018], *Criminal Law Review* Vol. 9, pp. 711–731 at p. 713.

85. CPS and Metropolitan Police, A Joint Review of the disclosure process in the case of *R v Allan*, January 2018, at p. 7 available here: https://www.cps.gov.uk/sites/default/files/documents/publications/joint-review- disclosure-Allan.pdf [Last accessed September 1, 2018].

86. Since 2010, frontline police officers have fallen by 20,000. See https://www.bbc.co.uk/news/uk-47225797 [Last Accessed December 2020].

87. Smith, The "Near Miss" of Liam Allan, 711–731.

88. House of Commons Justice Committee, Disclosure of evidence in criminal cases, Eleventh Report of Session 2017–2019, at p. 47. Availablehere: https://publications.parliament.uk/pa/cm201719/cmselect/cmjust/859/859.pdf [Last Accessed September 1, 2018].

89. HMCPSI, Making it fair—a joint inspection of the disclosure of unused material in volume Crown Court cases, (2017) at para 1.3.

90. The lawyer had a client who he believed to be unfit to plead but as a result. The client was later declared fit to plead but had lost his sentence discount as the plea was not entered at the earliest opportunity.

91. This phrase was repeated throughout the empirical research and Lawyer 007 explained how he witnessed junior lawyers being bullied by a magistrate.

92. Andrew Keogh speaking at the Eldon Lecture Series (2001), Northumbria University School of Law, "Criminal Case Management—Is the Game Over?" the quote is taken from p. 1 of the transcript.

93. For example, see *R (on the application of the DPP) v Chorley Justices & Anor* [2006] EWHC 1795 per Thomas LJ at para 24.

94. In *Tibbs* (The Times, February 28, 2000) the Court of Appeal stated that is was not suitable to merely use the general legal description of the defense, that is, accident or self-defense. The form needs extend to the facts the defendant will rely on at trial.

95. J. Plotnikoff and R. Wolfson, *A Fair Balance? Evaluation of the Operation of Disclosure Law*, (2001) RDS Occasional Paper no 76, at p. 77.

96. Ibid.

97. H. Quirk, "The Significance of Culture in Criminal Procedure Reform: Why the Revised Disclosure Scheme Cannot Work," [2006] *E&P* Vol. 10(1), 42–59 at 57.

98. F. Garland and J. McEwan "Embracing the Overriding Objective: Difficulties and Dilemmas in the New Criminal Climate" [2012] *E&P* Vol. 16, 233–262 at p. 243.

99. Ibid.

100. The protection afforded by *Newell* [2012] EWCA Crim 650 is welcomed but it can be viewed as somewhat opaque. The court decided the Crown could not use a statement made in a PCMH to prove the defendant's evidence at trial was inconsistent with the completed form. The prosecution could not use the statement to the detriment of the appellant. This would be unfair to the defense. However, if the spirit of the rules is not complied with the court may allow such evidence to be admitted at trial (per Sir Anthony May P at para. 37).

101. As per *Newell* [2012] EWCA Crim 650.

102. J. Plotnikoff and R. Wolfson, *A Fair Balance? Evaluation of the Operation of Disclosure Law,* Home Office, RDS Occasional Paper No. 76 (2001).

103. R. L. Denyer, "The Defense Case Statement," [2009] *Criminal Law Review* Vol. 340 at p. 343.

104. HM Crown Prosecution Service Inspectorate (HMPSI), *An Audit of the Crown Prosecution Service Handling of Judges' Orders in the Crown Court* (HMCPSI: London, 2011).

105. *Newell* [2012] EWCA Crim 650.

106. Rt. Hon Lord Justice Gross and Rt Hon Lord Justice Treacy, *Further Review of Disclosure in Criminal Proceedings* (Judiciary of England and Wales 2012).

107. Andrew Keogh speaking at the Eldon Lecture Series (2001), Northumbria University School of Law, "Criminal Case Management—Is the Game Over?" the quote is taken from p. 1 of the transcript.

108. [2010] EWCA Crim 1928.

109. S.11 Criminal Procedure and Investigations Act 1996, See also, J McEwan "From Adversarialism To Managerialism: Criminal Justice In Transition," *Legal Studies*, Vol. 31, no. 3, at p. 528, which states trial judges seem reluctant to discipline the defense through measures such as adverse inferences which penalize the defendant.

110. *R v Writtle* [2009] EWHC 236 and *R v Bryant* [2005] EWCA Crim 2079.

111. *Newell* [2012] EWCA Crim 650 per Sir John Thomas P at para 25.

112. *Firth* [2011] EWHC 388 (Admin) and *Newell* [2012] EWCA Crim 650.

113. [2012] EWCA Crim 650.

114. M. McConville and L. Marsh, *Criminal Judges: Legitimacy, Courts and State Induced Guilty Pleas in Britain* (2014) (Northampton: Edward Elgar) at p. 181.

115. A. Owusu-Bempah, "Defense Participation through Pre-Trial Disclosure: Issues and Implications" [2013] *E&P* Vol. 17, 183–201 at 200.

116. Ibid.

117. J. McEwan, "Adversarialism to Managerialism: Criminal Justice in Transition" (2011) 31 *Legal Studies* 519.

118. Andrew Keogh speaking at the Eldon Lecture Series (2001), Northumbria University School of Law, "Criminal Case Management—Is the Game Over?." The quote is taken from p. 1 of the transcript.

119. J. McEwan and F. Garland, Embracing the Overriding Objective: Difficulties and Dilemmas in the New Criminal Climate" [2012] *E&P*, Vol. 16(3), 233–262 at p. 245.

120. Ibid.

121. Chapter 3 examined the issue that prior to the s.5 Criminal Procedure and Investigations Act 1996, the defense only had to close alibi witnesses and expert evidence.

122. P. Hungerford-Welch, *Criminal Procedure and Sentencing,* (2014), 8th Edition, Routledge at para 4.4.5.

123. Criminal Procedure and Investigations Act 1996 (Code of Practice for Arranging and Conducting Interviews of *Witnesses* Notified by the Accused), available here: http://www.legislation.gov.uk/uksi/2010/1223/contents/made

124. Criminal Procedure and Investigations Act 1996 (Code of Practice for Arranging and Conducting Interviews of *Witnesses* Notified by the Accused), available here: http://www.legislation.gov.uk/uksi/2010/1223/contents/made para 3.1

125. A. Edwards " Criminal Defense Witness Notices" May 6, 2010, *Law Society Gazette*, available here: http://www.lawgazette.co.uk/55292.article

126. The term "panic" was espoused by both Lawyers 006 and 007.

127. A. Edwards "Criminal Defense Witness Notices" May 6, 2010, *Law Society Gazette*, http://www.lawgazette.co.uk/55292.article.

128. [2007] EWHC 1836 (Admin).

129. [2007] EWHC 1836 (Admin) per Mitting J at para 37.

130. *R (Law Society of England and Wales) v Lord Chancellor and the Legal Services Commission* [2012] EWHC 794 (Admin).

131. Owusu-Bempah, "Defense Participation through Pre-Trial Disclosure" 195.

132. See Lawyer 019's early example of a client with mental health concerns.

133. R. Gordon, "The Independence of Lawyers" [1988] *Boston Law Review* Vol. 1, 10.

134. Participant 002.

135. Rule 1.1 CrimPR 2015.

136. *The Oxford Dictionary of Current English*, 1990 p. 628.

137. M. McConville and L. Marsh, *Criminal Judges: Legitimacy, Courts and State-Induced Guilty Pleas in Britain* (Cheltenham: Edward Elgar Publishing, 2014) at p. 168.

138. Ibid., at p. 169.

139. [2003] EWCA Crim 3357.

140. [2006] EWHC 1795.

141. Fifteen of twenty-three lawyers indicated that in order to progress the case, they may be viewed as betraying their client by "snitching."

142. W. Bradley Wendell, *Ethics and Law: An Introduction* (Cambridge: Cambridge University Press, 2014) at p. 8.

143. The Trial at large of Her Majesty, Caroline Amelia Elizabeth, Queen of Great Britain; in the House of Lords on Charges of Adulterous Intercourse 3 (London 18210 as cited in M.H. Freedman, "Henry Lord Brougham Advocating at the Edge for Human Rights" [2007] Hofstra L. Rev. Vol. 36: 311, [2007] at p. 311.

144. 15/23 lawyers made explicitly reference to a letter or form which was provided to the client to explain the situation.

145. H. Quirk, "Twenty Years On, the Right of Silence and Legal Advice: The Spiraling Costs of An Unfair Exchange," [2013] *NILQ* Vol. 64(4), 465–484 at 482.

146. Ibid.

147. Ibid.

148. ECHR Article 6(2) states that "Everyone charged with a criminal offence shall be presumed innocent until proven guilty according to law."

149. Sanctions for noncompliance are set out in sub-rule 3.5(6) "If a party fails to comply with a rule or a direction, the court may—(a) fix, postpone, bring forward, extend, cancel or adjourn a hearing; (b) exercise its powers to make a costs order; and (c) impose such other sanction as may be appropriate."

150. No published data exist concerning the use of WCO being issued against the prosecution. I have contacted Jonathan Solly, secretary of the Criminal Procedure Rules Committee, who confirmed there are no records of such a sanction. Solly put

me in touch with Bob Weston, a Knowledge Information Liaison Officer at HMCTS, who said he would look into this issue. He confirmed that no data exist on the use of CPS sanction. He suggested I make a FoI request but at the time of writing no information has been received.

151. For an in-depth analysis of the theoretical sanctions, please see chapter 5 pages 109–144.

152. [2012] EWCA Crim 319.

153. Data taken from "Trial Effectiveness Tool" Criminal Justice Quarterly Statistics January to March 2019, available here: www.gov.uk/government/statistics/criminal-court-statistics-quarterly-january-to-march-2019 [last accessed March 2020].

154. Available here: https://www.justiceinspectorates.gov.uk/hmcpsi/inspections/disclosure-of-unused-material-in-the-crown-court-a-follow-up/ [Last accessed December 2020].

155. Ibid., at p. 7.

156. Ibid.

157. Ibid., at p. 8.

158. M. McConville and L. Marsh "Adversarialism goes West: Case Management in Criminal Courts" (2015) July, *E&P* 172–189.

159. J. Richardson, *Archbold 2015*, Sweet and Maxwell at p. ix.

160. Ibid.

161. Andrew Keogh speaking at the Eldon Lecture Series (2001), Northumbria University School of Law, "Criminal Case Management—Is the Game Over?"

162. Leveson L. J., "Essential Case Management: Applying the Criminal Procedure Rules, Senior Presiding Judge for England and Wales," December 2009: https://www.judiciary.gov.uk/wp-content/uploads/JCO/Documents/Protocols/applying-crim-procedure-rules- dec-2009.pdf [Last accessed December 2020].

163. S.6C Criminal Procedure and Investigations Act 1996.

164. See A. Edwards "Criminal Defense Witness Notices" (May 6, 2010), *Law Society Gazette*, http://www.lawgazette.co.uk/55292.article and P. Hungerford-Welch, "Prosecution Interviews of Defense Witnesses" [2010] *Criminal Law Review* Vol. 9, 690–701.

165. The CPS has been overstretched for a number of years. In 2010 in Bristol, a case collapsed because CPS lawyers were "swamped with work." See http://www.bbc.co.uk/news/uk-england-bristol-11650159 [last Accessed December 2020].

166. See Rt. Hon Lord Justice Gross and Rt Hon Lord Justice Treacy, *Further Review of Disclosure in Criminal Proceedings* [2012] Judiciary of England and Wales, available here: http://www.judiciary.gov.uk/wpcontent/uploads/JCO/Documents/Reports/disclosure_criminal_courts.pdf and Magistrates' Court Disclosure Review, May 2014, Judiciary of England and Wales.

167. M. Redmayne, "Criminal Justice Act 2003: Disclosure and its Discontents (1)," [2004], *Criminal Law Review*, Vol. 441–462 at 453.

168. See *Jisil* [2004] EWCA Crim 696, *Munsone* [2007] EWCA Crim 1237.

169. Rule 3.5(6)(c) CrimPR 2016.

170. Rule 1.1. CrimPR 2016.

171. Rule 1.1(e) CrimPR 2016.

172. W. Bradley Wendell, *Ethics and Law: An Introduction* (Cambridge: Cambridge University Press, 2014) at p. 8.

173. [2012] EWCA Crim 319.

174. Lawyers 002, 003 and 004 in particular.

175. A. Edwards "The Role of Defense Lawyers in a 'Rebalanced' System" in E. Cape and R. Young, *Regulating Police: The Police and Criminal Evidence Act 1984, Past, Present and Future* (Hart Publishing, 2008) at p. 252.

176. By the police and then taken to trial by the CPS.

177. [2011] EWHC 388 (Admin).

178. [2012] EWCA Crim 650

179. [2012] EWCA Crim 650 at para. 36. The court in the first instance should have used s.78 PACE to exclude the evidence.

180. H. Quirk, *The Rise and Fall of the Right of Silence* (Oxon: Routledge, 2017) at p. 172.

181. *R v Howell* [2003] EWCA Crim 01 as cited in H. Quirk, *The Rise and Fall of the Right of Silence* (Oxon: Routledge, 2017) at p. 172.

182. H. Quirk, *The Rise and Fall of the Right of Silence* (Oxon: Routledge: 2017) at p. 175.

183. Although Lawyer 013 was adamant that there was no dilution of the presumption.

184. It should be noted that these values are not exclusive to the adversarial process. The inquisitorial approach also allows for them.

185. Quirk, *The Rise and Fall of the Right of Silence* at 179.

186. Owusu-Bempah, "Defense Participation through Pre-Trial Disclosure," 195.

187. see C. Mosidis, *Criminal Discovery: From Truth to Proof and Back Again* (Sydney: Institute of Criminology, 2008).

Chapter 6

The "Efficient" Criminal Justice Process and the Dilution of Adversarialism

This book has sought to examine whether the disclosure regimes of the CPIA 1996[1] and the case management provisions of the CrimPR[2] have fundamentally altered the role of the criminal defense lawyer. This encompasses the first two research questions which the thesis set out to answer.[3] Further to this, the semi-structured nature of the interviews allowed the lawyers to talk about their obligations with relative freedom. This freedom permitted the participants to talk in-depth about the impact the changes had for the adversarial nature of our criminal justice process.[4] It was earlier suggested that the primary duty of the lawyer was to advance the best interests of his client.[5] Chapter 2 illustrated that the lawyer could be viewed as a "gladiator of the accused,"[6] a "fearless knight,"[7] or a "hired gun."[8] These impressions express the notion that the defense lawyer acts as the accused's protector from the state, who prioritizes the best interest of his client. Theoretically, the defense lawyer becomes an "extension of the client's will"[9] as it is the defense lawyer who presents the accused's case in court; the lawyer says "all that the client would say for himself (were he able to do so)."[10] The theoretical conception of the lawyer acting as a "fearless knight" on behalf of his client is supported by judicial precedent. For instance, Lord Reid indicated that the defense lawyer has three obligations, the duty to the client, the court, and the administration of justice.[11] However, whilst Lord Reid acknowledged that the duty to the client is paramount, it is clear that the duty is also contentious. Lord Reid acknowledged the existence of other competing duties, and that they often conflict and offered no weighting to the aforementioned duties. Nevertheless, a person can only have a single "primary" or "paramount" duty, posing the question "which duty would be prioritized by the lawyer?"

Five lawyers suggested that their "primary" duty was to their client, eighteen prioritized their client but accepted that this was tempered by other factors. Two prioritized the court and one elected to prioritize the duty court and the prosecution. This can be contrasted to the theoretical conception, who purely advanced the best interest of the client and ignored any other competing interests in pursuit of the adversarial ideology. The traditional conception established earlier in chapter 2 illustrates that the lawyer acts as the advocate of the accused and, as such, prioritizes that duty. It became clear from the research that this view was not universally accepted by the participants.

Chapter 2 highlights that there has been piecemeal legislative since 1967. The legislative amendments subtly altered the pretrial obligations of the defense lawyer, the advent of which was the defense disclosure obligations in terms of alibi[12] and expert evidence.[13] These provisions are relatively uncontentious and whilst they challenge the traditional adversarial stance of not having to disclose evidence in advance of trial, the erosion is relatively insignificant. A less subtle and more pronounced change came with the advent of the CPIA 1996 and the notion of the defense case statement.[14] Consequently, the defendant is now required to disclose "in general terms the nature of his defense . . . the matters he takes issue with the prosecution's case . . . and why he takes issue."[15] This disclosure was voluntary in the magistrates' court,[16] but was necessary in order to receive secondary prosecution disclosure, so there was an incentive to comply with the regime. The voluntary aspect of disclosure has now been effectively circumvented by the CrimPR by requiring the court to further the overriding objective, by actively managing the case.[17] This case management goal is achieved by the "early identification of the real issues."[18] The voluntary nature of defense disclosure in summary proceedings in the CPIA has been usurped by the provisions contained in the CrimPR and represents a shift in the notion of traditional adversarialism in England and Wales.

Arguably, this challenges the due process protections such as the privilege against self-incrimination and the burden of proof. These due process protections have been severely weakened by the shifting landscape, and the traditional adversarial notion that "the accused should not be required to actively participate or assist in proceedings against him" has been diluted.[19] By returning to a regime that draws parallels to the "accused speaks" mode of trial, the defendant is compelled to participate in proceedings which means that the pursuit of efficient fact-finding has taken precedence over fairness and defense rights.[20] This insistence on defendant participation and the dilution of adversarialism has been augmented by fact the courts have actively embraced the mantra of efficiency, without hesitation.[21]

THE CURRENT POLITICAL CONTEXT

As discussed earlier, the 1990s were a time of great political interest in the criminal justice process. The right to silence provisions contained in the CJPOA 1994 were an admission that the accused had "too many rights" and some needed to be removed.[22] This was the first stage of rebalancing of the criminal justice process and it led to the overhaul of the disclosure regime via the CIPA 1996, which was extended to the magistrates' court by the CrimPR. The legislative changes contributed to a culture that conflates non cooperation with guilt and if the processes are not complied with, the defense lawyer can be confronted with the following statement: "Well, your client knows if he's done it."[23] This disregards the "golden thread" of criminal law which states that it is the duty of the prosecution to prove the guilt of the accused. The golden thread does not state it is the duty of the prosecution to prove the prisoner's guilt with great assistance and cooperation of the accused. Ultimately, this crime control culture shows little sign of abating and whilst it was politicians who spearheaded the changes in the 1990s, it appears the courts hastened the modern changes. Quirk suggests that the Court of Appeal have "developed a normative expectation that the defendant should co-operate fully in the criminal justice process."[24]

Quirk cites the example of *Howell*[25] as the supporting case that suggests there is a shift in the presumption of innocence. The court intimated that the innocents have nothing to hide and therefore it is expected that they will fully cooperate with the police investigation and prosecution; as an "innocent person will generally be expected to seize the chance of denying allegations."[26] However, this approach affords no thought to the notion that the police station would be an unfamiliar and often hostile environment for suspects and therefore the suspect in the police may be extremely confused and/or frightened. Likewise, many suspects are poorly educated, inarticulate, or suffer from learning disabilities and/or mental health problems. It is here the role of the defense lawyer should be to protect the suspect, especially, if they are vulnerable. However, the forced cooperation seeks to ensure that the suspect participates in providing evidence that could be used to convict him. Ultimately, this culture of cooperation is "incompatible with the principles of adversarialism and sits uneasy with the presumption of innocence and assists the prosecution in discharging the burden of proof."[27] The clear drive behind these non-adversarial traits is the desire to become more efficient but little thought is given to the impact on the rights of the defendant. There are further proposals to increase efficiency through the digitization of the criminal courts with pleas being entered online[28] with the vision of "modernis[ing] and upgrade our justice system so that it works even better for everyone from judges and legal professionals, to witnesses, litigants and the vulnerable victims of crime."[29] It is unfortunate that the defendant is not considered here. After all, the defendant has the right to a fair and impartial trial and is protected by the presumption of innocence. Yet, the 2018 reform proposals do not even recognize the existence of the defendant and this approach is somewhat unfortunate. The "tough on crime" approach of successive Conservative Home Secretaries in the 1990s has continued and recent reform prioritizes other court users above that of the defendant. If the reforms in the 1990s represented the fact the defendant had too many rights, the continuation of these reforms further dilutes what protections were remaining. The accused enters the police station and is presumed guilty and he has to actively assist the prosecution in their goal of convicting him. Leng suggests, the changes made to the silence and disclosure provisions in the 1990s meant that we could be "losing sight of the defendant."[30] However, the culture of cooperation means that the criminal justice system has lost sight of the fundamental rights of the defendant, in pursuit of an efficient criminal justice process.

THE EFFICIENT PROCESS: BETTER CASE MANAGEMENT AND EARLY GUILTY PLEAS

This thesis has illustrated that prior to the disclosure obligations underpinned by the CPIA 1996,[31] there were very few constraints on the ability of the defense to pursue what was in the defendant's best interest. However, the advent of managerialist goals means that the primary concern of the accused is not to win its own case but to ensure the guilty are convicted and the case is dealt with efficiently. Both of which are alien to an adversarial setting.[32] In 2015, it was found that there was "undoubted room for improvement"[33] in the sphere of case management. Sir Brian Leveson's *Review of Efficiency in Criminal Proceedings*[34] found that all parties needed to work to "identify the issues so as to ensure that court time is deployed to maximum effectiveness and efficiency."[35] With this *Review*, the goals of efficiency and effectiveness were further consolidated with the genesis of the Better Case Management Initiative (hereafter, BCM).[36] This links a number of initiatives which aim to increase the efficiency with which cases are processed through the criminal justice system. The overarching aims of BCM are:

- Robust case management
- Reduced number of hearings
- Maximum participation and engagement with every participant within the system
- Efficient compliance with the CrimPR, Practice, and Court Directions

To achieve these goals, BCM introduced a new case management initiative, the uniform Early Guilty Plea Scheme. The CPS state that obtaining a guilty plea at the earliest opportunity has "huge advantages,"[37] one being efficiency, as the police, court, and prosecution will make economic savings. Furthermore, an early guilty plea reduces victim anxiety, ensuring they do not unnecessarily have to endure long waits, lengthy trials or come to court to give evidence. However, the lawyers interviewed did not view this economic saving in a positive light. For example, as Lawyer 004 stated: "my understanding is that it's a money saving exercise . . . the courts are insistent on a plea at the first hearing, despite us only seeing the client for twenty minutes and there are myriad of outstanding issues, like disclosure [of evidence in advance of trial]."

Lawyer 002 (senior partner, 40 years' experience) was more explicit in his condemnation of the pressures faced by defense lawyers: "we have circumvented the basis of criminal justice practice by a set of arbitrary rules . . . with the purpose to get more convictions." The lawyer added that "this 'speedy justice' is not based on statute, and merely looks to convict more people." These lawyers believe that this non-statutory policy is circumventing the adversarial nature of our criminal justice process. There is a benefit to a defendant entering an early guilty plea—should they do so, they will be entitled to a sentence discount. There is no statutory provision that dictates how much discount can be given for a guilty plea. The court must consider the stage in the proceedings the offender indicates his intention to plead guilty[38] and the amount of discount was previously at the discretion of the court. The Sentencing Guidelines Council recommend a one-third discount for a guilty plea at the first opportunity; a one-quarter discount for a plea after the date of trial has been set; and finally, a one-tenth discount should the defendant enter a plea of guilty at the door of the court or once the trial has started.[39] However, the Sentencing Council has attempted to amend the level of discount on offer. In February 2016, the council issued a consultation which is intended to encourage a greater number of defendants to enter a guilty plea at the "first reasonable opportunity." The new proposals will provide a tiered approach to the level of discount offered. The first tier provides the maximum discount of one-third should the defendant indicate a guilty plea at the first hearing that they are asked to plead. The second tier has a discount of one-fifth should the defendant enter a guilty plea at a later opportunity but before the trial commences. The third-tier states that, should the defendant enter a guilty plea on the first day of their trial, they will only receive a discount of one-tenth. Finally, should the defendant enter a guilty plea partway through the trial, they will not be eligible for any sentence discount. This reduction of the second tier and the zero discount for a "cracked trial" is an implicit indication that the provisions are about seeking more guilty pleas rather than the accused standing by his right to test the evidence at trial: thereby, subscribing to the goal of an economic and efficient criminal justice process.

The concept of an Early Guilty Plea (EGP) scheme is not, in itself, a controversial one. Where a case is straightforward, a defendant accepts their guilt, and the evidence is both substantial and undisputed, it seems justifiable to encourage a guilty plea at the initial stages, provided the circumstances of the defendant do not negate his free and informed choice. In circumstances where these conditions are not met, the scheme poses problems. The scheme states that the discount is not a reward but an incentive, this is questionable because a defendant may view the discount as neither a reward for "doing the right thing" nor an incentive to assist the prosecution. However, it could be viewed as a temptation to reduce the risk of conviction for an offence they have not committed or an inducement to sacrifice their legitimate fair trial rights, such as the privilege against self-incrimination and the fact it is the duty of the prosecution to discharge the burden of proof.

Furthermore, any guilty plea should be grounded in sound legal advice based on the weight of evidence the prosecution holds. However, there is clear evidence that pretrial disclosure by the CPS is often inadequate in practice, and this poses a difficulty for defense lawyers, when looking to advise client's as to an appropriate plea.[40] At present, there is little regulation of disclosure prior to the first hearing and the lack of regulation is important because it is the only point at which a defendant would be eligible for the maximum discount. The prosecution is only required to disclose Initial Details of the Prosecution Case (IDPC) if the defense request it (Rule 8.2(2)).

The scope of this disclosure is narrow, particularly for defendants brought to court in custody: prosecutors are mandated to share details of circumstances of the offence and the criminal record of the defendant, and little else. This poses a very serious question: how are defense lawyers expected to give sound legal advice as to plea when they are only advising on a partial picture of the evidence? This point is analogous to the completion of the case management forms with only a partial picture of the facts. Lawyer 001 (solicitor, sixteen years' experience) stated "you're being forced into completing a form with only a partial picture." If entering an EGP falls under "robust case management," it is difficult to see a lawyer being able to adequately advise on plea with such little information in front of him. This difficulty was illustrated by Lawyer 007 who did not believe the overriding objective was to deal with cases justly[41] but to be "a management tool in a system that assumes guilt and just wants to process guilty cases." The assumption of guilt is something that is deeply non-adversarial and if the assumption is true, it erodes the very fabric of the adversarial criminal justice process. Lord Sankey classed the presumption of innocence as the golden thread; it is one that is unbreakable. He said, "Throughout the web of the English Criminal Law one golden thread is always to be seen that it is the duty of the prosecution to prove the prisoner's guilt."[42]

Undue Pressure

The dangers of being pressured to enter a guilty plea and were demonstrated in the case of *R v (on the application of the DPP) v Leicester Magistrates' Court.*[43] The claimant applied for judicial review to reopen his conviction for common assault. The defendant was a care working in a children's home and the offence involved an alleged physical assault on a fourteen-year-old boy in his care. At his first appearance in court, he intended to enter a not guilty plea on the basis of self-defense. However, he changed this on the first day of his trial. He asserted that his solicitor had pressured him into entering an EGP; he was convicted and, as a result, was no longer able to find work in the social care sector. Whilst the magistrates' court can make an order to reopen a conviction when it is in the interests of justice (under s.142 Magistrates' Courts Act 1980), it can only be exercised where there has been a mistake or a situation akin to a mistake. A subsequent change of heart or regret at entering a guilty plea will not suffice as a mistake and as such the defendant's conviction stood. This is a matter of interpretation. One could argue that "regret" over changing a plea due to inappropriate pressure from lawyers is tantamount to a mistake. Clearly, the defendant's first inclination was to plead not guilty, but he was persuaded to plead otherwise. In the same way that false confessions are subsequently considered to be mistaken when extracted under police pressure, there seems no logical reason why a "change of heart" about a guilty plea in such circumstances should be considered any differently. In contrast, where a defendant enters a guilty plea and has a vague or ill-defined "regret" based on nothing more than the desire to avoid conviction, it seems more reasonable to prevent the overturning of convictions. There is a further danger to advising on a plea without sufficient prosecution disclosure. In response to a consultation issued in February 2016,[44] *The Law Society* suggested that lawyers will have to be careful when offering advice on plea as they will be potentially liable in negligence if inadequate advice is given.[45]

Newman found that undue pressure did not merely stem from the pressures from their client's interests; especially in those firms that were termed "sausage factories," which prioritized profit-making in the quickest time period possible.[46] Newman presented an unsatisfactory image of what he witnessed and suggested that most lawyers held a presumption of guilt in respect of their clients; the lawyer "assumed" the client would enter a plea of guilty and helped to facilitate such a plea,[47] even when the client wanted to enter a not guilty plea.[48] None of the participants interviewed for this study suggested that they would pressurize a client to enter a plea which suited their own needs.[49] Despite this, there is a concern that following Newman's findings and the *Leicester* magistrates' case that undue pressure may not only come from the judiciary but from the client's own lawyer.

Robust Case Management and the Intervening Judge

As discussed in chapter 2, the creation of the adversarial criminal trial demoted the judge from an active participant to that of a pilot who was responsible for guiding the trial to completion.[50] This remained the approach until the early part of the twenty-first century when tension arose between the judiciary's approach to case management and the passive demeanor of the judiciary. Lord Justice Auld[51] provided the catalyst for a change in the role of the judge. This change in role led to a number of participants in this study believing that the adversarial fabric has been torn, being replaced by a process that is distinctly non-adversarial. Traditional adversarialism means that the trial judge should refrain from entering the arena of the adversarial battle unless he has to clear up a particular point of law for the jury. In 1957, Denning LJ gave a notable description of the adversarial judge. The Court of Appeal case of *Jones v National Coal Board*[52] centered on the fact that the judge intervened too frequently during cross-examination and it determined that the judge should intervene as infrequently as possible as the heart of cross-examination lies in the unbroken sequence of question and answer.[53] Excessive judicial interruption weakens the effectiveness of cross-examination, and in this instance the defense were unduly hampered. The trial judge frequently initiated discussions with counsel and often interrupted witnesses during their answers to a question; he had effectively taken the task of examination out of the hands of the advocate. This behavior was deemed to fall outside the realm of their role. Denning LJ said the role of the judge is to "hearken" to the evidence; he can ask questions to clear up a point and keep the advocates in good order to ensure they follow procedure and avoid repetition. If he goes beyond these tasks, he "drops the mantle of a judge and assumes the role of an advocate; the change does not become him well."[54] Furthermore, Denning reiterated this stance when stating that "patience and gravity of hearing is an essential part of justice; and an over speaking judge is no well-tuned cymbal."[55]

Lawyer 002[56] (senior partner, thirty-two years' experience) intimated that the trial is evolving. He said that "the whole ethos of the modern trial is 'your client knew whether or not he did the act' and if he knows, you should therefore complete the forms in an expedited manner and comply with the CrimPR." It was this issue that raised a concern with many[57] of the lawyers who were interviewed. Lawyer 010 suggested that the "creation of the CrimPR and its case management provisions, considerably erode the privilege against self-incrimination" as the defense has to disclose "so much information pre-trial." The lawyer went on to suggest that it is impossible to not incriminate the defendant when completing the forms as failure to comply would look like the ultimate example of guilt. Lawyer 004 (solicitor, eight years' experience) also "certainly believed" that the robust case management and its early identification of the real issues impinged on the privilege against self-incrimination. Lawyer 009 (senior partner, twenty-nine years' experience) pointed to the changing face of adversarialism when speaking about the robust case management. The lawyer said, "the identification of the real issues and case management is about saving money. The system is better when the accused is allowed to stay silent." This point raises an interesting argument: are the case management provisions effectively forcing the accused to speak? It appears almost impossible to stay entirely silent and a knock-on effect of this managerial regime is the return to the "accused speaks" trial.

Arguably, the implementation of the CrimPR, coupled with the judiciary assuming a more interventionist role, might suggest that the pendulum is moving toward reestablishing the importance of uncovering the truth in criminal trials as opposed to discharging the burden of proof. This can be illustrated in the post-Auld review criminal trials. In *Gleeson*,[58] the court ruled that the defense tactic of an ambush defense will no longer be tolerated. This is an example of the court emphasizing the discovery of the "truth" over proving the allegation; as in the first instance, the prosecution could not prove the offence was committed by the defendant. It could only be proven once the indictment had been amended. Essentially, this is an erosion of the penalty shoot-out theory of criminal procedure. The Crown had one shot at goal, and if the striker missed, however unlucky, he did not get another chance.[59] Additionally, this provision arguably breaks the golden thread of criminal procedure. Whilst it appears that the prosecution still has to prove guilt beyond a reasonable doubt, it is clear the defendant now has to assist the prosecution in convicting himself, should there be a flaw in the case of the prosecution.

Whilst it appears that despite the notion of efficiency and effectiveness coursing through the criminal justice process, the "tolerance of prosecution errors is alarmingly apparent."[60] The CPS were allowed an adjournment to "get its case in order."[61] However, it is difficult to see an adjournment being granted to the defense to "get their case in order." In *Rochford*,[62] there was a lack of detail in the defense statement and the judge indicated that failure to complete the case statement in more detail would be treated as contempt of court for both the defendant and the lawyer. As such, tolerance and patience appear to be given to the prosecution but in the quest for truth and efficiency, the defense appear to be given a very unsympathetic and different treatment.

Truth or Proof: The dilution of the Adversarialism in Pursuit of the Overriding Objective

Undoubtedly, the criminal trial is continually evolving, which we have seen has previously occurred. The very essence of adversarialism arose when the courts fought hard to preserve the "accused speaks" form of trial. Retaining this form of trial would allow the court to benefit from treating the defendant as an "informational resource" and have him openly talking at trial, with control of the proceedings remaining with the judiciary. Adversarial theory holds that the trial is a dispute between two competing sides, which are in a position of equality. The argument takes place before a passive and neutral adjudicator. The evidence is predominately oral, and it is the responsibility of the adjudicator to ensure that the parties stay within the rules. Each side is responsible for the presentation of their individual case, the trial being the forum in which the guilt or innocence of the defendant is resolved.[63] Arguably, the trial in the new millennium has departed from this traditional stance of adversarialism; what has gone relatively unreported is the potential impact this change holds for justice and fair trial rights. The accused speaks trial reflected the notion that the trial was designed to establish the truth of a particular accusation. The implementation of the CrimPR alongside the judiciary assuming a more interventionist role might suggest that the pendulum is moving toward reestablishing the importance of the "truth" in criminal trials as opposed to "proof." Never before has the judiciary or magistracy had such explicit directions as to what constitutes their role of active case management. Furthermore, the voluntary nature of the defendant's participation as dissipated and he is effectively compelled to make disclosures in "pursuit of efficient fact-finding."[64]

Some of the component parts challenge the notion of adversarialism in England and Wales. It is conceivable to suggest that the case management forms are akin to completing a defense case statement under the CPIA 1996;[65] effectively the case management forms erode the voluntary nature of the statutory legislation. Whilst defense disclosure is not an entirely novel proposition, has the defendant had to disclose so much information.[66] However, the modern-day "accused speaks" trial has a notable difference from its earlier counterpart; the accused is now speaking through written case management disclosures, as opposed to orally disclosing information. It has been claimed that defense disclosure does not weaken a fundamental adversarial foundation that the burden of proof rests solely on the prosecution. When first suggesting enhanced defense disclosure in the 1980s, the Roskill Committee suggested why this issue would never manifest: "The prosecution would still have to prepare their case fully . . . including making early disclosure of their evidence . . . we recognize that the burden of proof would be affected if the prosecution were allowed to alter the nature of their case once the defense had been disclosed. To avoid this possibility, any proposal would therefore have to involve the prosecution's case being 'fixed' before the defense could show his hand. If the prosecution sought to change their ground . . . or, if it were not too late, to ensure that the prosecution adhered to the original case."[67]

This approach is admirable because it acknowledges that the burden of proof would be significantly diluted if the prosecution were permitted to amend their case once the defense has been disclosed. However, the "sea change" which started with the Auld Review and permeated through the judiciary and magistracy to enact a change in culture almost ignores the due process safeguard highlighted by the committee. The modern judge will permit the prosecution to alter an indictment to ensure cases are not frustrated by prosecutorial error.[68] Whilst this satisfies the goal of an efficient and expeditious criminal process, the decision is one that is certainly non-adversarial. For example, in *Chabaan*,[69] the Court of Appeal stated the trial judge was entirely correct; time is not unlimited, but the dual goals of efficiency and case management should not be fulfilled by the potential prejudice to the defendant. The evolution of role as an active case manager has further confused the role of the judge. It appears there is some difficulty in ascertaining the boundaries in which they operate. In *Cordingley*,[70] the judge was discourteous and rude and in *Copsey*,[71] the Court of Appeal deemed the judge's interventions all too frequent. The judge asked many questions during the trial, rendering the boundaries of the role rather opaque. What is clear is that the modern-day judiciary and magistracy are no longer passive umpires, but active case managers who pilot the case along the "correct" flight path to ensure nobody veers off course.

Furthermore, active case management makes significant inroads into the due process nature of the adversarial criminal trial. Adversarial systems are not created to consider the interests of anyone other than the state and the defendant.[72] The objective of active case management is to increase the efficiency of the criminal trial process. However, the adversarial process is much like an obstacle course, with many evidential and procedural obstacles to overcome before the court can reach a safe and just decision. This is best illustrated by Packer. He created the Due Process Model (DPM) and its polar opposite counterpart, the Crime Control Model (CCM). In the DPM, the process allows the accused to have "his day in court," and this trial is the central component of the model.[73] The process should represent an obstacle course and each of its successive stages are designed to present formidable impediments to carrying the accused any further through the process.[74] Packer's opposing model CCM is almost managerial in nature and can be likened to a conveyor belt which moved an endless stream of never-ending caseload. Cross-examination has no real value in the model, facts are more easily established at the police station and the procedures followed need to be uniform.[75] Essentially, the CrimPR reflects this uniform approach and the active case management powers allow the judiciary to supervise the conveyor belt of criminal cases, ensuring the process does not slow down. The judiciary can pursue the goal of efficiency and expedited trials by adopting a role that intervenes in proceedings where a delay may occur. This can potentially lead to the curtailment of oral evidence by not allowing advocates to take an unlimited amount of time to present their case.[76] The judiciary can also substitute oral evidence by written evidence to expedite proceedings.[77] With such a shift in the legal landscape, one can understand why some lawyers are confused to their role and how to tackle the many tensions they face whilst providing an adequate service to their client.

The requirement of cooperation between the parties is a distinctly non-adversarial feature of the criminal justice process. Dempster[78] suggests that cooperation is both unnecessary and unwelcome. He believes that the post-*Gleeson* approach is incorrect and states that "it is the Crown's job to draft an appropriate indictment, not the job of the defense to proofread it."[79] The very idea that trials should become more efficient and resources should be saved is commendable and one that should be embraced. However, in meeting this goal, the judiciary may act in a manner that might appear to be incongruent with the values and principles of an adversarial system. Having non-adversarial traits in a due process, adversarial system certainly appears to sit rather awkwardly; and the meeting of the overriding objective by active case management with an interventionist judiciary is distinctly non-adversarial. McEwan suggests that a new ethical code is needed if the criminal justice system is no longer adversarial.[80] There has been no official recognition that adversarialism has, or should be, abandoned. However, this has been suggested through piecemeal changes to the criminal justice process, and the increasing significance of judicial intervention since the turn of the century suggests a new form of process is being created.[81]

A cornerstone of this change is the return to the "Accused Speaks" trial, albeit the accused is speaking from written disclosure rather than orally. The importance of having the accused speak was best highlighted by the earlier Hawkins quote for "[the] guilty, when they speak for themselves, may often help disclose the truth, which probably would not so well be discovered from the artificial defense of others speaking for them."[82] The interventionist judiciary and the disclosure regime are forcing the accused to talk by having them "identify the real issues" at an early stage. The culture does not represent a shift in process toward inquisitorialism. Instead, the shift is toward managerialism, and at the heart of this shift is the interventionist judge who is not merely a guiding pilot;[83] but the pendulum has swung, and the judiciary is now also the controller of the trial process. With the adversarial landscape shifting, the role the actors play also changes. What has not been recognized is the impact the managerial agenda has for the role of the defense lawyer.

There has been a clear departure from the traditional notion of adversarialism. The goal of the criminal trial is to reconstruct historical events in respect of which neither party is in possession of all the facts.[84] Mosidis believes it is the problem of fact possession that reveals the tension between truth and proof in a criminal trial. He states that the essence of a criminal trial is a search for the truth rather than a sporting contest between the prosecution and defense.[85] It is this sporting contest that the CrimPR has assisted in eradicating. The criminal trial now resembles the "Accused Speaks" trial of the eighteenth century, where the defendant was viewed as "an informational resource of the court."[86] However, he is not an informational resource as used in the early days of the adversarial trial, where he would make oral admissions. The modern-day informational resource is forced to identify the "real issues" of his case. Should the defendant delay, the court will exert pressure in order to extract a plea, even if the defense lawyer does not hold all the facts. Furthermore, the defendant is ultimately compelled to breach his privilege against self-incrimination in order to satisfy the overriding objective.

This has drastically altered the adversarial process and as such it has altered the role of the defense lawyer. A minority of respondent lawyers still fitted the *Classic* conception of the defense lawyer, but the majority of the lawyers were identified as either *Conflicted* or *Procedural*—simply operationalized by their obligations to the court. These lawyers are not zealous defenders of their clients, despite their initial veneer of zealous advocacy.[87] The defense lawyer in the modern era is a lawyer who is cajoled and pressurized[88] to satisfy the overriding objective, regardless of how the quest for efficiency impacts upon their client. After all, their client "knows if he did it or not."[89]

The Current State of the Adversarialism: A Theoretical Analysis

If the due process provisions contained within PACE 1984 represented the high-water mark of due process protections, the thesis has illustrated that there have been piecemeal changes since that have eroded various protections and left the criminal justice system in a state of flux; it is ultimately masquerading as a due process system but this is a veneer. Therefore, crime control traits now permeate every facet of the process. Starting with the requirement to disclose expert evidence, the curtailment of the right to silence and then the genesis of the "new regime," it can be stated that the due process nature of the criminal justice process has been fundamentally altered. It is clear that the process is centered within a crime control agenda.

The primary purpose of the CCM is to repress criminal conduct. Lawyer 002 (senior partner, thirty-two years' experience) highlighted this goal when he explained that the whole system is about "convictions, ideally via a guilty plea." This ties into the second element of Packer's model, the process is a uniform conveyor belt. Ideally suspects are merely processed from charge to conviction. The EGP scheme is designed to mimic this process. The scheme takes a carrot and a stick approach to criminal procedure. The carrot is the availability of a lesser sentence should the defendant opt to enter an EGP. The stick is the idea that the defendant would receive a more severe sentence should they contest their innocence at trial and then be convicted. The process wants to save money and, therefore, this waste of resource needs punishing, as, after all, "the defendant knows if he's done it." The defendant is co-opted into the process and compelled to take part in order to achieve the efficiency goals. The goals of efficiency underpin the CCM and is one clear indicator that the criminal justice process of England and Wales resembles such a process. The alternative is the DPM, which resembled the process until the mid-1990s. This model takes the obstacle course approach to justice, that is, there are formidable hurdles in the way of a prosecution. As such, there is a presumption of innocence. However, in the modern criminal justice process it is hard to argue that this exists when you consider the all the pretrial disclosure obligations and couple that with a great deal of pressure to enter an EGP.

The Culture of the New Regime and the Lawyer-Client Relationship

Chapter 4 suggested that the lawyer-client relationship remained relatively intact, despite the raft of obligations which means that the defendant is effectively co-opted and compelled to participate in the proceedings against him. The participants suggested that their clients had little to no issue with the lawyers completing the case management forms and effectively showing part of their hand to the prosecution. As their "client care letter outlines all of our obligations both to the client and to the court . . . as such, clients are acutely aware of what we have to do."[90] As discussed throughout the thesis, the new obligations effectively mean the lawyer would have to "grass-up"[91] the accused in the case of any delays. The new obligations under the rules mean the courts have to be kept fully abreast of the progress of the case.[92] As the book has highlighted, the case management regime was born out of the idea of efficiency because "defense lawyers were frequently accused of failing to submit case statements, or of producing statements lacking and clear and detailed exposition of the case."[93] However, as chapter 5 suggested, both are almost equally at fault for disclosure failings. Yet, despite this face, the drive for efficiency being directed against the defense, the culture of adversarialism may be difficult to overturn in its entirety. Garland and McEwan suggest that it is "difficult to see how defendants can be persuaded that they have an interest in the smooth running of the criminal justice system."[94] Despite this difficulty, not a single one of the twenty-four participants suggested that their clients had any problem with the overriding objective of the CrimPR. This is surprising considering that it can be argued that the suspect is being to ignore the golden thread of criminal proceedings and assist the prosecution in building the case against him.

Quirk suggests that the CPIA 1996 disclosure regime ignored the different working practices and therefore cultures of the key actors in the process. She suggests that it first requires the police to fulfill an inquisitorial function, the prosecutor to view the evidence from a defense perspective and the defense to consider the interests of justice and ultimately the occupational culture of both prosecution and defense ought to be considered.[95] However, it is the very nature of this culture that has been almost entirely ignored during this procedural evolution to the new regime of criminal justice. Quirk suggests that the disclosure regime is "exacerbated by the flawed premise that prosecution and defense disclosure are equivalent or reciprocal; yet the two processes have discrete rationales, impose distinct responsibilities, raise divergent concerns and necessarily attract different sanctions."[96] Furthermore, the disclosure regime ignores the working practices and attitudes of the key actors at play; they are adversaries. The disclosure regime requires the adversarial police to fulfill an inquisitorial function; prosecutors to view material from the defense perspective and the defense to act in the administration of justice, rather than the best interest of his client. Finally, the defendant is effectively compelled to cooperate in the prosecution's quest to convict them.[97] By ignoring the cultural workings of the criminal justice system, it leaves a potential source of injustice. The source of this injustice stems from the cooperative nature of the process and begins in the police station and permeates through the criminal justice process. If adversarialism were to exist, "a partisan defense lawyer [is] essential."[98] However, from the moment the suspect is interviewed at the police station, it is clear that an adversarial defense is unlikely to materialize. Whilst the CrimPR expect a notion of cooperation between the "competing" sides, the defense lawyer is already regarded as "unwelcome"[99] in the police station interview. Despite, being unwelcome, there still is a great deal of cooperation required between the suspect (and by virtue of the fact he is in the room, his lawyer) and the police. Chapter 2 established the political context in which the disclosure provisions were enhanced, in the early to mid-1990s there was a push to reenforce a "crime control" mantra to dilute the protective due process provisions afforded by PACE 1984. As part of this push, the Criminal Justice and Public Order 1994 permitted the courts to draw adverse inferences from a suspect remaining silent. As such, Leng suggests that this created a "normative expectation"[100] that suspects would speak in the police station interview. This is a deeply non-adversarial trait which undermines the due process protection of remaining silent. As such, the importance of a partisan protector at the police station has grown in importance. In order to build a strong lawyer-client relationship, the client needs to feel protected by his lawyer and trust that he will fend off attacks from his adversaries. However, Quirk paints a very bleak picture of police station advice. She states that the lawyer "essentially played the role of the third interviewer."[101] Arguably, the silence provisions of the CJPOA have "made it much more difficult for legal representatives to act in an adversarial manner."[102] However, the evidence suggests that there was little regard for the lawyer-client relationship prior to the enactment of the silence provisions but if an adversarial defense did exist prior to the 1994 changes, it has now been made even more difficult to act in an adversarial manner.

Garland and McEwan suggest that the normative expectation of cooperation is lopsided because only one side are punished for a failing to cooperate, as such any attempt to establish a new culture will likely fail because it is difficult to change a culture if the system is not perceived to be fair to all actors and participants.[103] The findings of Garland and McEwan's study suggest that the goal of a cooperative, efficiency driven culture might be hampered by the fact lawyers on either side do not believe the court sufficiently rebuke its opponent for failings that frustrate the process. In their research, prosecution lawyers believed that the courts were harsh on them regarding the time limits they have to adhere to whilst the defense lawyers suggested the failure of the prosecution to complete paperwork in good time went largely unpunished.[104] Furthermore, prosecutors argued that the incomplete detail offered by the defense defeated the overriding objective; whereas the defense did not view this as problematic.[105] The empirical research conducted for this study suggested that some defense lawyers did not view this a problem. For example, Lawyer 008 wanted to supply as "minimal detail as possible." Lawyer 010 refused to go "chapter and verse into his client's defense." Lawyer 011 went a little further to explain that the detail of the case management is "very basic, not very detailed" as they are working from a skeleton; the prosecution have not provided adequate disclosure to ensure a full defense could be provided in the forms. These working difficulties suggest two important points. Firstly, there are failings on both sides—the prosecution supplies insufficient detail and the defense retort with a similar response. Secondly, the classic adversarial lawyers want to advance the best interest of their client and, as such, disregard the other duties that compete for priority. However, whilst the culture might be difficult to change for the classic lawyers it appears that the case management requirements appear less troublesome for the other types of lawyer. For example, Lawyer 005 did not think the forms were "too onerous

. . . we are not telling the CPS anything they do not already know." Lawyer 024 suggested that the rules and the accompanying culture change was "positive tool" for criminal practitioners. Arguably, the lawyers who embrace the culture change are allowing a shift from adversarialism to a new form of process. The benefits of a true adversarial process are clear; as Steinburg suggests an adversarial lawyer is needed because this benefits society as it offers all who fall into the criminal justice system a robust defense from state prosecution.[106] Garland and McEwan point out that defense lawyers are under pressure to be ready for trial without sufficient time to prepare and as a result they have to disregard their clients' interest in favor of the system.[107] This non-adversarial culture was reflected in the empirical findings of chapter 5. When questioned only four lawyers suggested that their primary duty was to the client. The breakdown and full analysis of this can be found in chapter 5 but it is worth reminding the reader of the breakdown of primary duties (figure 6.1):

The culture has already changed from zealous advocacy, in which defense lawyers advance the client's best interest to the explicit obligation of considering the court and the prosecution. It has been suggested that adversarialism did not really exist in reality,[108] but nevertheless, the criminal process was created with a culture of adversarial due process safeguards, which includes the burden of proof resting on the prosecution, the privilege against self-incrimination and the presumption of innocence. Packer's model of due process would liken these safeguards to the "obstacles" on the "course" of criminal procedure that he described. However, it appears that a new culture exists where fundamental safeguards can be circumvented by an overriding objective "to deal with cases justly." Garland and McEwan suggest the "culture change envisaged by the Court of Appeal may be unattainable."[109] Yet when examining the primary duty of the defense lawyer, in this thesis,

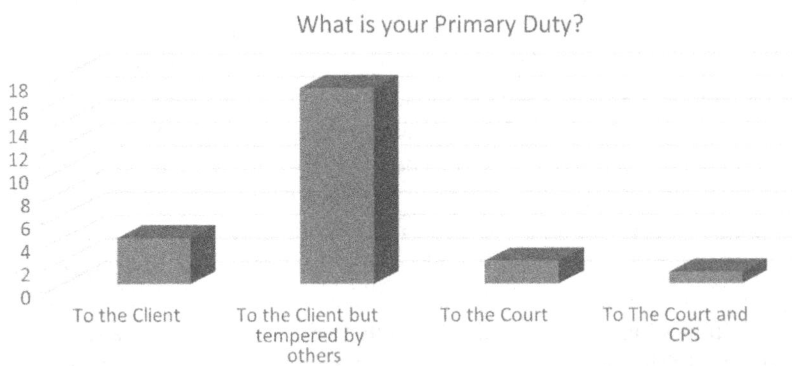

Figure 6.1 Data compiled by author survey.

coupled with empirical work from the 1990s, it could be argued that culture of criminal defense has embraced the overriding objective and the accompanied efficiency drivers. The adversarial culture of England and Wales is no more. This section opened with the idea that the lawyers interviewed believed the lawyer-client relationship remained intact because they disclosed all their competing obligations in a standard client care letter. However, what appears to be happening is the fact that the traditional notion of adversarialism does exist in classic form and it has not for some time. Ultimately, it is arguable that lawyer-client relationship remains intact because the notion of an adversarial culture was merely a veneer; this can be evidenced by the tiny pocket of *classic adversarial lawyers* in the study and literature from the mid-1990s which highlighted the general lack of adversarialism.

CONCLUSION

This chapter concluded, on the basis of the fieldwork, that three different distinctive types of lawyer currently practice in England and Wales. What this chapter has sought to do is to address the arena in which the three types of defense lawyers' practice. Traditionally, England and Wales had an adversarial criminal justice process, but this chapter raises a number of issues relating to the dilution of the adversarial nature of this process. This was examined through the lens of disclosure, the EGP, and the judge as the robust case manager. All of these features are distinctly alien to the adversarial process which is predicated on the battle between the all-powerful state and the zealous defender of the accused. When considering the impact of the early guilty plea regime, it has been established that the defense are given inadequate access to prosecution information prior to the first hearing.[110] This can affect the ability of the defense lawyer to advise on an appropriate plea. Equally, a defendant may be pressured by his lawyer to enter a guilty plea or be tempted to do so because of the sentence discount. In such cases, there is a risk that the overriding objective of the CrimPR will be undermined—that is, to deal with cases justly, which includes acquitting the innocent and convicting the guilty.[111] Whilst it is important to consider the effects of lengthy criminal proceedings on victims and witnesses, it is often the defendant who is forgotten in any reform. The rise of the CrimPR and its implicit goals of managerialism has arguably diluted the adversarial nature of the criminal justice process and has given rise to emphasizing the importance of cooperation throughout proceedings.

There is undoubtedly an agenda, for better or worse, to encourage defendants to enter EGPs, and it seems that should the defendant regret doing so, a remedy will rarely be offered by the courts.[112] It is imperative to ensure that any decision to enter a guilty plea is based on full and accurate evidence from the police and prosecution, made available at an early stage. This is arguably commensurate with the objectives of the CrimPR and the general culture change that has seen a drift from away from pure adversarialism, where each party conceals their argument for as long as possible. If cooperation is to be encouraged, it should be done on an equal basis. This would ensure that the defense lawyer can adequately advise the client as to plea. Moreover, it would reassert the adversarial tradition of English and Welsh criminal justice by moving away from a system that is reliant on a defendant "knowing" when to plead guilty toward a system which requires the prosecution to discharge the burden of proof by revealing the totality of their case from the beginning of the process. A further shift from traditional adversarialism can be seen when one considers the impact of robust case management and the role of the intervening judge. The implementation of these ideas sits rather awkwardly in the adversarial process. The managerial model dislikes party control and this control is now taken away from the state and defense lawyers and transferred to the court.

The judge in the twenty-first century plays a far more prominent role than his twentieth-century predecessor. The judge is no longer described as passive and is undoubtedly the key figure throughout the trial process. He is more than a pilot, more than an umpire. He is the manager, with the goal of concluding the trial in the most expedient manner possible. Should either side not comply with the directions given by the "manager," they may face a number of sanctions. The court can fix, postpone, bring forward, cancel, or adjourn a hearing. It can make a costs order and, ultimately, it can impose any other sanction as may be appropriate. The interventionist judiciary has its goals underpinned by the CrimPR. The traditional adversarial trial has diminished in importance and it is no longer the forum in which the prosecution and defense zealously represent their clients. With the erosion of the ambush defense, the creation of both the defense case statement under section 5 of the CPIA 1996 and the analogous requirement under the CrimPR, the adversarial battle has been replaced with each party knowing the "real issues" of the opposition's case. This is in stark contrast to the initial development of the disclosure regime. As previously discussed, prosecution disclosure was the antidote to the potential unfairness caused by the inequality of resources between the prosecution and defense.[113]

In the modern criminal trial, a duty of cooperation permeates the trial process and has fundamentally altered the culture of criminal procedure. This is illustrated by the creation of timetables and each side informing the judiciary of any significant failures of themselves or their opponent. This has effectively reconstructed the role performance of defense lawyers, so they are partners and cooperators with the prosecution. This partnership and cultural evolution are clear, and the role of the judiciary should be viewed through the same lens. It is the judiciary which facilitates this change by performing the pivotal role of case manager. The very idea that trials should become more efficient and that resources should be saved is commendable and one that should be embraced, but not at the cost of due process protections. However, it is apparent that the due process protections are ridden over roughshod by the judiciary who now view their role as interventionist case managers.

The interventionist judiciary, and case management provisions, alongside the disclosure regime, are forcing the accused to "speak," albeit these are not oral representations; but by having them "identify the real issues" at an early stage, the accused is "speaking." The price of this is the return to an "accused speaks" format, leading to the dilution of core adversarial features in England and Wales such as the burden of proof, the privilege against self-incrimination, and the notion of zealous advocacy. This leaves the defense lawyer in the modern era in a perilous position. His pretrial obligations not only alter his role but the very arena in which he operates. McConville and Marsh suggest that the CrimPR represent a platform which has allowed a departure from due process protections toward a process that maximizes the opportunities for the prosecution to obtain knowledge.[114] This has seen a dramatic reversal of "fearless advocate,"[115] or "gladiator of the accused."[116] The *Conflicted* and *Procedural* lawyers did not share the worry that the adversarial lawyers were dying, and the arena was shifting.

However, the lack of concern might be misplaced. The defense lawyer in the modern era is a key cog in the drive for efficiency; the adversarial criminal justice process has been vastly diluted, so much so that defense lawyers are properly described as "the handmaidens of the prosecution and left hand of the court."[117] The dilution of adversarialism means that its due process protections offer little for those accused of crimes. However, there is a clear and present danger to the notion of "justice," if the courts of England and Wales continue to prioritize efficiency and economy over the interests of fairness. Considering the manner of the transformation of criminal justice in the twenty-first century, this prioritization shows no signs of abating.

NOTES

1. s.5 Criminal Procedure and Investigations Act 1996.
2. Part III Criminal Procedure Rules 2016.
3. Research Question 1 What relevant legislation has changed over the last twenty years? Research Question 2: What are the theoretical and practical consequences of the changing legislation for the defense lawyer?

4. This was the third and final research question, which had a dual purpose: first, it sought to examine the ramifications of the lawyer-client relationship and it also looked at what are the implications of the developments for the notion of adversarialism in England and Wales?

5. See chapter 3 for an in-depth examination of the classic conception of the defense lawyer at pages 49–75.

6. R. Du Cann, *The Art of the Advocate* (Penguin Publishing: London, 1964) at p. 46.

7. D. Nicholson and J. Webb, *Professional Legal Ethics* (Oxford: Oxford University Press, 1999) at p. 182.

8. M. Cain and C. Harrington *Lawyers in the Post-Modern World* (Oxford University Press: Buckingham, 1994) at p. 55.

9. W. Simon, "The Ideology of Advocacy: Procedural Justice and Professional Ethics" [1978], *Wisconsin Law Review* Vol. 42.

10. D. Pannick *Advocates* (Oxford University Press: Oxford, 1992) at p. 92.

11. *Rondell v Worsley* [1969] 1 AC 191.

12. S.11 Criminal Justice Act 1967 see chapter 4.1 for the genesis of the defense disclosure regime.

13. S.2(3) Criminal Justice Act 1987.

14. S.5 Criminal Procedure and Investigations Act 1996.

15. S.5(6)(c) Ibid.

16. S.6 Ibid.

17. Rule 3.2(1) Criminal Procedure Rules 2016.

18. Rule 3.2(1)(a) Ibid.

19. A. Owusu-Bempah, *Defendant Participation in the Criminal Process* (London: Routledge, 2017) at p. 101.

20. Ibid., at p. 49.

21. The courts had adopted the efficiency mantra proposed by Auld LJ *Review of the Criminal Courts* prior to the implementation of the CrimPR. See *R v Chaaban* [2003] EWCA Crim 1012, *R v Jisil* [2004] EWCA Crim 696, *R v Gleason* [2004] 1. Cr. App. R 29, discussed at length in chapter 5.

22. H. Quirk, *The Right of Silence in England and Wales: Sacred Cow, Sacrificial Lamb or Trojan Horse?* in J. Jackson and S. Summers, *Obstacles to Fairness in Criminal Proceedings: Individual Rights and Institutional Forms* (Hart: Oxford, 2018) at p. 77.

23. Lawyer 007.

24. Quirk, *The Right of Silence in England and Wales*, at p. 96.

25. [2002] EWCA Crim 1 [10].

26. Quirk, *The Right of Silence in England and Wales*, at p. 97.

27. Ibid.

28. HM Courts and Tribunals Service, *Justice Matters: Reform Update, May 2018, available here:* https://assets.publishing.service.gov.uk/government/uploads/system/uploads/attachment_data/file/711535/H MCTS_Reform_Update_May_2018 .pdf p. 9.

29. Ibid., at p. 4.

30. R. Leng, "Losing Sight of the Defendant: The Government's Proposals on Pre-Trial Disclosure" [1995] *Criminal Law Review* Vol. 704, at p. 711.

31. s.5-6 Criminal Procedure and Investigations Act 1996.

32. J. McEwan "From Adversarialism to Managerialism: Criminal Justice in Transition" [2011] *Legal Studies* Vol. 31, no. 519 at p. 532.

33. Gross LJ, *Review of Disclosure in Criminal Proceedings*.

34. Sir Brain Leveson, *Review of Efficiency in Criminal Proceedings* (London, Judiciary of England and Wales, 2015) https://www.judiciary.gov.uk/wp-content/uploads/2015/01/review-of-efficiency-in-criminal- proceedings-20151.pdf.

35. Ibid., at p. 12.

36. Courts andTribunals Judiciary, *Better Case Management* available at www.judiciary.gov.uk/publications/better-case-management

37. Seeparagraph3:http://www.cps.gov.uk/southwest/cps_southwest_news/news_articles/in_the_dock_early_guilty_plea_schem e_speeds_up_justice_for_victims/

38. S.144(1)(a) Criminal Justice Act 2003.

39. See Sentencing Guidelines Council, Reduction in Sentence for a Guilty Plea (2007) available here: https://www.sentencingcouncil.org.uk/wp-content/uploads/Reduction_in_Sentence_for_a_Guilty_Plea_- Revised_2007.pdf.

40. Twenty-four lawyers commented that the prosecution does not adhere to the regime and are effectively unchecked. When the defense do not adhere to the regime, they are frequently threatened with sanction by the court.

41. Rule 1.1(1) Criminal Procedure Rules 2016.

42. Per Lord Sankey in *Woolmington v DPP* [1935] AC 462 at 481.

43. (Unreported, February 9, 2016).

44. Sentencing Council, *Reduction in Sentence for a Guilty Plea Guideline Consultation*, February 2016, available here: https://www.sentencingcouncil.org.uk/wp-content/uploads/Reduction-in-sentence-for-a- guilty-plea-consultation-paper-web.pdf [Last Accessed September 15, 2016].

45. The Law Society, *Response of the Law Society of England and Wales to the Sentencing Council consultation on the Reduction in Sentence for an Early Guilty Plea,* May (2016) at p. 6, available here: http://www.lawsociety.org.uk/policy-campaigns/consultation-responses/sentencing-council-consultation-on- the-reduction-in-sentence-for-a-guilty-plea-guideline-law-society-response/ [Last Accessed September 15, 2016].

46. D. Newman, *Legal Aid Lawyers and the Quest for Justice* (Hart: Oxford, 2013) at p. 30.

47. Ibid., at p. 112.

48. Ibid., at p. 115, where the client says he's not guilty and the lawyer says "look, if you plead guilty, then I'll explain why later, okay?"

49. However, as well as interviews, Newman carried out observations which allowed him to contrast his interview findings by observing "how" lawyers worked.

50. For a full examination of the judge's role during the "accused speaks" trials please see pp .48–54.

51. L. J. Auld, *Review of the Criminal Courts of England and Wales* (HMSO: 2001).

52. *Jones v National Coal Board* [1957] 2 Q.B. 55

53. Ibid per Denning LJ at p. 65.

54. Ibid., at p. 64.

55. F. Bacon, *Essays, Civil and Moral.* Vol. III, Part 1. The Harvard Classics. (New York: P.F. Collier & Son, 1909–14), Chapter 56 Of Judicature as cited by Denning LJ ibid.

56. Lawyers 006, 007, and 009 explicitly commented that they have heard magistrates use a similar phrase. Four other lawyers intimated they had heard colleagues have encountered a similar phrasing.

57. Whilst it was a clear issue for the five *Classic Adversarial Lawyers*, six *Conflicted Adversarial Lawyers* also raised this issue.

58. [2003] EWCA Crim 3357

59. J. Chalmers, F. Leverick and L. Farmer, *Essays in Criminal law in Honour of Sir Gerald Gordon*, 2010 (Edinburgh: Edinburgh University Press) p. 323.

60. M. McConville and L. Marsh *Criminal Judges, Legitimacy, Courts and State-Induced Guilty Pleas in Britain"* (Edward Elgar: Cheltenham, 2014) p. 175.

61. *R (on the application of Payne) v South Lakeland Magistrates' Court* [2011] EWHC 1802 (Admin) at para 39.

62. [2010] EWCA Crim 1928.

63. McEwan "From Adversarialism to Managerialism,"" at p. 520.

64. A. Owusu-Bempah, *Defendant Participation in the Criminal Process* (Routledge: London, 2017) at p. 163.

65. Andrew Keogh argues the case management form is analogous to the defense statement in the Crown Court. See A. Keogh "Criminal Case Management—Is the Game Over?, Eldon Lecture Series, (2011) Northumbria University School of Law.

66. Previously, defense alibi witnesses had to be disclosed by virtue of S.11 Criminal Justice Act 1967 and in fraud trials the defendant had to outline his defense in general terms. However, if the defense to the fraud charge was based on alibi or expert evidence then fuller disclosure was required.

67. The Fraud Trials Committee, Chairman: The Right Honorable Lord Roskill, P.C, (HMSO: 1986) at p. 104 at para 6.75.

68. See *Gleeson* [2004] 1.Cr. App. R. 29.

69. [2003] EWCA Crim 1012.

70. [2007] All ER (D) 131.

71. [2008] EWCA Crim 2043.

72. McEwan "From Adversarialism to Managerialism" at p. 520.

73. H. L. Packer, *The Limits of the Criminal Sanction* (California: Stanford University Press), 1968, at p. 157.

74. Ibid., at p. 163.

75. Ibid.

76. Rule 3.10 (d)(ii) CrimPR 2016.

77. *D and Others* [2007] EWCA Crim 2485.

78. 1099 J. Dempster, "Show Your Hand or Have It Cut Off," Criminal Bar Association Newsletter, March 1, 2005.

79. See *Gleeson* [2004] 1.Cr. App. R. 29.

80. F. Garland and J. McEwan, "Embracing the Overriding Objective: Difficulties and Dilemmas in the New Criminal Climate" [2012] *The International Journal of Evidence and Proof* Vol. 16 (233–262) at p. 262.

81. Inter alia the dilution of the right to silence, the growing importance of the pretrial investigation in deciding criminal matters. See J. Jackson, "Police and Prosecutors after PACE: The road from case construction to case disposal" in E. Cape and R. Young, *Regulating Policing: The Police and Criminal Evidence Act 1984: Past, Present and Future*, 2008 (Hart) 255–277.

82. W. Hawkins, *A Treatise of the Pleas of the Crown*, Vol. II (London 1721) cited in no. 1 at p. 171.

83. W. Silverman, "The Trial Judge: Pilot, Participant or Umpire?" 11. *Alta L Rev* 40 1973 at p. 63.

84. C. Mosidis, *Criminal Discovery: From Truth to Proof and Back Again*, 2008, Institute of Criminology: Sydney at p. 250.

85. Ibid.

86. W. Hawkins, *A Treatise of the Pleas of the Crown*, Vol II (London, 1721) cited in. J. H. Langbein, *The Origins of the Adversary Criminal Trial* (Oxford: Oxford University Press, 2003) p. 171.

87. The veneer exists since the majority of the lawyers suggested that their primary duty is to their client.

88. Although there were four lawyers who were termed as "classic adversarial" lawyers and their answers indicated that they would not buckle to such pressure.

89. As espoused by Lawyer 007.

90. Lawyer 016.

91. See p. 230 for examination of the lawyers considering the implications of "grassing up" their client.

92. CrimPR Rule 1.2(1)(c).

93. Garland and McEwan "Embracing the Overriding Objective," 233–262 at 243.

94. Ibid., at p. 254.

95. H. Quirk, "The Significance of Culture in Criminal Procedure Reform: Why the Revised Disclosure Scheme Cannot Work" [2006] *E&P* Vol. 10(1), 42–59 at pp. 42–43.

96. Ibid., at p. 44.

97. Ibid.

98. Quirk, *The Rise and Fall of the Right of Silence* p89

99. Ibid., at p. 90.

100. See Leng, "The Right to Silence in Police Interrogation."

101. Quirk, *The Rise and Fall of the Right of Silence* at p. 3.

102. Ibid., at p. 118.

103. Garland and McEwan "Embracing the Overriding Objective," at p. 260.

104. Ibid.

105. Ibid., at p. 245.

106. H. B. Steinberg, "The Responsibility of the Defense Lawyer in Criminal Cases" [1960], *Syracuse Law Review* Vol. 12, 442.

107. Garland and McEwan "Embracing the Overriding Objective," at 242.

108. McConville et al. study found that lawyers held a low opinion of their clients and Newman found that some law firms acted as "sausage factories" rather than viewing the client as someone who needed "shielding."

109. Garland and McEwan "Embracing the Overriding Objective," at 262.

110. See The Judiciary of England and Wales, Magistrates' Court Disclosure Review (May 2014), see also J. Plotnikoff and R. Wolfson, *A Fair Balance? Evaluation of the Operation of Disclosure Law*, Home Office, RDS Occasional Paper No. 76 (2001) and H. Quirk, "The Significance of Culture in Criminal Procedure Reform: Why the Revised Disclosure Scheme Cannot Work," *The International Journal of Evidence & Proof*, 10(1), pp. 42–59.

111. Rule 1.1 CrimPR 2016.

112. *R v on the application of the DPP) v Leicester Magistrates' Court* (Unreported, February 9, 2016).

113. D. Corker and S. Parkinson, *Disclosure in Criminal Proceedings* (Oxford: Oxford University Press, 2009) at p. 6.

114. M. McConville and L. Marsh *Criminal Judges, Legitimacy, Courts and State-Induced Guilty Pleas in Britain* (Edward Elgar: Cheltenham, 2014) at p. 165.

115. Ibid., at p. 179.

116. R. Du Cann, *The Art of the Advocate* (Penguin Publishing: London, 1964) at p. 46.

117. M. McConville and L. Marsh, *Criminal Judges, Legitimacy, Courts and State-Induced Guilty Pleas in Britain* (Edward Elgar: Cheltenham, 2014) at p. 165.

Appendix

Cases and Legislation

CASES

Aravinthan Visarathnam v Brent Magistrates' Court [2009] EWHC 3017 (Admin)
Arthur J.S. Hall and Co v Simmons [2000] UKHL 38, [2002] 1 AC 615
Balogun v DPP [2010] EWHC 799 (Admin).
Blunt v Park Lane Hotel Ltd [1942] 2 KB 253 *Brett v DPP* [2009] EWHC 440.
D and Others [2007] EWCA Crim 2485.
Dallison v Caffery [1965] 1 QB 348.
ex p Lloyd (1822) Mont 70.
Firth v Epping Magistrates' Court [2011] EWHC 388 (Admin)
Jones v National Coal Board [1957] 2 QB 55.
Malcolm v DPP [2007] EWHC 363.
R (on the application of the DPP) v Chorley Justices [2006] EWHC 1795.
R (On the Application of Drinkwater) v Solihull Magistrates' Court [2012] EWCA 765
R v (on the application of the DPP) v Leicester Magistrates' Court (Unreported, February 9, 2016).
R (on the application of Payne) v South Lakeland Magistrates' Court [2011] EWHC 1802 (Admin)
R v Barnes [1971] Cr.App.R 100.
R v Bryant and Dickson [1946] 31 Cr App R 146.
R v Bryant [2005] EWCA Crim 2079.
*R v Buffrey*14.Cr. App R (S) 511.
R *v Clarke* (1930) 22 Cr App R 58.

R v Clewer (1953) 37 Cr.App.R 37.
R v Grafton [1992] Crim LR 826.
Re P(A Barrister) (No 1 of 1991) [1993] QB 293.
Rondel v Worsley [1969] 1 AC 191 HL. *R v Chaaban* [2003] EWCA Crim 1012.
R v College 8 St. Trials 549 (1681)
R v Ensor [2009] EWCA Crim 2519.
R v Essa [2009] EWCA Crim 43.
R v Gleeson [2004] 1. Cr. App. R. 29.
R v Haringey Justices, ex p DPP [1996], 1 All RT 828\.
R v Keane [1994] 2 All ER 478.
R (Kelly) v Warley JJ [2007] EWHC 1836.
R v Jisl [2004] EWCA Crim 696.
R v Lady Alice Lisle 11 St. Tr. 297 (Winchester Assizes 1685).
R v Lawson [1990] Crim LR 62.
R (Law Society of England and Wales) v Lord Chancellor and the Legal Services Commission [2012] EWHC 794 (Admin).
Medcalf v Mardell [2003] 1 AC 120 (HL).
R v Melvin and Dingle (Unreported, 20 December 1993).
R v *MclKenny and Others* [1991] 93 CR AR 287.
R v Musone [2007] EWCA Crim 1237.
R v Newell [2012] EWCA Crim 650.
R v Samuel [1988] QB 615.
R v O'Connell (1844) 7 I.L.R. 261.
R v Olivia [1965] 1 WLR 1028.
R v Rochford [2010] EWCA Crim 1928.
R v Sharp [1993] 3 All ER 225.
R v SVS Solicitors [2012] EWCA Crim 319.
R (Tinnion) v Reading Crown Court [2009] EWHC 2930 (Admin).
R v Titus Oates 10, St. Tr 1079 (K.B 1685).
R v Ward [1993] 2 All ER 577.
R v Walter Thomas, 2 Bulstrode 147, 80 Eng. Rep 1022 (K.B 1613).
The People (at the Suit of the Director of Public Prosecutions v Phelim McGuinness
[1978] IR 189.
Three Rivers DC v Bank of England (Disclosure) (No. 4) [2004] UKHL 48.
Tibbs (The Times, February 28, 2000) *Woolmington v DPP* [1935] AC 462.
Writtle v DPP [2009] EWCA 236 (Admin).
Yuill v Yuill [1945] 1 All ER 18.

LEGISLATION

Courts Act 2003
Courts and Legal Services Act 1990 Criminal Evidence Act 1898
Criminal Justice Act 1967
Criminal Justice and Public Order Act 1994
Criminal Procedure and Investigations Act 1996
Criminal Procedure Rules 2016
Human Rights Act 1998
Legal Services Act 2007
Police and Criminal Evidence Act 1984
The Prisoner's Counsel Act 1836
Solicitors Act 1974
Treason Act 1696

Bibliography

Abel R, *Lawyers: A Critical Reader* (New York: New Press, 1997).

Alschuler A, *How to Win the Trial of the Century: The Ethics of Lord Brougham and the OJ Simpson Defense Team* (1997–1998) 29 *McGeorge Law Review*.

Ambos K, 'International criminal procedure: "Adversarial", "Inquisitorial" or Mixed?' (2003) 3 International Criminal Law Review.

Arber S, *Designing Samples*, in N. Gilbert (ed.) *Researching Social Life* (London: Sage, 1993).

Archer, G., 'Ethical Obligations of the Lawyer' in F. Zacharias and B. Green *Reconceptualizing Advocacy Ethics* (2005) 74 *Geo. Was. L.R.* 28.

Archbold J. *Archbold: Criminal Pleading, Evidence and Practice* (London: Sweet & Maxwell, 1997).

Arguedas C, *Duties of a Criminal Defense Lawyer* (1996–97) 30 *Loy. L.A.L. Rev.*

Arksey H, and Knight P. *Interviewing for Social Scientists* (London: SAGE, 1999).

Ashworth A, and Redmayne M, *The Criminal Process* (3rd Edition, Oxford: Oxford University Press, 2003).

Ashworth A, 'The Techniques of Sentencing' (1984) *Crim LR* 519.

Atkinson D, and Moloney T, *Blackstone's Guide to the Criminal Procedure Rules 2005* (Oxford: Oxford University Press 2005).

Atkinson G. *Criminal Litigation: Practice and Procedure* (Guildford: College of Law, 2006).

Atkinson P, and Silverman D, 'Kunera's Immortality: The Interview and the invention of the Self,' (1997) 3 *Qualitative Inquiry* 197.

Atkinson R, and Flint J, 'Accessing Hidden and Hard-to-Reach Populations: Snowball Research Strategies,' (2001) *Social Research Update.*

Bachman R, and Schutt R.K, *Fundamentals of Research in Criminology and Criminal Justice* (2nd Edition, London: Sage, 2012).

Baldwin J, McConville M., *Courts, Prosecution and Conviction* (Oxford: Clarendon Press, 1981).

Baldwin J, McConville M, *Plea Bargaining: Legal Carve-Up and Legal Cover-Up* (1978) 5 *British Journal of Law and Society* 2.

Baldwin J, 'Police Interview Techniques: Establishing Truth or Proof?' (1993) 33(3) *The British Journal of Criminology* .

Barker E, *The Making of a Moonie: Brainwashing or Choice* (Oxford: Blackwell 1984).

Beattie J, *Crime and the Courts in England 1660–1800* (New Jersey: Princeton University Press, 1986).

Baksi C, 'Fraud Case Judge Slams Solicitor-Advocates for Incompetence,' (2009) *Law Society Gazette* 23 April.

Beattie J, 'Scales of Justice: Defense Counsel and the English Criminal Trial in the Eighteenth and Nineteenth Centuries,' (1991) 9 *Law & History Review*.

Bentham J, *The Works of Jeremy Bentham* (John Bowring edition, William Tait: Edinburgh, 1843), Vol II.

Bingham T, *The Rule of Law* (London: Allen Lane, 2010).

Boon A, Levin J. *The Ethics and Conduct of Lawyers in England and Wales* (Oxford: Hart Publishing, 1999).

Bottoms A, *Theory and Empirical Observations in Criminology* in King R.D, and Wincup E, *Doing Research on Crime and Justice* (Oxford University Press, 2008).

Bradney A, *How to Study Law* (5th edition, London: Sweet and Maxwell, 2005).

Bradley C.M, 'he Convergence of the Continental and Common Law Model of Criminal Procedure,' (1996) 7 *Criminal Law Forum* 471

Braun V, and Clarke V, 'Using Thematic Analysis in Psychology', (2006) *Qualitative Research in Psychology* 3(2), 77–101,

Bress D, *Professional Ethics in Criminal Trials: A View of Defense Counsel's Responsibility* (1965–1966) 64 Mich. L.R.

Bridges L, and McConville M, 'Keeping Faith With Their Own Convictions: The Royal Commission on Criminal Justice' (1994) 57 Mod. L. Rev. 75.

Briggs C.L, *Learning How to Ask: A Sociolinguistic Appraisal of the Role the Interview in Social Science Research* (London: Cambridge University Press, 1986).

Brougham H, *The Life and Times of Henry Lord Brougham* (London: Blackwood, 1871).

Bryman A., Burgess R. *Analysing Qualitative Data* (London: Routledge, 1994).

Burgess G, *In the Field: An Introduction to Field Research* (London: Routledge 1984).

Burns R, *Introduction to Social Research Methods* (2nd Ed, Melbourne: Longman Cheshire, 1997).

Carlen P, 'Remedial Routines for the Maintenance Control in Magistrates' Courts, (1974) *British Journal of Law and Society* 101.

Cain M, Harrington C, *Lawyers in a Post-Modern World* (Buckingham: Open University Press, 1994).

Cairns D.J.A, *Advocacy and the Making of the Adversarial Criminal Trial 1800-1865* (London: Clarendon Press, 1998).

Cape E. *The Rise (and Fall?) of a Criminal Defence Profession* (2004) Crim LR.

Cape E. *Rebalancing the Criminal Justice Process: Ethical Challenges for Criminal Defence Lawyers* (2006) 9 Legal Ethics 1.

Card R, and Ward R, *The Criminal Procedure and Investigations Act 1996* (Jordan's Publishing, Bristol, 1996).

Cape E. *Defending Suspects at the Police Station* (London: Legal Action Group, 2006).

Cape E, and Young R, *Regulating Police: The Police and Criminal Evidence Act 1984, Past, Present and Future* (Hart Publishing, 2008).

Cape E, Hodgson J, et al. *Suspects in Europe* (Oxford: Intersentia, 2007).

Cape E, Namoradze Z, Smith R, Spronken T, *Effective Criminal Defence in Europe* (Antwerp-Oxford: Intersenti, 2010).

Chalmers J, Leverick F, and Farmer L, *Essays in Criminal law in Honour of Sir Gerald Gordon* (Edinburgh: Edinburgh University Press, 2010).

Chakrabarti E. 'A Thinning Blue Line? Police Independence and the Rule of Law' (2008) 2(3) Policing 367-74 at 369.

Choo A, *Evidence* (Oxford: Oxford University Press, 2006).

Corker D, and Parkinson S, *Disclosure in Criminal Proceedings* (Oxford University Press: Oxford, 2010).

Cornwell J, *Hard-earned lives: Accounts of health and illness from East London* (London: Tavistock, 1984).

Costley C, Elliott G, and Gibbs P, *Doing Work Based Research: Approaches to Enquiry for Insider-Researchers* (Sage: London 2010).

Cranston R, *Legal Ethics and Professional Responsibility* (Oxford: Oxford University Press, 1995).

Curtis C, *The Ethics of Advocacy* (1951–1952) 4 Stanford L.R.

Damaska M.R, *The Faces of Justice and State Authority: A Comparative Approach to the Legal Process* (New Haven: Yale University Press, 1986).

Damaska M.R, *Evidence Law Adrift* (New Haven: Yale University Press, 1997).

Damaska M.J, 'Evidentiary Barriers to Conviction and Two models of criminal procedure' (1973) U. PA. LR 507.

Dare T, *The Counsel of Rogues: A Defence of the Standard Conception of the Lawyer's Role* (Ashgate: Surrey, 2009).

Delmas-Marty M, and Spencer J, *European Criminal Procedures* (Cambridge: Cambridge University Press, 2002).

Dempster J, 'Show your Hand or Have it Cut Off', March 2005, Criminal Bar Association Newsletter, 1.

Denscombe M, *The Good Research Guide: For Small Scale Social Research Projects* (2nd Edition, Maidenhead: Open University Press, 2003).

Denecke A. *The Dilemma of the Virtuous Lawyer or When Do You Have to Blow the Whistle On Your Client?* (1979) Ariz. St. L.J.

De Vries H. *Civil Law and the Anglo-American Lawyer* (New York: Oceana Publications 1976).

Dingwell R, 'Accounts, Interviews and Observations' in Miller G, and Dingwell R, (Eds) *Context and Method in Qualitative Research* (London: Sage, 1997).

Drever E, *Using Semi-Structured Interviews in Small-Scale Research: A Teacher's Guide*, The Scottish Council for Research in Education (Glasgow: University of Glasgow, 1995).

Doak J. *Victims' Rights in Criminal Trials: Prospects for Participation* (2005) 32 Journal of Law and Society 2.

Dos Passos J. *The American Lawyer: As He Was, As He Is, As He Could Be* (New York: The Banks Law Publishing Co. 1997).

Du Cann R, *The Art Of The Advocate* – (London: Penguin, 1993).

Du Plessis J, *The Accusatorial System – Too Much A Game?* (1991) 108 South African Law Journal.

Duff P, 'Disclosure in Scottish criminal procedure: another step in an inquisitorial direction?,' (2007) 153 International Journal of Evidence and Proof.

Duff R, *Trials and Punishments* (Cambridge University Press, 1986).

Ede R, Shepherd E, *Active Defence* (London: The Law Society, 1997).

Ede R, Edwards A, *Criminal Defence: The Good Practice Guide* (London: The Law Society, 2002).

Edwards A, 'Criminal Defence Witness Notices' 6th May 2010, London Law Society Gazette Edwards A, 'Case Management Forms' (2011) *Crim L Rev* 546.

Ellis T, and Savage S. P, *Debates in Criminal Justice* (London Routledge 2012).

Ellison L, *The Adversarial Process and the Vulnerable Witness* (Oxford: Oxford University Press, 2001).

Ellison L, 'The Protection of Vulnerable witnesses in Court: An Anglo-Dutch Comparison' (1999) 3 *International Journal of Evidence and Proof.*

R. Ericson, "The State and Criminal Justice Reform" in R. Ratner and J. McMullan (Eds) *State Control: Criminal Justice Politics in Canada* (Vancouver: University of British Columbia Press, 1987).

Evans E. P, *The Criminal Prosecution and Capital Punishment of Animals* (London, Heinemann, 1906).

Ferdico J. N, Frandella H and Totten C, *Criminal Procedure for the Criminal Justice Professional* (Cengage Learning: California 2012).

Field. R and P.A. Thomas, *'Justice and Efficiency? The Royal Commission on Criminal Justice* (Oxford: Blackwell, 1994).

Field S, and Thomas P, 'Justice and Efficiency? The Royal Commission on Criminal Procedure,' (1994) 21 The Journal of Law and Society.

Field S. *Early Intervention and the 'New' Youth Justice: A Study of Initial Decision-Making* – (2008) Crim LR 177.

Field S, 'State Citizen and Character in French Criminal Process,' (2006) *Journal of Law and Society* 33(4).

Freedman M, *Lawyers' Ethics in an Adversary System* (Indianapolis: Bobbs-Merrill, 1975).

Freedman M, and Smith A, *Understanding Lawyers Ethics* (4th Edition, New Providence: NJ, 2010).

Freedman M, *Are There Public Interest Limits on Lawyers' Advocacy?* (1977) 2 J. Legal Prof.

Freedman M, *Henry Lord Brougham, Written By Himself* (2006) 19 Geo. J. Legal Ethics. Freedman M, *Henry Lord Brougham and Zeal* (2005–2006) 34 Hofstra L. Rev.

Freiberg A, *Post-Adversarial and Post-Inquisitorial Justice: Transcending Traditional Penological Paradigms* (2010) Faculty of Law, Monash University, Research Paper No. 2010/1.

Fried C, *The Lawyer as Friend: The Moral Foundations of the Lawyer-Client Relation* (1975-1976) 85 Yale L.J.

Fuller L, Randall J, *Professional Responsibility: Report of the Joint Conference* (1958) 44 *American Bar Association Journal.*

Fuller L, 'The Forms and Limits of Adjudication' (1978) 92 Harv LR 353.

Fuller L, Randall J, Professional Responsibility: Report of the Joint Conference, *American Bar Association Journal* (1958), 44, 1159–1162.

Glenn H, *Legal Traditions of the World* (Oxford: Oxford University Press, 2000)

Gilbert N, *Researching Social Life* (London: SAGE 2001).

Gillham B, *Research Interviews: The Range of Techniques* (Berkshire: Open University Press 2005).

Goffman E, *The Presentation of self in Everyday Life* (London: Anchor Publishing, 1959).Hakim C, R*esearch Design: Strategies and Choices in the Design of Social Research* (Routledge, 1987).

Haar C, *The Golden Age of American Law* (New York: George Braziller, 1965).

Hammersely M, *What's wrong with Ethnography?* (London: Routledge, 1992).

Henn M, Weinstein M, Foard N, *A Short Introduction to Social Research* (London: SAGE, 2006).

Harding C, et al. *Criminal Justice In Europe: A Comparative Study* (Oxford: Oxford University Press 1995).

Hodgson J, *Conceptions of the Trial in Inquisitorial and Adversarial Procedure* in A. Duff, *The Trial on Trial Volume 1, Truth and Due Process* (1st edition, Hart, Oxford, 2001).

Hodgson J, 'The Police, The Prosecutor and the Juge d'instruction: Judicial Supervision in France, theory and Practice,' (2001) *British Journal of Criminology* 41.

Hodgson J, 'Suspects, Defendants and Victims in the French Criminal Process: The Context of Recent Reform,' (2002) 51 Int. and Comp. L.Q.

Hodgson J, 'Codified Criminal Procedure and Human Rights: Some Observations on the French Experience' (2003) Crim. L.R.

Hodgson J, *The Future of Adversarial Criminal Justice in 21*st *Century Britain* (2010) 35 N.C.J. Int. L. & Com. Reg.

Hoffman D, *A Course of Legal Study* – (Baltimore: Joseph Neal, 1836).

Holland A, et al. *Cordery on Solicitors* (London: LexisNexis Butterworths, 2008).

Hugman R, Smith D, *Ethical Issues in Social Work* (London: Routledge, 1995).

Hungerford-Welch P, *Criminal Procedure and Sentencing* (8th Edition, London: Routledge, 2014).

Hungerford-Welch P, *Summary Trial – Too Summary?* (2011) Criminal Justice Matters, No.84 June.

Jackson J, Two Methods of Proof in Criminal Procedure (1988) *MLR* 5, 549.

Jackson J, *Judge Without Jury: Diplock Trials and the Adversary System* (Oxford: Clarendon, 1995).

Jackson J, and Summers S, *Obstacles to Fairness in Criminal Proceedings: Individual Rights and Institutional Forms* (Hart: Oxford, 2018).

Jorg N, Field S, and Brants C, Are Inquisitorial and Adversarial Systems Converging? In *Criminal Justice in Europe: A Comparative Study* (Clarendon Press, Oxford, 1995).Kaplan J. *Criminal Justice* (New York: Foundation Press, 1973).

K . Krippendorff *Content Analysis: An Introduction to its Methodology* (2nd Ed. Sage: California, 2004).

Kumar R, *Research Methodology: A Step by Step Guide for Beginners* (4th Ed, London: Sage, 2015).

Langbein J, *The Origins of Adversary Criminal Trial* (Oxford: Oxford University Press, 2003).

Langbein J, 'The Criminal Trial Before Lawyers' (1978) 45 *U Ch LR* 263.

Langer M, 'The Rise of Managerial Judging in International Criminal Law,' (2005) 53 Am. J. Comp. L.

The Law Society, *The Guide to the Professional Conduct of Solicitors* (London: The Law Society 1999).

Legal Aid Board, *Legal Aid Handbook 1998/99* (London: Sweet & Maxwell, 1998).

Leng R, and Taylor R, *Blackstone's Guide to the Criminal Procedure and Investigations Act 1996* (Blackstone's Press, London 1996).

Leng R, 'Losing Sight of the Defendant: The Government's Proposals on Pre-Trial Disclosure,' (1995) Crim L.R 704.

Leng R, 'The Right to Silence in Police Interrogation: A Study of Some of the Issues Underlying the Debate,' (1993) *RCCJ Research Study* No 10.

Levi M, The Future of Fraud Prosecutions and Trials: Reviewing Roskill,' (1986) 7(4) *Company Law*, 139–146.

M. Levi, 'The Investigation, Prosecution and Trial of Serious Fraud,' (1993) RCCJ Research Study No.14 .

Luban D, *Lawyers and Justice* (Princeton: Princeton University Press, 1988).

Luban D, *The Ethics of Lawyers* (Aldershot: Dartmouth Publishing 1994).

May T, *Social Research* – Buckingham: Open University Press, 1994).

Maguire M, *Researching Street Criminals* in King R.D, and Wincup E, *Doing Research on Crime and Justice* (2nd Edition, Oxford: Oxford University Press, 2000).

McConville M, Sanders A, Leng R, *The Case for the Prosecution: Police Suspects and the Construction of Criminality* (London: Routledge, 1991).

McConville M., et al. *Standing Accused: The Organisation and Practices of Criminal Defence Lawyers in Britain* (Oxford: Oxford University Press, 1994).

McConville M, Wilson G, *The Handbook of Criminal Justice Process* (Oxford: Oxford University Press, 2002).

McConville M, Chui W. H, *Research Methods for Law* (Edinburgh: Edinburgh University Press, 2007).

McConville M and Marsh L, *Criminal Judges: Legitimacy, Courts and State Induced Guilty Pleas in Britain'* (Edward Elgar: Northampton, 2014).

McConville M, 'An Error of Judgment,' (1993) Legal Action, September.

McConville M, and Marsh L, 'Adversarialism Goes West: Case Management in Criminal Courts,' (2015) 19(3) E&P.

McEwan J, 'Truth, Efficiency and Co-operation in Modern Criminal Justice,' (2013) 1 *Current Legal Problems*, 66(1)

McEwan J, 'From Adversarialism to Managerialism: Criminal Justice in Transition,' (2011) 31(3) *Legal Studies*, Wiley.

McEwan J, *The Adversarial and Inquisitorial Models of Criminal Trial* in the Trial on Trial Volume 1: Truth and Due Process (Hart: Oxford, 2001).

Miles M, Huberman M, *Qualitative Data Analysis: An Expanded Sourcebook* (London: SAGE, 1994).

Milsom S, *Historical Foundations of the Common Law* (London: Butterworths. 1981).

Monette D.R, Sullivan T.J, and DeJong C.R, *Applied Social Research: Tools for Human Services* (Fort Worth: Holt, Rienheart and Wilson 1984).

Mosidis C, *Criminal Discovery: From Truth to Proof and Back Again* (Sydney Institute of Criminology Series: Sydney, 2008).

Murphy P, *Murphy on Evidence* (Oxford: Oxford University Press, 2005).

Napley D, *The Technique of Persuasion* (4th ed. Sweet and Maxwell: London, 1991).

Newman D, *Legal Aid Lawyers and the Quest for Justice* (Hart: Oxford, 2013).

Newman D, 'Still Standing Accused: Addressing the Gap between work and talk in firms of criminal defence lawyers,' (2012) 19 *International Journal of the Legal Profession* 1

Newman D, and Ugwudike P, 'Defence Lawyers and Probation Officers: Offenders' Allies or Adversaries? (2014) *International Journal of the Legal Profession* 183

Nicolson D, Webb J, *Professional Legal Ethics* (Oxford: Oxford University Press, 1999).

O'Dair R, *Legal Ethics: Text and Materials* – (London: Butterworths, 2001).

Owusu-Bempah A, *Defendant Participation in the Criminal Process* (Routledge: London, 2016).

Owusu-Bempah A, 'Defence Participation through Pre-Trial Disclosure: Issues and Implications,' (2013) 17 E&P 183.

Pakes F, *Comparative Criminal Justice* (2nd Edition, Willan Publishing, 2010).

Packer H.L, *The Limits of the Criminal Sanction* (California: Stanford University Press, 1968).

Padfield N, *Text and Materials on the Criminal Justice Process* (Oxford: Oxford University Press 2008).

Pannick D, *Advocates* (Oxford: Oxford University Press, 1992).

Plowden P, *Criminal Litigation in Practice* (Newcastle-Upon-Tyne: Northumbria Law Press, 2006).

Plowden P, 'Make Do and Mend, or a Cultural Evolution?,' (2005) *The New Law Journal*, March.

Quirk H, *The Rise and Fall of the Right of Silence* (Oxon: Routledge, 2017).

Richardson J, *Archbold* (London: Sweet and Maxwell, 2015).

Quirk H, 'The Significance of Culture in the Criminal Procedure Reform: Why the Revised Disclosure Scheme Cannot Work,' (2006) 10 Int. Journal of Evidence and Proof 1.

Quirk H, 'Twenty Years On, the Right of Silence and Legal Advice: The Spiraling Costs of An Unfair Exchange,' (2013) 66(4) *NILQ*, 465–484.

Quirk H, *The Right of Silence in England and Wales: Sacred Cow, Sacrificial Lamb or Trojan Horse?* in J. Jackson and S. Summers, *Obstacles to Fairness in Criminal Proceedings: Individual Rights and Institutional Forms* (Oxford: Hart Publishing, 2018).

Redmayne M, 'Criminal Justice Act 2003: (1) Disclosure and its Discontents,' (2004) CrimLR 441.

Rhode D, *An Adversarial Exchange on Adversarial Ethics: Text, Subtext and Context* (1991) 41 J. Legal Ed.

Reichel P, *Comparative Criminal Justice Systems* (New Jersey: Pearson/Prentice Hall, 2005).

Rubin H.J, and Rubin I.S, *Qualitative Interviewing: The Art of Hearing Data* (3rd Edition, London: Sage, 2012).

Rueschemeyer D, *Lawyers and their Society* (Massachusetts: Harvard University Press, 1973) Sanders A, and Young R, *Criminal Justice* (3rd Edition, Oxford: Oxford University Press, 2007).

Seipp D. J, *Crime in the Year Books*, in Law Reporting in England 15, 22 (Chatal Stebbings ed. 1995).

Sharswood G, *An Essay on Professional Ethics* (Michigan: University of Michigan, 1860).

Silverman D, *Doing Qualitative Research: A Practical Handbook* (London: Sage 2000).

Stephen J.F, *History of the Criminal Law*, Volume I (Kessinger Publishing, 1883).

Smith A, Montross W, *The Calling of Criminal Defense* (1998–1999) 50 *Mercer L.R.*

Smith T, 'Trust, Choice and Money: Why the Legal Aid Reform "U-Turn" is Essential for Effective Criminal Defence,' (2013) *Crim L.R.* Issue 11.

Smith T, 'Justice for Sale: An Empirical Examination of the Attitudes of Criminal Defence Lawyers Toward Legal Aid Reform,' (2014), *Plymouth Law and Justice Review* 1.

Smith T, The "Near Miss" of Liam Allan: Critical Problems in Police Disclosure, Investigation Culture, and the Resourcing of Criminal Justice. (2018) 9 *Criminal Law Review*, 711–731.

Stephen J.F, *A General View of the Criminal Law in London,* Volume II (London, 1883).

Spradley J.P, *The Ethnographic Interview* (New York: Holt 1979).

Summers S, *Fair Trials* (Oxford: Hart Publishing, 2007).

Thornton P, Mallaliey A, and Sceivener A, *Justice on Trial: Report of an Independent Civil Liberty Panel on Criminal Justice* (London: Civil Liberties Trust, 1993).

Walker C, and Starmer K, *Miscarriages of Justice* (London: Blackstone 1999).

Wendell W.B, *Ethics and Law: An Introduction* (Cambridge University Press: Cambridge, 2014).

Webley L, *Qualitative Approaches to Empirical Legal Research* in P. Crane and H. M. Kritzer, (ed.), *The Oxford Handbook of Empirical Legal Research* (Oxford: Oxford University Press, 2010).

Williams G, *The Proof of Guilt* (London: Stevens and Sons, 1963).

Travers M, *The Reality of Law* (Ashgate: Dartmouth, 1997).

Zacharias F, Green B, *Reconceptualizing Advocacy Ethics* (2005) 74 Geo. Wash. L. Rev.

Zacharias F, Green B, *Reconsidering Brougham* (2006) 74 Geo. J. Legal Ethics.

Zander M, *Lord Justice Auld's Review of the Criminal Courts: A Response* (2001).

Vogler R, *A World View of Criminal Justice* (Ashgate Publishing, 2005).

Zander M, *Cases and Materials on the English Legal System* (10th Edition, Cambridge University Press, Cambridge, 2007).

Zedner L, *Criminal Justice* (Oxford University Press, 2004).

Index

About the Author

Ed Johnston is a Senior Lecturer in Law at the Bristol Law School, University of the West of England. Ed's research interests are in the areas of pretrial disclosure, the role of the defense lawyer, and rise of managerialism in an adversarial setting. Ed is the co-author of *Criminal Procedure and Punishment* and *The Law of Disclosure: A Perennial Problem in Criminal Justice*. Ed has published widely concerning issues within criminal justice, in particular at the pretrial stage. Ed also runs the YouTube channel, *Criminal Justice Natters*.

Ed lives in Somerset with his partner, Wolfy, and their two children Erin and Jacob.

CPSIA information can be obtained
at www.ICGtesting.com
Printed in the USA
BVHW010824240821
615013BV00020B/140

9 781793 612922